Jaap Huisman

Jacqueline van der Kloet

V+K Publishing, Blaricum

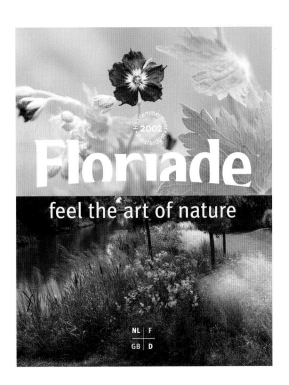

Floriade

feel the art of nature

Haarlemmermeer
2002
Amsterdam

NL | F
GB | D

NL | F
GB | D

Floriade

feel the art of nature

© 2001 V+K Publishing, Blaricum
In cooperation with Floriade 2002

ISBN 90 74265 29 4

Bij het Dak | Près de la Coupole
Near the Roof | Am Dach

Naast de Berg | **À côté de la Colline**
By the Hill | Am Hügel

Aan het Meer | **Au bord du Lac**
On the Lake | Am See

Voorwoord · Préface

Preface · Vorwort

Eens in de tien jaar presenteert Nederland zich aan de rest van de wereld in één van haar glansrollen als wetenschappelijk en wereldwijd toonaangevend kenniscentrum op het gebied van de tuinbouw. Op een ca 65 hectare groot visitekaartje van 'Holland Tuinbouwland' zal Nederland in het teken staan van een kleurrijk en internationaal evenement: Floriade 2002. De eerste wereldtuinbouwtentoonstelling van de éénentwintigste eeuw zal in 2002 – van 6 april tot en met 20 oktober – haar ongeveer drie miljoen nationale en internationale bezoekers op spectaculaire en aangename wijze inspireren om zuinig te zijn op onze leefomgeving en daar gelijktijdig vele ideeën voor aandragen. Het hoofdthema van de Floriade 2002, 'feel the art of nature', doelt op genieten van de natuur, terwijl tegelijkertijd de duurzaamheid en kwaliteit van onze leefomgeving wordt nagestreefd. In elk van de drie parkdelen zal 'feel the art of nature' terugkeren, steeds op een andere manier.

Dit boek kan u al vast een voorproefje geven van wat u in de leukste tuin van Nederland kunt zien en beleven. In het geval u al een bezoek aan de Floriade heeft gebracht, biedt dit boek u een uitstekende mogelijkheid om al uw mooie herinneringen aan de Floriade nog eens opnieuw te beleven aan de hand van de verhalen en de talrijke foto's die in dit boek te vinden zijn.

Ik wens u veel lees- en kijkgenoegen toe!

John L. Reinhard
Algemeen Directeur
Stichting Floriade 2002

Les Pays-Bas se présentent une fois tous les dix ans au reste du monde dans l'un de leurs rôles les plus brillants de leader mondial en tant que centre de connaissances et d'expertise en matière d'horticulture. Arborant le titre de 'Hollande, Pays d'horticulture' sur une gigantesque carte de visite d'environ 65 hectares, les Pays-Bas seront sous le signe d'un événement international riche en couleurs: la Floriade 2002.

La première exposition mondiale de l'horticulture du 21ème siècle, qui se tiendra du 6 avril au 20 octobre 2002, inspirera ses quelque trois millions de visiteurs nationaux et internationaux, de façon spectaculaire et attrayante, à préserver l'environnement dans lequel nous vivons tous et présentera en mÍme temps de nombreuses nouvelles idées à cette fin.

Le thème central de la Floriade 2002: 'Vivre l'art de la nature', appelle à savourer les plaisirs de la nature tout en sauvegardant la durabilité et la qualité de notre milieu de vie. L'adage 'Vivre l'art de la nature' se retrouvera dans les trois parties du parc, sous des interprétations différentes à chaque fois.

Avant la visite de la Floriade, cet ouvrage vous donne d'ores et déjà un avant-goût de ce que vous pouvez voir et vivre dans le jardin le plus passionnant des Pays-Bas. Après la visite, les récits et les innombrables illustrations contenus dans l'ouvrage vous permettront de revivre vos plus beaux souvenirs de la Floriade.

Je vous souhaite une excellente lecture!

John L. Reinhard
P.D.G.
Association Floriade 2002

Once every ten years, the Netherlands stars in one of its most glittering roles – that of a centre of horticultural knowledge with a worldwide popular and scientific reputation. The 65-hectare showpiece of Holland as 'the Land of Horticulture' is certain to bring the whole country into the limelight of that most colourful of international events: Floriade 2002.

For a large part of 2002 – from 6 April to 20 October – the first worldwide horticultural show of the twenty-first century will spectacularly and pleasurably inspire some three million visitors from home and abroad to cherish and protect our environment – and at the same time it will offer countless new ideas on ways to do so. The leitmotif of Floriade 2002, 'Feel the art of Nature', implies enjoying the fruits of nature while appreciating the need for the sustainability and quality of the natural environment. The 'Feel the art of Nature' theme returns in a different guise in each of the three main parts of the Floriade Park.

One aim of this book is to give you an enticing preview of the fascinating things you will see and experience in Holland's most gorgeous garden. And, once you have enjoyed your visit to Floriade, it will enable you to relive all those delightful moments though its sumptuous photos and illuminating background information. Wishing you much pleasure both in reading about and visiting Floriade 2002,

John L. Reinhard
General Director
Floriade 2002 Foundation

Alle zehn Jahre präsentieren sich die Niederlande dem Rest der Welt in einer ihrer Glanzrollen als wissenschaftliches und weltweit tonangebendes Wissenschaftszentrum auf dem Gebiet des Gartenbaus. Auf einer ca. 65 ha groflen Visitenkarte von 'Holland Gartenbauland' stehen die Niederlande im Zeichen einer farbenfrohen internationalen Veranstaltung, der Floriade 2002.

Die erste Weltgartenbau-Ausstellung des 21. Jahrhunderts wird vom 6. April bis zum 20. Oktober 2002 ihre etwa drei Millionen nationalen und internationalen Besucher auf eine spektakuläre und angenehme Weise inspirieren, sparsam mit unserer Lebensumgebung umzugehen und dazu gleichzeitig auch viele Ideen beitragen. Das Hauptthema der Floriade 2002, 'feel the art of nature', richtet sich auf das Genieflen der Natur, während zur gleichen Zeit die Dauerhaftigkeit und Qualität unserer Lebensumgebung angestrebt wird. In jedem der drei Parkteile wird 'feel the art of nature' immer auf eine andere Weise wiederkehren. Dieses Buch kann Ihnen schon einmal einen Vorgeschmack davon geben, was Sie im schönsten Garten der Niederlande sehen und erleben können. Für den Fall, dass Sie die Floriade schon besucht haben, bietet es Ihnen eine ausgezeichnete Möglichkeit, Ihre schönen Erinnerungen an die Floriade anhand der Geschichten und der zahlreichen Fotos, die in diesem Buch abgebildet sind, erneut zu erleben.
Ich wünsche Ihnen viel Vergnügen beim Lesen und Schauen!

John L. Reinhard
Allgemeiner Direktor
Stiftung Floriade 2002

Verleid in de leukste tuin van Nederland

Séduit par le jardin le plus passionnant des Pays-Bas

Temptation in Holland's Most Gorgeous Garden

Verführung im schönsten Garten der Niederlande

Het gevoel begint

In de lucht hangt een Boeing 747, roerloos als een buizerd lijkt het wel, klaar om te landen. Op de grond beweegt over de vrije busbaan, de Zuidtangent, het busverkeer in een continue stroom. Afgezonderd daarvan voert de N205 auto's aan. Verkeersstromen glijden door een oneindig laagland. We bevinden ons op het vermoedelijk laagste punt van Nederland, dat je oneerbiedig het schrobputje van het land zou kunnen noemen, omdat hierin van alles samenvloeit: water, economische bedrijvigheid, mensenmassa's, akkerbouw, volkshuisvesting en een ongelofelijke hoeveelheid infrastructuur. We bevinden ons op een plek waar meer dan 150 jaar geleden nog het water tegen de oevers klotste, water dat werd bedwongen en dat vervolgens plaats maakte voor stevig boerenland met een vette klei die berucht en beroemd is. Berucht om zijn

The start of a feeling

A Boeing 747 hovers in the sky, seemingly as motionless as a buzzard, waiting for clearance to land. An endless stream of buses zooms along Zuidtangent, the road reserved for public transport. Alongside it, the N205 highway bears its separate torrent of car traffic. Traffic streams flow through a boundless lowland. We are at what is probably the lowest point of the Low Countries, at what we could irreverently call the drain of the Netherlands. Here, everything flows together: water, industry, crowds, agriculture and housing, not to mention an improbable number of main roads. Not 150 years have passed since the waves rippled over the shallow seas at this place. But the Dutch mastered the water, draining the shallows and salt marshes to make way for farmlands of sticky clay: the polder of Haarlemmermeer. The clay is renowned and notorious –

L'impression se profile

Un Boeing 747 plane dans les airs, presque immobile comme une buse à l'affût d'une proie, prêt à se poser. En bas, les bus défilent en courant continu sur la voie qui leur est réservée, la Zuidtangent. A côté, les voitures déferlent sur la N205. Les flux de circulation glissent à travers un plat pays s'étendant jusqu'à l'horizon. Nous sommes au point vraisemblablement le plus bas de la Hollande, que nous pourrions appeler un peu irrespectueusement le puisard du pays puisque s'y concentrent toutes sortes de choses: l'eau, les activités économiques, la population, l'agriculture, l'habitat et une infrastructure d'une ampleur incroyable. Nous sommes où, il y a plus de 150 ans, l'eau clapotait encore contre les rives avant d'être refoulée pour faire place à cette bonne terre agricole dont l'argile grasse est à la fois redoutée et renommée; redoutée pour sa rusti-

Das Gefühl stellt sich ein

Am Himmel hängt eine Boeing 747, regungslos wie ein Bussard und bereit zum Landen. Auf der Erde bewegt sich über die freie Busbahn, die Südtangente, der Busverkehr in einem andauernden Strom fort. Zusätzlich transportiert die N205 Autos. Verkehrsströme gleiten über ein unendliches flaches Land. Wir befinden uns am vermutlich niedrigsten Punkt der Niederlande, den man respektlos den Abfluss des Landes nennen könnte, weil in ihm alles mögliche zusammenfließt: Wasser, wirtschaftliche Betriebsamkeit, Menschenmassen, Ackerbau, Wohnungswesen und eine unglaubliche Menge Infrastruktur. Wir befinden uns an einer Stelle, an der vor über 150 Jahren noch das Wasser gegen die Ufer schwappte – Wasser, das gebändigt wurde und danach Platz machte für solides Bauernland mit einem fetten Lehmboden, der berühmt und berüchtigt ist. Wegen seiner Widerspen-

weerbarstigheid, beroemd vanwege zijn vruchtbaarheid. Graan voor Visch heette heel toepasselijk een boerderij in deze omgeving. Waar eerst aal werd gevangen, ploegen nu combines door het koren. Maar zoals de schepen zijn verdreven, hebben ook combines het tij tegen. Steeds meer wordt er van het boerenland afgeknabbeld. Een vijfde baan voor Schiphol. Een nieuwe uitbreiding – de zoveelste – van Hoofddorp. Een extra bedrijvenpark. Een recreatiegebied en een televisiefabriek naast de Ringvaart. En dan nu, alsof de kok lang geaarzeld heeft met het menu, wordt het hoofdgerecht opgediend: de leukste tuin van Nederland. Een tuin die ligt op het kruispunt van Europa. Op het laagste punt van Europa, wie zal het zeggen.

In deze polder met vaarten waaraan geen eind lijkt te komen, nachtmerries voor fietsers omdat hun eindeloosheid gepaard gaat met een nooit aflatende wind, zien we het silhouet van de tuin vanuit de verte opdoemen. Dat kan met gemak want nergens lijkt de horizon zo'n rechte streep als in de Haarlemmermeer. Voordat we de tuin binnengaan, lijken de bouwsels van die skyline zonder betekenis, hooguit mystiek van uiterlijk. We zien een uitgestrekt geel veld, gevuld met blauwe panelen dat als een opgetilde waterplas boven de aarde lijkt te zweven. Daar vlak naast de glinstering van een tuinderskas: dat is nog de meest

cité et renommée pour sa fertilité. Témoin en fut longtemps une ferme des environs avec un nom tout à fait de circonstance: 'Graan voor Visch', ce qui signifie que le poisson avait été échangé pour des céréales. En effet, les moissonneuses-batteuses émergeaient des champs où se pêchaient autrefois les anguilles. Mais de même que les bateaux disparus, les moissonneuses-batteuses connaissent aussi des temps difficiles. Au fil du temps, on empiète de plus en plus sur les terres agraires: pour une cinquième piste d'atterrissage à Schiphol, pour l'énième élargissement d'Hoofddorp, pour une zone d'activités en plus, pour un parc de loisirs et pour une énorme usine de postes télé près de la Ringvaart. Et maintenant, comme si le chef avait longtemps hésité sur le menu, voilà que nous est servi le plat de résistance: le jardin le plus passionnant des Pays-Bas. Un jardin situé au carrefour de l'Europe. Qui sait? Peut-être au point le plus bas d'Europe.

Dans ce polder irrigué de cours d'eau et qui semble s'étendre à l'infini, un vrai cauchemar d'ailleurs pour les amateurs de promenades en vélo qui doivent affronter un vent sans répit, se dessine au loin la silhouette du jardin. Rien d'étonnant à cela car l'horizon n'est nulle part ailleurs aussi rectiligne que dans l'Haarlemmermeer. Avant d'entrer dans le jardin, les édifices dressés dans ce profil semblent dépourvus de sens, d'un aspect

Bij het Dak, subtropische vallei

Près de la Coupole, vallée subtropicale

Am Dach, subtropisches Tal

Near the Roof, subtropical valley

renowned for its fertility, and notorious for the difficulty of tilling it. *Graan voor Visch*, or 'Grain instead of Fish', is the apt name of a farm in this vicinity. Where people used to fish for eels, combine harvesters now ply the waving corn.
But just as the ships were banished to deeper waters, the tide is now turning against the combine harvesters. More and more farmland is being nibbled away for other purposes. Schiphol International Airport is expanding to provide a fifth runway. The town of Hoofddorp is adding yet another suburb to its margins. Another new industrial park is on its way. A recreation zone and a TV factory are planned alongside the Ringvaart, the canal that girdles the polder. And now, as though the chef had been holding back on the diners for extra effect, comes the *pièce de résistance* – the most sumptuous garden in Holland. It is a garden at Europe's lowest point, and a point which is also a crossroads.

The flat land of the polder is sliced through by straight ribbons of water, which vanish to an infinite horizon – a nightmare for cyclists on the roads alongside them, struggling against an unrelenting headwind. The silhouette of the garden and its buildings looms up from afar. We cannot miss it because apart from that the horizon is a pure horizontal line. Until we enter the park, the structures that rise above the plain are totally

stigkeit berüchtigt, wegen seiner Fruchtbarkeit berühmt. 'Korn für Fisch' hieß sehr treffend ein Bauernhof in dieser Umgebung. Wo man früher Aal gefangen hat, bewegen sich jetzt Mähdrescher durch das Getreide. Aber so wie die Schiffe verschwunden sind, haben auch die Mähdrescher die Zeit gegen sich. Immer mehr wird von dem Bauernland abgeknabbert. Eine neue Erweiterung – die soundsovielste – von Hoofddorp. Ein zusätzlicher Unternehmenspark; ein Erholungsgebiet sowie eine Fernsehfabrik neben der Ringvaart. Und nun schließlich, als habe der Koch mit dem Menü lange gezögert, wird das Hauptgericht aufgetischt: der schönste Garten der Niederlande. Ein Garten, der auf der Kreuzung von Europa liegt. Auf dem niedrigsten Punkt Europas – wer hätte so etwas erwartet!

In diesem Polder mit Kanälen, die endlos scheinen – ein Albtraum für Fahrradfahrer, weil ihre Endlosigkeit mit einem nie abflauenden Wind einhergeht –, sehen wir in der Ferne die Silhouette des Gartens auftauchen. Das geht ganz einfach, denn nirgendwo erscheint der Horizont als eine solche gerade Linie wie im Haarlemmermeer. Bevor wir den Garten betreten, scheinen die Bauten dieser Skyline ohne Bedeutung, machen höchstens einen etwas mystischen Eindruck. Vor unseren Augen breitet sich ein ausgedehntes gelbes Feld aus, das mit blauen Flächen gefüllt wie eine hochgehobene Wasserpfütze über der Erde zu schweben scheint. Direkt daneben das Glitzern

logische, die hadden we hier verwacht. Raadselachtiger wordt het met een enorme groene bult, die verwantschap vertoont met een piramide. Erbovenop een plateau dat wordt afgeschermd door een reusachtig oranje doek, en een soort hengel die daardoorheen beweegt. Met een hoedje aan het uiteinde, een feestelijk gebaar naar de wijde wereld. We kunnen het niet haarscherp ontwaren, de nieuwsgierigheid is gewekt, we hebben ons laten verleiden. We moeten erin, in de leukste tuin van Nederland, Floriade 2002, een van de grootste internationale tuinbouwtentoonstellingen ter wereld. Waren we via het luchtruim gekomen, dan hadden we het kunnen lezen, in letters gevormd door struiken, geboomte, en bloembedden. En we lazen, op een talud aan een vaart, het woord 'Floriade'. Het signaal van een feest in kleur, geur en smaak.

Vreemd hoe dat gaat. We stappen uit de bus of de auto, gaan de toegangspoort door en raken raakt ogenblikkelijk in de ban van het schouwspel. De bloemenzee, de restaurantjes die geuren verspreiden, de valleien en de hellingen, en de bordjes die ons leiden naar namen vol geheimzinnigheid. *'Bij het Dak'. 'Naast de Berg'. 'Aan het Meer.'* Ogenblikkelijk zijn we de alledaagse werkelijkheid vergeten, omdat we ons hebben overgegeven aan de Tuin. Ineens is daar een oase van groei

un peu mystique. Nous découvrons un grand champ jaune rempli de panneaux bleus, comme si un plan d'eau avait été soulevé et planait au-dessus du sol. Juste à côté, le scintillement d'une serre d'horticulture nous surprend moins, logique... n'est-ce pas ! Ce qui est plus énigmatique, c'est de découvrir une énorme butte verte à l'allure d'une pyramide. Tout en haut, un plateau recouvert d'une immense toile orange où s'agite une sorte de gaule coiffée d'un chapeau à son extrémité et adressant comme un salut solennel au monde entier. Difficile de savoir vraiment ce dont il s'agit mais la curiosité est éveillée, nous sommes déjà séduits. Tout nous incite à entrer dans le jardin le plus passionnant des Pays-Bas qu'est la Floriade 2002, l'une des plus grandes expositions horticoles internationales qui soit au monde. Si nous étions venus par les airs, nous aurions même pu lire ce que nous découvrons maintenant sur la berge d'un cours d'eau: le mot 'Floriade' qui, en lettres immenses formées d'arbres, d'arbustes et de massifs de fleurs, nous anonce une fête des couleurs, des senteurs et des saveurs.

Comme c'est étrange de descendre de car ou de voiture, de passer le porche d'entrée et de tomber à l'instant même sous le charme de l'entourage. Les arômes de la mer de fleurs et des restaurants nous caressent les narines; les vallées, les collines et les panneaux nous guident vers des

'Floriade', gevormd door struiken, geboomte, en bloembedden
'Floriade', formées d'arbres, d'arbustes et de massifs de fleurs
'Floriade', aus Sträuchern, Bäumen und Blumenbeeten geformt
'Floriade', marked out in shrubs, trees and flowerbeds

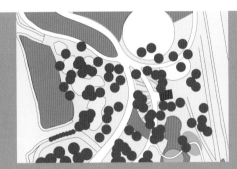

Aan het Meer
Au bord du Lac
Am See
On the Lake

inscrutable or at best enigmatic. We see a huge yellow field, crowded with blue panels that seem to float above the ground like a levitating lake. Next to it, there is the glitter of a greenhouse – well, that at least is the kind of thing we expected. The enormous green bump is a bit odd though. It has a platform on top, covered by a huge orange tarpaulin with a kind of fishing rod waving above it. The rod has what looks like a little hat at the tip, raised in a cheerful greeting to the world at large. We cannot make out exactly what it all is but our curiosity is aroused. The temptation is too hard to resist. Down the garden path we go, in Holland's most gorgeous garden – Floriade 2002, one of the world's biggest international horticultural shows. Had we flown in by air, we could have read the name marked out in shrubs, trees and flowerbeds on a sloping bank - 'Floriade', the byword for a feast of colour, perfume and taste.

Funny how it goes. You get off the bus or out of the car, walk up to the entrance gate, and suddenly you are in the grip of a spectacular show. The sea of flowers, the tempting aromas from the restaurants, the unexpected dips and slopes, and the signs that point us towards enigmatic-sounding destinations: 'near the Roof', 'by the Hill' and 'on the Lake'. We instantly forget our everyday preoccupations and submit to the charms of the Garden. Here we are in an oasis of growth and greenery amid the

eines Gewächshauses: das ist noch am logischsten, das haben wir hier auch erwartet. Rätselhafter wird es durch eine riesige grüne Beule, die einer Pyramide ähnelt. Darauf befindet sich ein Plateau, das durch ein riesiges orangefarbenes Tuch abgeschirmt wird und eine Art Angel, die sich dazwischen bewegt. Mit einem Hut an der Spitze, eine festliche Geste an die ganze Welt. Wir können es nicht genau erklären, aber die Neugierde ist geweckt, wir haben uns schon verführen lassen. Wir müssen hinein, in den schönsten Garten der Niederlande, die Floriade 2002, eine der größten internationalen Gartenbauausstellungen der Welt. Wären wir über den Luftraum gekommen, dann hätten wir es auf der Erde, in Buchstaben aus Sträuchern, Bäumen und Blumenbeeten geformt, sehen können. Und wir hätten auf einer Böschung an einem Graben das Wort Floriade gelesen, das Signal für ein Fest der Farbe, des Duftes und des Geschmackes.

Merkwürdig, wie das so geht. Man steigt aus dem Bus oder dem Auto, man geht durch die Eingangstür und gerät auf der Stelle in den Bann des Schauspiels. Das Blumenmeer, die Restaurants, aus denen Düfte strömen, die Täler und die Abhänge und die Schilder mit ihren geheimnisvollen Namen. *'Am Dach', 'Am Hügel', 'Am See'.* Man hat den Alltag sofort hinter sich gelassen, weil man sich dem Garten hingegeben hat. Plötzlich befindet man sich in einer Oase des Wachstums und der Blüte in einer Umgebung, die

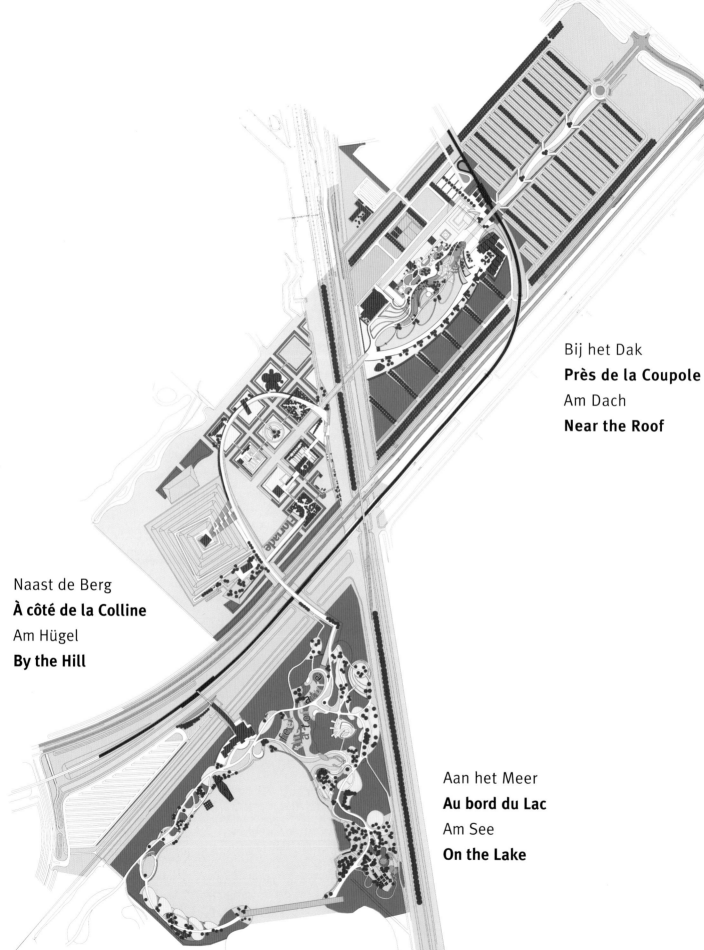

Bij het Dak
Près de la Coupole
Am Dach
Near the Roof

Naast de Berg
À côté de la Colline
Am Hügel
By the Hill

Aan het Meer
Au bord du Lac
Am See
On the Lake

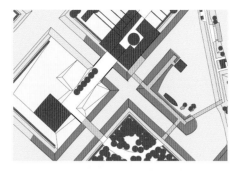

Naast de Berg, de Groene Stad
À côté de la Colline, la Ville Verte
Am Hügel, der Grünen Stadt
By the Hill, the 'Green City'

Bij het Dak, noordelijke ingang
Près de la Coupole, l'entrée nord
Am Dach, nördlichen Eingang
Near the Roof, northern entrance

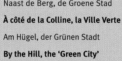

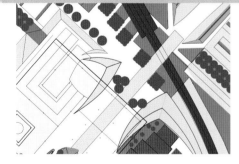

Aan het Meer, Bijzondere
Bolgewassenvallei
Au bord du Lac, Vallée des
bulbes insolites
Am See, das Tal der seltenen
Zwiebelgewächse
On the Lake, Valley of Bulb
Specials

en bloei in een omgeving die voornamelijk uitblinkt door asfalt en steen. Daar horen dan ook de wetmatigheden van de tuin bij, zoals bijvoorbeeld de kleuren die in elk gedeelte de toon zetten. Geel als hoofdtint bij het Dak, rood in het gebied aan de voet van de Berg en blauw uiteraard bij het Meer.

Het eerste dat het oog treft is een stapel van dertig reusachtige keien, stuk voor stuk veertigduizend kilo zwaar, door tientonners uit een groeve in Duitsland aangevoerd. De keien lekken. Het water dat hieruit 'ontspringt' – een kunstwerk van Ton Kalle – zal ons begeleiden. Kalle is een van de kunstenaars die heeft gereageerd op het polderlandschap. Als commentaar op die weerbarstige klei koos hij voor stoer graniet, de hardste steen ter wereld. Het is een rudimentaire, abstracte stapeling die net als de meeste andere beelden met het landschap vergroeid zijn. We volgen het beekje dat vanaf de stenenmassa vloeit in de Arcadië-vallei, die omzoomd wordt met wilde planten. Daar stopt de stroom even. Maar als we de coupure in de Geniedijk doorsteken, een overblijfsel van de Stelling van Amsterdam die in de 19e eeuw werd gebouwd ter verdediging van de hoofdstad, komen we het water weer tegen. Nu is het verspreid in sloten en vaarten, waarover notarisbootjes varen. Hier herkennen we het typisch Nederlandse polderlandschap, geome-

noms pleins de mystère: *'Près de la Coupole'*, *'A côté de la Colline'*, *'Au bord du Lac'*. D'un seul coup, le quotidien est oublié et l'ambiance du Jardin nous prend dans ses bras. Nous voilà subitement dans une oasis de verdure et de fleurs au milieu d'une région où notamment le bitume et la pierre sont omniprésents. Rien d'étonnant donc à ce que le parc témoigne d'une certaine conformité, ne serait-ce par exemple que dans les couleurs qui donnent le ton à chaque partie. Le jaune est la couleur dominante aux alentours de la Coupole, le domaine au pied de la Colline est celui du rouge et le bleu règne évidemment en bordure du Lac.

Le regard se pose d'abord sur un amas de trente pierres gigantesques, chacune pesant quarante mille kilos. Elles ont été transportées d'une carrière d'Allemagne par des géants du transport routier. Un filet d'eau s'écoule des blocs de pierre et va nous accompagner dans notre promenade. Cette œuvre d'art est signée Ton Kalle, l'un des artistes qui s'est inspiré du paysage des polders et a choisi la robustesse du granit, la pierre la plus dure, pour donner répartie à la rusticité de l'argile. C'est un amoncellement rudimentaire et abstrait qui, comme la plupart des autres sculptures, s'identifie avec le paysage. Nous suivons le cours d'eau qui naît des rochers et coule vers la vallée Arcadië bordée de plantes sauvages où il semble s'interrompre. Mais nous le retrouvons dès que nous

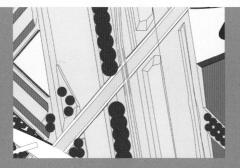

Coupure in de Geniedijk
La coupure dans la Geniedijk
Den Durchbruch im Geniedijk
The gap in the Geniedijk

14

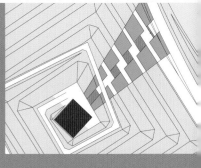

Big Spotters' Hill: ontleend aan de piramide van Cheops in Egypte
Big Spotters' Hill: calquées sur la pyramide Cheops en Egypte
Big Spotters' Hill, ausgehend von die Cheops-Pyramide in Ägypten
Big Spotters' Hill: based on the Pyramid of Cheops in Egypt

wider desert of asphalt and brick. The logic of the garden prevails here, for example the colours that set the mood for each section. Yellow is the dominant hue near the Roof, red marks the area by the Hill and – perhaps you guessed – blue is the keynote on the Lake.

The first thing to strike the eye is a heap of thirty gigantic rocks. Apparently they weigh some forty tons each, and they were brought in on lowloaders from a quarry in Germany. Then we notice that the rocks are leaking water. The water that trickles from this 'spring' – a sculpture by Ton Kalle – will keep us company for a while. Kalle is one of several invited artists to make work that relates to the topography of the natural surroundings. Thumbing his nose at the sticky clay of the polder, he chose that hardest of rocks, granite. His sculpture is a rudimentary, abstract mound that, like most of the other works of art, seems to become a natural part of the landscape. We follow the stream, which flows out of the heap of rocks into the Arcadië Valley, which is lined with wild flowers. Then the stream disappears. But once we pass through the gap in the Geniedijk, a remnant of a wide ring of nineteenth-century defensive works known as the 'Stelling van Amsterdam', the water appears to greet us again. Now it is spread out in ditches and waterways, along which small cabin-boats chug back and forth. Here we

sich hauptsächlich durch Asphalt und Stein auszeichnet. Dazu gehören dann auch die Gesetzmäßigkeiten des Gartens, wie zum Beispiel die Farben, die in jedem Teil den Ton angeben. Gelb als Hauptton beim Dach, rot im Gebiet am Fuße des Hügels und blau natürlich beim See.

Das Erste, was einem auffällt, ist ein Stapel von dreißig riesigen Steinen, die alle vierzigtausend Kilo schwer sind und von Zehntonnern aus einem Steinbruch in Deutschland antransportiert worden sind. Die Steine lecken. Das Wasser, das aus ihnen 'entspringt', ist ein Kunstwerk von Ton Kalle und wird uns begleiten. Kalle ist einer der Künstler, der auf die Polderlandschaft reagiert hat. Als Kommentar auf diesen widerspenstigen Stein wählte er wuchtiges Granit, den härtesten Stein der Welt. Es ist eine rudimentäre, abstrakte Anhäufung, die wie die meisten anderen Skulpturen mit der Landschaft verwachsen sind. Wir folgen dem Bach, der von der Steinmasse aus in das von wilden Pflanzen umsäumte Arcadië-Tal fließt. Da macht der Strom kurz Halt. Aber wenn wir den Durchbruch im Geniedijk überqueren – ein überbleibsel der einstigen Festung Amsterdams, die im 19. Jahrhundert zur Verteidigung der Hauptstand erbaut wurde -, treffen wir wieder auf Wasser. Jetzt ist es verteilt in Gräben und Kanälen, auf denen elegante Boote fahren. Hier erkennen wir die typisch niederländische Polderlandschaft: geometrisch, grün und glatt. Die Ufer

trisch, groen en glad. De oevers zijn omzoomd met riet en lisdodde, de eilanden zijn grotendeels bebouwd, waardoor er associaties opkomen met Amsterdam of Venetië. Overleven met en dankzij het water, dat is voorbehouden aan de volkeren die onder de zeespiegel hun domicilie kiezen. De Floriade is daar in miniatuur-versie een afspiegeling van. Dat patroon van eilanden kent een contrapunt, in de vorm van Big Spotters' Hill waarvan de inhoud en vorm is ontleend aan de piramide van Cheops in Egypte. Een piramide met die referentie, het is wel het laatste waaraan je denkt in de Haarlemmermeer, want zelden is de tegenstelling tussen dergelijke omgevingen zo groot. Klei versus woestijnzand, de polder tegenover de woestijn en dus de diepte als contrast met de hoogte. *Never the twain shall meet*, en toch is het gelukt die eindjes aan elkaar te knopen in de Haarlemmermeer. Het verbindende element is de mens, die een artificieel bouwsel heeft gewrocht op een plaats die daar ogenschijnlijk niet geschikt voor is.

Maar we zouden het water en de bijbehorende beplanting volgen. In het eilandenrijk bij de Berg is het alomtegenwoordig. Maar nu gaan we een brug over die de Zuidtangent en de N205 overbrugt, en belanden in het parkdeel Aan het Meer. De populieren en wilgen zijn al wat ouder, omdat ze als omlijsting dienden van de zandput dat hier in de jaren zeventig gegraven werd. Het is dus een toevallig bos met een al

franchissons la coupure dans la Geniedijk, un vestige du Stelling d'Amsterdam qui avait été construit au 19ème siècle pour protéger la capitale. L'eau poursuit sa course sur plusieurs bras et canaux où voguent de belles petites embarcations. Nous reconnaissons alors le paysage typique des polders hollandais: géométrique, vert et uniforme. Les rives sont bordées de roseaux et de typhas; les îles sont en grande partie construites, évoquant Amsterdam ou Venise. Survivre avec l'eau et par l'eau, c'est le sort des peuples qui choisissent de s'établir en dessous du niveau de la mer. La Floriade nous en donne l'interprétation en miniature. Au dessin des îles se superpose en contrepoint la silhouette de la colline Big Spotters' Hill dont la composition et la forme ont été calquées sur la pyramide Cheops en Egypte. Qui aurait imaginé trouver une pyramide d'une telle référence dans l'Haarlemmermeer, le paysage offre rarement de contraste aussi flagrant: l'argile opposée au sable, le polder face au désert et le bas-relief accentué par cette proéminence. *'Les deux resteront à jamais inconciliables'* (*Never the twain shall mee*), et pourtant les extrêmes se rencontrent dans l'Haarlemmermeer. Le lien a été établi par l'Homme, créateur d'un ouvrage artificiel dans un lieu apparemment inopportun.

Mais revenons à notre idée première: suivre l'eau et la végétation aquatique qui ont fait leur territoire du royaume des îles à côté de la Colline.

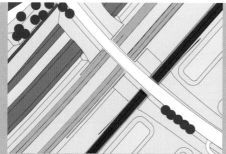

De Zuidtangent en N205
La Zuidtangent et la N205
Die Südtangente und die N205
The Zuidtangent and N205

15

recognize the typically Dutch polder landscape, geometrical, green and flat. The banks are fringed with reeds and bulrushes, and the Islands are built up, raising associations of Amsterdam or Venice. Living with the water and surviving in spite of it: that is the fate of a people that chooses to live below sea level. The Floriade is a condensed version of Holland's water-rich landscape. The Islands form a counterpoint to Big Spotters' Hill. The design of this towering mass of sand was based on the Pyramid of Cheops in Egypt. A pyramid with such antecedents is perhaps the last thing we would expect in Haarlemmermeer. The contrast between the two environments could hardly be greater – clay as opposed to sand dunes, the silver-veined polder as opposed to the waterless desert, and the lowlands in contrast to the heights. Never the twain shall meet, but somehow they have been brought together here in Haarlemmermeer. The linking element is humanity, which has wrought an artificial structure in a place that is at first sight inappropriate for it.

But we were going to follow the watercourses and the plants alongside them. Around the Islands, by the Hill, water is everywhere. Taking the footbridge over Zuidtangent and the N205 highway brings us into the 'on the Lake' section of the park. The Poplars and Willows were here long before the Floriade came. They once bordered a sand quarry that was excavated here in the 1970s and later filled with water. So it is a random

werden von Riet und Rohrkolben gesäumt und die Inseln sind größtenteils bebaut, was Assoziationen an Amsterdam oder Venedig erweckt. Überleben mit und Dank des Wassers, das ist den Völkern vorbehalten, die ihr Domizil unter dem Meeresspiegel aufgeschlagen haben. Die Floriade ist davon eine Spiegelung in Miniaturversion. Das Muster der Inseln besitzt einen Kontrapunkt in der Form von Big Spotters' Hill, dessen Inhalt und Form die Cheops-Pyramide in Ägypten nachahmen. Eine Pyramide ist wohl das letzte, an das man im Haarlemmermeer denken würde, denn selten ist der Gegensatz zwischen solchen Gegebenheiten dermaßen groß. Lehm versus Wüstensand, der Polder gegenüber der Wüste sowie die Tiefe als Kontrast zur Höhe. 'Never the twain shall meet', und dennoch ist das Kunststück hier im Haarlemmermeer gelungen. Das verbindende Element ist der Mensch, der ein künstliches Bauwerk an einer Stelle erschaffen hat, die dafür offensichtlich nicht geeignet ist.

Aber wir wollen dem Wasser und der dazugehörenden Bepflanzung folgen. Im Inselreich bei der Brücke ist es allgegenwärtig. Aber jetzt überqueren wir eine Brücke, die die Südtangente und die N205 überbrückt und landen im Parkteil des Sees. Die Pappeln und Weiden sind schon etwas älter, weil sie als Umrahmung der Sandgrube dienten, die hier in den siebziger Jahren gegraben wurde. Es handelt sich also um einen zufälligen Wald mit einem ebenso zufälligen See, die zuerst beide dem Verkehr dienten und danach

even toevallig meer, eerst dienstbaar aan weg en waterstaat, daarna aan de recreatie. Dat bos schreeuwde om een tweede leven, toe als het was aan snoeimes en hak, en gelukkig kwam de Floriade als geroepen.

Dat meer en het bos zijn erfstukken die dankbaar zijn gebruikt voor de Floriade. Ze zijn afgestoft en opgedoft, zoals je dat met antiek doet. Zo is het ook met het moeras in een uitloper van het meer, waar geboomte zijn wortels in het dras heeft staan, waar muggen zoemen en de orchideeën tot leven komen. Als de mens niets doet, stippelt de natuur gewoon zijn eigen koers uit. Het water van het meer is behandeld tegen de blauwalg die het milieu verstikt en tot botulisme zou kunnen leiden. Stille wateren hebben niet alleen diepe gronden maar ook verraderlijke naturen. Hoewel ze lijken te leven, zijn ze dood. Dit water is tot leven gewekt, aan de oevers liggen dikke plakken natuursteen, die uit een groeve in de Ardennen zijn gehouwen. Er is een inham met de grootste collectie waterlelies die ooit in een tuin is verzameld. Water is er dus vooral, stilstaand als een moeras, glinsterend als een vijver, feeëriek zoals we dat ons in een oriëntaalse tuin kunnen voorstellen. Het is daarmee het vanzelfsprekende middelpunt van de Aziatische inzendingen die hier aan de boorden zijn neergestreken, met bamboe-paviljoens, bonsai en grint en allerhande exotische bloemen. Waarmee is

Nous passons maintenant sur un pont chevauchant la Zuidtangent et la N205 pour arriver dans la partie du parc appelée Au bord du Lac. Les peupliers et les saules y sont d'âge mûr car ils encadraient déjà la carrière de sable creusée dans les années soixante-dix. Ce bois, comme le lac d'ailleurs, se trouvait donc là par hasard et a d'abord été exploité par le service des Ponts et Chaussées avant de se vouer aux activités récréatives. Languissant dans l'attente d'un coup de sécateur ou de la hache, il réclamait une seconde vie: la Floriade arrivait à pic.

Le lac et le bois font partie des héritages utilisés avec gratitude pour la Floriade. Ils ont été retapés et bichonnés comme de précieuses antiquités. Cela vaut aussi pour le marais en prolongement du lac, là où les arbres ancrent leurs racines dans le sol marécageux, où bourdonne le vrombissement des moustiques, où les orchidées s'ouvrent à la vie. Sans intervention de l'Homme, la nature suit son cours. L'eau du lac a été traitée contre les algues bleues qui asphyxient le milieu ambiant et peuvent engendrer le botulisme. Il n'est pire eau que l'eau qui dort, elle est traîtresse car elle semble vivre mais c'est en fait une eau morte. Elle a donc été revivifiée. Sur les rives s'alignent des blocs de pierre naturelle venant d'une carrière des Ardennes. Dans une crique se prélasse la plus grande collection de nénuphars qui puisse être rassemblée dans un jardin. Encore et encore de l'eau, stagnante comme dans un marécage, scin-

De zuidelijke ingang
L'entrée sud
Den südlichen Eingang
The southern entrance

wood around an equally random lake, first serving the needs of the civil engineers and later those of recreation. The trees were in desperate need of thinning and pruning, and seemed doomed to be felled. But then came the Floriade to give them a new lease of life. The Lake and the wood are inheritances of which the Floriade has made grateful use. They have been dusted off and spruced up, like long unused furniture. The marshy area in one arm of the Lake has shared the same good fortune. It is a place where the tree roots are anchored in mud, where the air buzzes with mosquitoes, and where wild orchids flourish. Left to itself, nature follows its own wisdom.

The Lake has been cleaned up and its shores paved with thick slabs of stone brought from quarries in the Ardennes. There is a side pool housing the largest collection of waterlilies ever brought together in a garden. Water is here in every form – static as a marsh, glistening like a pool and as magical as we might picture it in a Oriental water garden. The Asian contributions to the Floriade have alighted on these banks, complete with bamboo pavilions, bonsai trees, ornamentally raked gravel and countless unfamiliar blooms. The Lowlands can sometimes rise to surprisingly exotic heights.

We have now wandered several kilometres from the northern entrance and have lost the link with the everyday world. Visitors who opted for the

der Erholung. Dieser Wald schien schon Hippe und Spitzhacke ausgeliefert zu sein, und deshalb kam die Floriade wie gerufen. Der See und der Wald sind Erbstücke, die man für die Floriade dankbar benutzt. Sie wurden abgestaubt und herausgeputzt, wie man es auch mit Antiquitäten macht. Ähnlich ist es auch mit dem Morast in einem Ausläufer des Sees, wo Bäume ihre Wurzeln im Sumpf haben, Mücken schwirren und die Orchideen zum Leben erweckt werden. Wo der Mensch nicht eingreift, nimmt die Natur einfach ihren Lauf.

Das Wasser des Sees wurde gegen die Blaualge behandelt, die die Umwelt erstickt und zu einer Vergiftung des Oberflächenwassers führen kann. Stille Wasser gründen nicht nur tief, sondern haben auch verräterische Naturen. Obwohl sie zu leben scheinen, sind sie tot. Dieses Wasser wurde zum Leben erweckt; an den Ufern liegen dicke Natursteinplatten, die aus einem Steinbruch in den Ardennen gebrochen wurden. Es gibt eine Bucht mit der größten Kollektion Seerosen, die je in einem Garten versammelt wurde. Es gibt aber vor allem Wasser, entweder still stehend wie ein Morast oder aber glänzend wie ein Teich, genauso märchenhaft, wie wir es uns von einem orientalischen Garten vorstellen. Es ist damit der selbstverständliche Mittelpunkt der asiatischen Einsendungen, die hier an den Ufern mit Bambus-Pavillons, Bonsai und Kies und allerhand exotischen Blumen einen Platz gefunden haben. Womit der Beweis erbracht ist, dass

aangetoond dat je het polderland wel degelijk tot grote verrassende hoogte kunt tillen.

Inmiddels zijn we al kilometers verwijderd van de noordelijke ingang en zijn we de schakel met alledag verloren. Ook de bezoekers die juist de zuidelijke ingang hebben genomen, zijn het contact kwijt, zoveel indrukken snellen tegelijk op je af. We hebben ons in de vallei bij het Dak even in de Mediterrannee gewaand, vonden ons in de Groene Stad even terug in het oer-Hollandse polderlandschap, totdat we door de exotica bij het Meer werden betoverd. *Feel the art of nature*, het motto van de Floriade, is door de aderen gaan stromen.

tillante comme sur un étang, féerique comme on se l'imagine dans un jardin oriental. C'est d'ailleurs aussi le foyer des présentations asiatiques venues s'installer sur le rivage, avec des pavillons en bambou, des bonsaïs, des graviers et toutes sortes de fleurs exotiques. Le tout prouve que la terre des polders peut bel et bien être 'exhaussée' jusqu'à un niveau surprenant.

Nous sommes maintenant à des kilomètres déjà de l'entrée nord et avons tout oublié du quotidien. Même ceux qui viennent d'arriver par l'entrée sud ont perdu le contact avec la vie de tous les jours tant le décor a d'emprise sur eux. Dans la vallée près de la Coupole, nous nous imaginons en Méditerranée et nous retrouvons le bon vieux paysage des polders dans la Ville Verte jusqu'à ce que nous soyons ensorcelés par le cadre exotique au bord du Lac. '*Feel the art of nature*', le slogan de la Floriade coule dans nos veines et se fait le nôtre.

De Aziatische inzendingen
Les présentations asiatiques
Die asiatischen Einsendungen
The Asian contributions

southern entrance will be just as far from reality, because wherever you go you are overwhelmed by new impressions. In the valley next to the Roof, we found ourselves in Mediterranean surroundings, in the 'Green City' we were back in an old Dutch Master and finally on the Lake we were enchanted by the exotic atmosphere. 'Feeling the art of nature', as the Floriade motto puts it, has swamped our senses.

das Polderland durchaus zu großen, überraschenden Leistungen fähig ist. Inzwischen befinden wir uns schon einige Kilometer vom nördlichen Eingang entfernt und haben mittlerweile auch unseren Alltag ganz hinter uns gelassen.

Den Besuchern, die den südlichen Eingang genommen haben, geht es ebenso, so viele Eindrücke strömen auf einen ein. Wir haben uns im Tal beim Dach kurz am Mittelmeer gewöhnt, fanden uns in der Grünen Stadt eben zurück in der urholländischen Polderlandschaft, bis uns die Exotik am See bezaubert hat. 'Feel the art of nature', das Motto der Floriade, strömt jetzt durch unsere Adern.

Een subtropische vallei in de Haarlemmermeer? Agaves en oleanders? Een laan met platanen? Niemand zou dat tien jaar geleden voor moge- lijk hebben gehouden, maar de realiteit van 2002 is een andere. Wat je van ver haalt is niet alleen lekker, het gedijt ook nog op de Hollandse klei. Het geheim zit in het dak. Dat is niet zomaar een dak. Hoewel in de onmetelijke Haarlemmermeer reuzen al gauw tot dreume- sen worden gereduceerd, is er geen ontkomen aan: dit dak met zon- nepanelen meet 28 duizend vierkante meter, veruit het grootste ter wereld. Dat staat voor halve verstaanders gelijk aan vier voetbalvel- den. (Hoe banaal het ook klinkt: het is daarmee een gedoodverfde kandidaat voor het Guiness Book of Records). Het formaat van de ten- toonstelling en de locatie leenden zich voor een vorstelijke uithaal. Zonnestroom verwarmt de Floriade, dankzij deze innovatie van Nuon.

Une vallée subtropicale dans l'Haarlemmermeer? Des agaves et des lau- riers roses? Une allée de platanes? Qui l'aurait imaginé, il y a dix ans... Pourtant, en 2002 c'est la réalité ! Comme le dit un adage néerlandais: 'Ce qui vient de loin s'apprécie bien' et, en plus, ces plantes aux origines lointaines se plaisent aussi sur l'argile hollandaise. Tout le secret est dans le toit, un toit pas comme les autres.
Si même les géants prennent vite l'allure de gamins dans l'immensité de l'Haarlemmermeer, une chose ne saurait échapper aux regards: une ver- rière de panneaux solaires dont la surface de 28.000 m² en fait de loin la plus grande du monde. Pour les moins ferrés des chiffres: la surface de quatre terrains de football. L'ampleur de l'exposition et l'emplacement se prêtaient tout à fait à un geste grandiose.
La Floriade est chauffée par l'énergie solaire captée grâce à cette innova-

A subtropical valley in Haarlemmermeer? Agaves and oleanders? An avenue lined with plane-trees? Nobody would have thought it possible ten years ago, but the reality of 2002 is a different one altogether. Exotic delights do surprisingly well when rooted in dour Dutch clay. The secret is in the Roof – although roof is a word that hardly does it justice.
Giants are easily cut down to size in the immensity of Haarlemmermeer, but here there is no way around it: this roof clad with solar panels has an area of over 28 thousand square metres. For those who like such analo- gies, that is equal to four football pitches. (It wouldn't be too hackneyed to say it is a cert for the Guinness Book of Records.) The size of the exhibi- tion and the location lent themselves to a grand gesture.
Solar energy heats the Floriade thanks to this innovation by the electricity company, Nuon. Solar power belongs with windmills, tidal power and

Ein subtropisches Tal im Haarlemmermeer? Agaven und Oleander? Eine Platanenallee? Vor zehn Jahren hätte das niemand für möglich gehalten, aber die Realität von 2002 ist eine andere. Was man von weit her holt, ist nicht nur schmackhaft, es gedeiht darüber hinaus auch noch auf holländi- schem Lehmboden. Das Geheimnis befindet sich im Dach. Hierbei handelt es sich um kein gewöhnliches Dach.
Obwohl Riesen im unermesslichen Haarlemmermeer schon schnell zu Knir- psen reduziert werden, gibt es kein Entkommen: Dieses Dach besteht aus Solarzellen und ist 28.000 m² groß und damit mit Abstand das größte der Welt. Es entspricht etwa einer Größe von vier Fußballplätzen. (So banal es auch klingt, aber damit ist es ein todsicherer Kandidat für das Guiness Book of Records.) Sowohl das Format der Ausstellung als auch die Lage eignen sich für einen fürstlichen Empfang.

Daarmee hoort het samen met windmolens, waterkrachtcentrales en verbranding van biomassa tot de duurzame energie, die anders dan de fossiele energiebronnen (gas, kolen en kernenergie) geen aantasting betekent van de wereldvoorraad.

Duurzaamheid, de ongeschreven boodschap van de Floriade 2002, wordt niet gebracht op de geitenwollensokken-manier van de jaren tachtig uit de vorige eeuw. Immers, duurzaamheid veronderstelt een bewustzijn voor de kwaliteit van het leven en de bronnen die dat leven voeden. Dat blijft niet beperkt tot de zes maanden van de Floriade, de bloeitijd van de tuin, die reikt verder en blijft evenmin beperkt tot de plaats. De zonne-energie mag dan voor de duur van de Floriade de kassen, kiosken en restaurants van stroom voorzien (goed voor drie miljoen kilowattuur stroom), na afloop zal het Dak worden opgenomen in het elektriciteitsnetwerk van de Haarlemmermeer en een slordige 400 huishoudens kunnen verwarmen.

Natuurlijk is de achterliggende gedachte dat Nederland in de toekomst minder afhankelijk wil zijn van de fossiele energiebronnen zoals kolen en gas, maar en passant onderstreept het dak met gehard glas en ontelbare fotovoltaïsche zonnecellen dat de consument op een grauwe winterse dag niet op een houtje hoeft te bijten. Het tekort wordt aangevuld. Sterker nog: door de uitvinding van het zonnepanelendak van deze omvang is het op de Floriade mogelijk kwetsbare planten en gewassen uit de Middellandse Zee te presenteren.

Het is een aaneenschakeling van schuine glazen kappen met een patroon dat het gebladerte van bomen suggereert. Er wordt gefilterd licht op de flora geworpen. Nauwkeurig bezien zijn de panelen zo opgebouwd dat zo min mogelijk ruimte wordt verspild aan lijst en

tion de Nuon; classant ainsi cette forme d'énergie, au même titre que les éoliennes, les centrales hydro-électriques et la combustion de biomasse parmi les énergies durables qui, contrairement aux énergies fossiles (gaz, charbon et énergie nucléaire), ne portent pas atteinte aux réserves mondiales.

La durabilité est le message tacite de la Floriade 2002 dont l'interprétation n'est plus la même que celle de la vague écolo des années quatre-vingt du siècle dernier. En effet, la durabilité implique une prise de conscience de la qualité de la vie et des ressources qui l'alimentent. Elle ne se limite pas aux six mois de la Floriade, à la floraison du parc, mais va plus loin en temps et en lieu. En effet, si l'énergie solaire alimente en courant électrique les serres, les kiosques et les restaurants pendant la durée de la Floriade (ce qui représente un total de 3.000.000 kW), la Verrière fera après partie intégrante du réseau d'alimentation en électricité de l'Haarlemmermeer et servira à chauffer quelque 400 ménages.

L'idée à l'arrière-plan est bien sûr de rendre à l'avenir les Pays-Bas moins tributaires des énergies fossiles telles que le charbon et le gaz, mais le toit, composé de verre trempé et d'une multitude de cellules photovoltaïques, prouve en même temps que le consommateur n'a pas à se soucier de son approvisionnement pendant les sombres journées d'hiver puisque les manques sont vite comblés. Mieux encore: grâce à la réalisation d'un toit de panneaux solaires d'une telle ampleur, les végétaux fragiles des régions méditerranéennes peuvent être exposés à la Floriade.

C'est une succession de pans de verre inclinés dont la disposition rappelle le feuillage d'un arbre. La lumière filtrée est projetée sur la flore. A titre de précision: les panneaux sont constitués d'une mosaïque de cellules solaires et de particules de verre transparent avec un minimum de croi-

biomass combustion among the 'renewable' energy sources. They are unlike fossil fuel energy technologies (coal and oil power stations) because they do not use up the world's resources and they place much less strain on the environment.

Sustainability is the unspoken message of Floriade 2002, and it is now free of the back-to-nature image that dogged it in the 1980s. After all, green energy presupposes a consciousness of the quality of life and of the resources that sustain that quality. The message is not restricted to the six months of the Floriade, to just as long as the flowers are in bloom, but has a wider reach in time and space. The solar roof will power the greenhouses, kiosks and restaurants for the duration of Floridade with 2.3 Megawatts. After the show is over it will feed power to the Haarlemmermeer grid and meet the electricity needs of about 400 homes.

The idea behind all this is that the Dutch government plans to cut the country's consumption of energy generated from fossil fuels such as coal and natural gas. Meanwhile, the solar energy roof, with its armoured glass and countless solar cells, is a demonstration to the public that renewable energy doesn't mean having to suffer on a grim day in the middle of winter. What solar power cannot provide is made up from other sources. Due this enormous solar roof, moreover, it has now become possible include many sensitive Mediterranean species in the exhibition for the first time. The roof shelters them from the unkinder climate of Holland.

The roof consists of an array of sloping glass panels each bearing a specially-designed pattern of solar cells which suggest the leaves of a tree. Daylight filters between these 'leaves' onto the flora below. The frames of the panels and the connecting lines have been made as slender as

Sonnenstrom erwärmt die Floriade dank dieser Innovation des Energiekonzerns Nuon. Damit gehört er zusammen mit Windmühlen, Wasserkraftwerken und Verbrennung von Biomasse zur dauerhaften Energie, die anders als die fossilen Energiequellen (Gas, Kohle und Kernergie) keine Gefahr für den Weltvorrat bedeutet.

Dauerhaftigkeit ist die ungeschriebene Botschaft der Floriade 2002, die jedoch nicht in der alternativen Art und Weise der achtziger Jahre des letzten Jahrhunderts verkündet wird. Denn Dauerhaftigkeit setzt ja ein Bewusstsein für die Lebensqualität voraus und für die Quellen, die dieses Leben nähren. Das beschränkt sich nicht auf die sechs Monate der Floriade, die Blütezeit des Gartens, sondern sie reicht weiter und bleibt ebenso wenig auf den Ort beschränkt. Die Sonnenenergie mag dann für die Dauer der Floriade die Gewächshäuser, Kioske und Restaurants mit Strom versorgen (gut für 3 Millionen Kilowattstunden Strom); nach Ablauf wird das Dach in das Elektrizitätsnetzwerk von Haarlemmermeer aufgenommen und etwa 400 Haushalte erwärmen können: Dank des Daches können etwa 1000 Haushalte davon profitieren. Der dahinter liegende Gedanke ist natürlich, dass die Niederlande in der Zukunft weniger abhängig von den fossilen Energiequellen wie Kohle und Gas sein wollen, aber das Dach mit den Solarzellen zeigt dem Konsumenten nebenbei, dass er an einem grauen Wintertag keinen Hunger zu leiden braucht. Der Mangel wird ausgeglichen. Man könnte sogar sagen, dass es durch die Erfindung eines Sonnenkollektordachs in dieser Größe auf der Floriade möglich ist, empfindliche Pflanzen und Gewächse aus dem Mittelmeerraum zu präsentieren.

Es besteht aus einer Anreihung von schrägen Glashauben mit einem Muster, das an das Blattwerk von Bäumen erinnert. Es fällt ein gefiltertes Licht auf die Flora. Genau betrachtet sind die Kollektoren so aufgebaut,

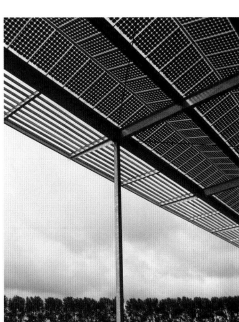

aluminiumlijntjes volgens de eenvoudige logica dat overal waar toevoer-
lijntjes zijn, geen zonnestroom kan worden opgewekt. Het rendement
van het dak moet per slot van rekening optimaal zijn. En dat niet alleen:
er moet de suggestie van een natuurlijke biotoop worden opgeroepen.
Het gevoel, de geur, de reuk en de aanraking, dat zijn de zintuigen die
geprikkeld worden, het zijn sensaties die de mens nader tot de natuur
brengt. Vergeten wordt in zo'n geval de techniek die sensaties mogelijk
maakt. Zoals er innovatief gewerkt is om de zonnepanelen een natuurlijk aanzien te geven, het fijnste soort silicium dat is gebruikt om het
grootst mogelijk effect te sorteren. En wie nog twijfelt aan rendement,
kan zich ter plekke laten overtuigen door educatieve displays over de
werking van het zonnepanelendak.
Dit overrompelende dak voedt een biotoop die van getemperd zonlicht
profiteert, en ook nog eens beschut ligt tegen de wind van zee.
De wereldreis is begonnen, een reis die in het teken staat van de
wisselwerking tussen mens en natuur. Onderweg zullen we de draag-
kracht van de zon nog tegenkomen, in de verlichting die reageert op
en met zonnecellen.

Als we de Arcadië-vallei overbruggen waar lage sparren voor enige
beschutting zorgen, vinden we, aan de rand van het Floriade-park een

**sillons et de poutrelles en aluminium, partant du principe logique que
tout élément opaque représente une perte d'espace où l'énergie solaire
n'est pas captée. Le but final du toit est en effet d'en tirer un maximum de
rendement. Et ce n'est pas tout: Il faut aussi y 'créer' un biotope naturel.
Les sens éveillés sont du domaine de la perception, des senteurs, du toucher; ce sont les sensations qui rapprochent l'être humain de la nature.
Mais n'oublions pas pour autant les efforts techniques déployés pour que
ces sensations puissent être perçues, par exemple: l'ingéniosité dont il a
fallu faire preuve pour que les panneaux solaires aient un aspect naturel,
l'utilisation du silicium le plus fin pour obtenir le meilleur effet possible.
Et quiconque douterait encore du rendement peut se laisser convaincre
par des visualisations éducatives expliquant le fonctionnement de la verrière de panneaux solaires. Ce toit impressionnant crée un biotope profi-
tant d'une douce lumière solaire tout en étant à l'abri des vents marins.
Le voyage autour du monde a commencé, sous le signe de l'interaction de
l'homme et de la nature. Nous verrons d'ailleurs plus tard d'autres formes
de mise à profit du soleil, par exemple dans l'éclairage déclenché et produit par des cellules solaires.**

**Quand nous traversons la vallée Arcadië, quelque peu protégés par des
épicéas de faible hauteur, nous trouvons une autre vallée en bordure du**

**possible, to reinforce the sensation of a subtropical forest canopy.
Vision, smell, taste and touch are the senses that bring us closer to
nature. And this is what the Floriade aims to do when it invites us to 'feel
the art of nature'. It is of course easy to forget the technology that makes
some of these sensations possible here. Not only is the innovative design
of the roof intended to give the most naturalistic possible feeling possible, but it uses the most advanced solar cell technology. Anyone who still
entertains doubts about the value of solar energy can wise up from the
educational displays that tell the story of the solar roof.
This awe-inspiring roof creates a biotope that is a mixture of sun and
shade, and where there is hardly any wind. Our world tour has begun,
a journey whose keynote is the interplay between mankind and nature.
We will come across the contribution of the sun again later, in the
automatic lighting which reacts to failing daylight and is powered by
solar cells.**

**Crossing the Arcadië Valley, where low fir trees provide some shelter,
we find another valley at the edge of the Floriade Park – the Valley of
the Senses. What's it like to be faced by plants that tower above you?
This is one of the many children's playgrounds where the youngsters
can literally enjoy the smell of nature.**

dass Zellen mit lichtdurchlässigen Glasstückchen abgewechselt werden,
wobei möglichst wenig Platz für Rahmen und Aluminiumlinien verschwen-
det wird, und zwar der einfachen Logik zufolge, wonach überall, wo Zufuhr-
linien sind, keine Sonne genutzt werden kann. Der Wirkungsgrad des
Dachs soll schließlich optimal sein. Und nicht nur das: Man möchte den
Eindruck eines natürlichen Biotops erwecken.
Fühlen, riechen, schmecken, berühren, das sind die Sinne, die stimuliert
werden, es sind Empfindungen, die der Mensch in der Beziehung zur Natur
erfahren will. In einem solchen Fall wird meistens die Technik vergessen,
die diese Empfindungen möglich macht. So wurde beispielsweise innovativ
gearbeitet, um den Solarpanelen ein natürliches Aussehen zu geben,
indem man die feinste Siliziumsorte verwendete, um so den größten Effekt
zu erzielen. Und wer immer noch am Nutzen zweifelt, kann sich an Ort und
Stelle von Displays über die Wirkung des Sonnenkollektordachs überzeu-
gen lassen.
Dieses imposante Dach erzeugt einen Biotop, der von gedämpftem Sonnenlicht profitiert und außerdem vor dem Meerwind geschützt ist. Die Weltreise
hat angefangen, eine Reise, die im Zeichen der Wechselwirkung zwischen
Mensch und Natur steht. Unterwegs werden wir der Leistungsfähigkeit der
Sonne noch begegnen, in der Beleuchtung, die auf die Solarzellen reagiert.

ander dal, de Vallei der Zinnen. Hoe is om oog in oog te staan met gewassen die groter zijn dan jezelf? Dit is een van de vele kinderspeelplaatsen waar de jeugd letterlijk kan ruiken aan de natuur. Een fysieke confrontatie, met hout, water of geurende bloemen.

Het Dak is een beschutte ontmoetingsplaats voor de professionals. Al meteen bij het begin van de reusachtige overkapping lopen we aan tegen het Floriade Green Trade Center waarin is opgenomen het Rabo Auditorium. De wanden zijn uit leem en stro opgetrokken. Het meubilair is al net zo *basic* als de constructie, hier voelen we letterlijk de band met de natuur, de geur van stro en hooi, de rauwe wanden van leem. Terug naar de natuur is ook het adagium dat de Nederlandse kwekers van vaste planten hanteren, als een groen verweer tegen een maatschappij die zich laat regeren door gsm en e-mail, in een tijd waarin de mens niet meer aan zichzelf toekomt. De sierteelt, met Boskoop als belangrijkste uitvalsbasis, waar het veen al eeuwen de ideale ondergrond is gebleken voor appelbomen en heesters, is een economische factor van belang. De Nederlandse bomenkwekers zijn de grootste exporteurs ter wereld: 70 procent van wat hier gekweekt wordt, vindt zijn weg over de grens, bijvoorbeeld naar de 'openbare groenmarkt' (plantsoenen en parken). Eens in de tien jaar fungeert de Floriade als enorme etalage van know how en ontwikkelingen in de

parc Floriade: la Vallée des Sensations. Quelle impression suscite le fait de se trouver en face de végétaux plus hauts que nous? C'est l'une des nombreuses aires de jeux où les enfants reniflent littéralement la nature et sont en contact physique avec le bois, l'eau ou les fleurs odoriférantes. La Verrière est aussi l'abri des rendez-vous professionnels. Dès le début de notre promenade sous cette couverture gigantesque, nous nous trouvons devant le Green Trade Center de la Floriade hébergeant l'Auditorium Rabo. Les parois sont en argile et en paille. Le mobilier est aussi élémentaire que la construction, nous percevons littéralement le lien avec la nature, l'odeur de la paille et du foin, le brut des parois d'argile. Le retour à la nature est aussi le leitmotiv des producteurs néerlandais de plantes vivaces, en signe de réticence verte contre une société se laissant gouverner par les téléphones portables et le courrier électronique, à une époque où l'être humain n'a plus de temps pour lui-même. L'horticulture ornementale, avec Boskoop comme principal centre où la tourbe, depuis des siècles, s'est avérée idéale pour les pommiers et les arbustes, est un facteur économique de grand intérêt. Les arboriculteurs néerlandais sont les plus grands exportateurs du monde: 70% de la production est expédié au-delà des frontières, par exemple sur le marché des espaces verts (parcs et massifs). Tous les dix ans, la Floriade fait office d'énorme vitrine du savoir-faire et des progrès de l'horticulture ornementale; c'est l'heure

It is a sensory confrontation wood, water and the perfume of flowers. **The Roof is a sheltered meeting point for the professionals. Immediately we enter the gigantic canopy, we run into the Floriade Green Trade Centre, which includes the Rabo Auditorium. The walls are made of mud and straw, and the furniture is just as basic. Here we literally feel a bond with nature, with the smell of the straw and the roughness of the daubed walls. 'Back to nature' would also seem to be the motto of the Dutch perennial plant breeders, an ecological answer to a society in the sway of mobile phones and e-mail – an age when people have no time to stop and think. Ornamental plant breeding takes place predominantly in a region centring around Boskoop, a village near Gouda, where for centuries the peaty soil has proved an ideal substrate for apple trees and ornamental shrubs. It is an industry of some importance to the Dutch economy, for these tree nurserymen are the largest exporters of their products in the world. Seventy percent of the plants bred here end up across the border, for example to satisfy the needs of the public gardens and parks market. Once every ten or so years, the Floriade acts as a gigantic shop window for know-how and innovations in ornamental plants. It a moment when this nation of merchants turns up with a batch of new products. The Floriade forms a bridge between the consumer and the 'wholesale' market. After all, a conifer is just as happy in a public garden as in a pri-**

Wenn wir das Arcadië-Tal überbrücken, wo niedrige Tannen für Schutz sorgen, finden wir am Rande des Floriade-Parks ein anderes Tal, das Tal der Sinne. Was ist es für ein Gefühl, wenn man vor Gewächsen steht, die größer sind als man selbst? Dies ist einer der zahlreichen Kinderspielplätze, wo die Jugend im wahrsten Sinne des Wortes an der Natur riechen kann. Eine physische Konfrontation mit Holz, Wasser oder duftenden Blumen.

Das Dach ist ein geschützter Treffpunkt für die Professionals. Schon sofort am Anfang der überdachung stoßen wir auf das 'Floriade Green Trade Center', in dem sich das Rabo-Auditorium befindet. Die Wände wurden aus Lehm und Stroh errichtet. Das Mobiliar ist genauso einfach wie die Konstruktion, hier fühlen wir buchstäblich das Band mit der Natur, den Geruch von Stroh und Heu, die rauen Wände aus Lehm. Zurück zur Natur lautet auch die Devise der niederländischen Züchter von Dauerpflanzen, die einem grünen Widerstand gegen eine Gesellschaft ähnelt, die sich von gsm und E-Mail regieren läßt, in einer Zeit, in der der Mensch nicht mehr zu sich selbst kommt. Der Anbau von Zierpflanzen, mit Boskoop als wichtigstem Zentrum, wo sich das Moor schon seit Jahrhunderten als idealer Untergrund für Apfelbäume und Sträucher erwiesen hat, ist ein wichtiger wirtschaftlicher Faktor. Die niederländischen Baumzüchter sind die größten Exporteure der Welt: 70 Prozent dessen, was hier gezüchtet wird, findet seinen Weg über die Grenze, zum Beispiel zum 'öffentlichen Grünmarkt'

sierteelt, het is het moment waarop de handelsnatie even de kop opsteekt met een nieuwe oogst aan producten.

Op de Floriade wordt een brug geslagen tussen de consument en de 'markt'. Uiteindelijk houden coniferen zich net zo goed op in het openbaar groen als in de particuliere tuin. Uit onderzoek is gebleken dat de consument zijn tuin weer wil gebruiken als afleiding van de dagelijkse stress. De tuin als centrum van bezinning, maar ook als dynamisch middelpunt, we zullen het op een andere plek in de Floriade tegenkomen waar enkele tuinen een ander appèl doen op het gevoel. Per seizoen tekent zich dan ook nog een nuancering af: tijdens de zomer volgen de vaste planten het ritme van de dag, terwijl het najaar logischerwijs een contemplatief beeld laat zien. Van een regenboog aan kleuren verschuift het accent naar vormen, geboetseerd door ingenieus snoeiwerk.

De Kas van de Toekomst

Geen Floriade of er worden uitvindingen getoond, die direct te maken hebben met de kwaliteit van onze omgeving of die een nieuwe visie tentoonspreiden over onze landschappelijke inrichting. Elke Floriade is daarin uniek, dus niet te vergelijken met de voorgaande afleveringen en bij voorkeur geen blauwdruk voor die van 2012. Internet, nog afwezig in 1992, kan de Floriade dichterbij brengen in Brazilië of Canada,

où le pays met à l'affiche sa bosse du commerce avec une nouvelle moisson de produits.

La Floriade jette un pont entre le consommateur et le 'marché' car en fin de compte, les conifères se plaisent aussi bien dans les espaces verts que dans les jardins des particuliers. Maintes analyses ont montré que l'individu cherche à s'évader du stress quotidien dans son jardin. Le jardin centre de réflexion mais aussi de dynamisme, la Floriade nous donnera l'occasion d'y revenir ailleurs, là où plusieurs jardins font un autre appel aux sensations. Chaque saison apporte en soi une nuance distincte: en été, les plantes vivaces suivent le rythme de la journée alors que l'image est logiquement plus contemplative à l'automne. L'accent posé d'abord sur un arc-en-ciel de couleurs passe ensuite sur les formes sculptées résultant de tailles ingénieuses.

La Serre de l'Avenir

Une Floriade ne saurait être sans qu'y soient exposées des innovations se rapportant directement à la qualité de notre environnement ou témoignant d'une nouvelle optique de l'aménagement du paysage. A ce propos, chaque Floriade est unique en son genre; celle-ci est donc incomparable aux éditions précédentes et de préférence, ne se révélera pas avoir été la matrice de la Floriade de 2012. Internet, phénomène encore absent en

vate one. **Research has shown that consumers need their gardens as a means of coping with the stress of daily life. The garden as a place to come to one's senses, but also as a dynamic focus, is something we shall meet at a different spot in the Floriade, where several gardens make a different appeal to the feelings. There are also gradual shifts with the seasons. In summer, the perennials follow the fixed rhythm of the day, but autumn logically presents a more contemplative picture. The emphasis shifts from a dazzling array of colour to shapes, sculpted by ingenious pruning.**

The Glasshouse of the Future

The Floriade would not be the Floriade without at least one new invention on display which has a direct bearing on the quality of our environment or which conveys a new outlook on the look of the Dutch landscape. Every Floriade is unique in that respect, dissimilar from the last and anything but a blueprint for the next (so we hold out hope for 2012). The Internet, which was nowhere to be seen in 1992, now brings the Floriade closer for the stay-at-homes in Brazil or Canada; it conjures the wealth of blooms through cyberspace so that we can study them without actually having to walk through the exhibition.

In the same way as Les Halles used to be the larder of Paris, with all the

(Grünanlagen und Parks). Alle zehn Jahre fungiert die Floriade als riesiges Schaufenster von Know-how und Entwicklungen im Anbau von Zierpflanzen; es ist der Moment, in dem sich die Handelsnation mit einer neuen Ernte an Produkten präsentiert.

Auf der Floriade wird eine Brücke zwischen dem Konsumenten und dem 'Markt' geschlagen. Letztendlich halten sich Nadelbäume genauso gut in öffentlichen Grünanlagen wie im privaten Garten. Untersuchungen haben ergeben, dass der Konsument seinen Garten wieder als Ablenkung vom täglichen Stress benutzen will. Der Garten als Zentrum der Einkehr, aber auch als dynamischer Mittelpunkt; wir werden ihm an einem anderen Ort in der Floriade begegnen, wo einige Gärten wieder anders an das Gefühl appellieren. Je nach Saison zeichnet sich dann auch noch eine Nuancierung ab: Im Sommer folgen die Dauerpflanzen dem Tagesrhythmus, während der Herbst logischerweise ein kontemplatives Bild zeigt.

Von einem Regenbogen an Farben verschiebt sich der Akzent zu Formen, die durch ingeniöses Stutzen modelliert worden sind.

Das Gewächshaus der Zukunft

Keine Floriade, auf der nicht Erfindungen vorgestellt werden, die in einem direkten Zusammenhang mit der Qualität unserer Umgebung stehen oder die ein neues Konzept unserer landschaftlichen Einrichtung vorstellen. Jede

het tovert de bloemenpracht virtueel zonder dat je daadwerkelijk op de tentoonstelling hoeft te wandelen.

Zoals de Hallen ooit de buik van Parijs waren waar al het voedsel voor de hoofdstad lag opgeslagen, zo is Nederland uitgegroeid tot de boomgaard/kas/weide van Europa. Op de kleinst denkbare oppervlak wordt een ongehoorde hoeveelheid gewassen geteeld die hun weg vinden over de hele wereld. Van paprika's tot snijbloemen, van tomaten tot bolgewassen. Dat is te danken aan een enorme efficiency die is bereikt, onder meer door het beter benutten van de milieucondities in een tuinbouwkas. De productiewaarde voor snijbloemen ligt op 5 miljard gulden per jaar, die voor potplanten op 2 miljard: Nederland is ook hierin veruit de grootste exporteur. Dat komt door die vergrote efficiency die bijvoorbeeld wordt bereikt door de fusies van enkele Zuid-Hollandse veilingen in een enorme Veiling Holland.

En opnieuw wordt er een hoofdstuk toegevoegd aan die ontwikkeling. De Kas van de Toekomst die de Land- en Tuinbouworganisaties van Nederland laten zien is op het eerste gezicht een conventionele kas. Gerbera's en tomaten geteeld op substraat, we kijken er niet meer van op. Kleigrond zien of voelen ze al jaren niet meer. Aan die conventionele kas zijn twee kassen toegevoegd die wel degelijk een andere presentatie op de tuinbouwteelt laten zien, een van kunststof glas en een van gehard glas. Essentieel is bijvoorbeeld het doelmatig gebruik van de ruimte, waardoor de looppaden tussen de tray's met gewassen zijn geschrapt. Niet de kweker beweegt maar het gekweekte beweegt dankzij een gemotoriseerd systeem, zodat de pluk in een hoek van de kas kan plaatsvinden.

1992, met la Floriade à portée des Brésiliens et des Canadiens qui pourront admirer cet univers florissant et se promenant virtuellement dans les allées de l'exposition.

Telles les Halles qui furent jadis le garde-manger de Paris où toutes les vivres de la capitale étaient stockés, les Pays-Bas sont devenus le verger / la serre / le champ de l'Europe. Une incroyable quantité de végétaux ayant leurs débouchés dans le monde entier sont cultivés sur la plus petite superficie concevable. Des poivrons aux fleurs coupées, des tomates aux bulbes... Et ce, grâce à une productivité phénoménale due entre autres à une meilleure mise à profit des conditions climatiques dans les serres horticoles. La production des fleurs coupées se chiffre à 5 milliards de florins par an, celle des plantes en pots à 2 milliards: les Pays-Bas sont aussi et de loin le plus grand exportateur de fleurs et plantes. C'est le résultat d'un summum de rationalisation dont l'un des exemples est la fusion de plusieurs marchés floraux de la Hollande méridionale en une seule grosse coopérative de vente: Veiling Holland.

Poursuivant cette marche vers le progrès, une nouvelle étape est franchie. La Serre de l'Avenir présentée par les organisations agricoles et horticoles des Pays-Bas est à première vue une serre conventionnelle. En effet, nous ne sommes plus surpris de voir des gerberas et des tomates poussant sur un substrat. Il y a belle lurette que les cultures ont abandonné l'argile. Mais à cette serre traditionnelle ont été ajoutées deux serres, l'une en Plexiglas et l'autre en verre trempé, qui nous montrent l'horticulture sous un autre angle. L'un des principes essentiels est de tirer un maximum de profit de l'espace disponible, c'est pourquoi les allées entre les clayettes de végétaux ont été supprimées. Ce n'est plus le producteur

capital city's food warehoused and traded there, the Netherlands has grown into the orchard, glasshouse and meadow of Europe. An incredible quantity of nursery products which eventually find their way all over the globe, are cultivated in the smallest possible area – bell peppers, cut flowers, tomatoes, bulbs. This success is due to the immense efficiency the industry has reached, for example by the clever control of glasshouse conditions. The value of cut flowers produced is some two thousand million Euros per annum, and potted plants reach nearly half that amount. The export volume of these products is also the highest in the world. The industry is also reaping benefits of scale due to company mergers: numerous small wholesalers in the South Holland region – known as the 'flower auctioneers' – teamed up to form a gigantic company called Veiling Holland.

Another chapter has now been added to this story. The Glasshouse of the Future is presented by the joint agricultural and horticultural organizations of the Netherlands. At first sight it is a conventional commercial greenhouse. Gerberas and tomatoes thriving on an artificial substrate – nothing new about that. After all, their roots have not touched ordinary soil for years. However, two glasshouses have been added on to the conventional one, and each has something new to show us. One has windows of plastic and the other of toughened glass. The first thing that strikes us in both glasshouses is the efficient use of space. The corridors between the trays have been eliminated. The nurseryman does not go to the crop but the crop comes to the nurseryman on a motorized production line. Work like planting and harvesting all takes place in one corner of the glasshouse. The panes of toughened glass are less prone to hailstorm

Floriade ist darin einzigartig, also in keiner Weise mit ihren Vorgängern zu vergleichen und vorzugsweise kein Blaudruck für die von 2012. Das Internet, das im Jahr 1992 noch abwesend war, kann die Floriade beispielsweise Brasilien oder Kanada näher bringen, es zaubert die Blumenpracht virtuell hervor, ohne dass man tatsächlich auf der Ausstellung spazieren muss.

Wie die Hallen einmal der Bauch von Paris waren, wo Nahrungsmittel für die Hauptstadt lagerten, so haben sich die Niederlande zu einer Art Obstgarten-Gewächshaus-Wiese von Europa entwickelt. Auf der denkbar kleinsten Oberfläche wird eine unvorstellbare Menge Gewächse gezüchtet, die in die ganze Welt exportiert werden, von Paprikas bis Schnittblumen, von Tomaten bis Zwiebelgewächsen. Dies verdankt man einer enormen Effizienz, die man unter anderem durch die bessere Nutzung von Umweltbedingungen im Gartenbau-Gewächshaus erreicht hat. Der Produktionswert für Schnittblumen liegt bei 5 Milliarden Gulden pro Jahr, der für Topfpflanzen bei 2 Milliarden: die Niederlande sind auch auf dem Gebiet der bei weitem größte Exporteur. Das kommt durch die erhöhte Effizienz, die beispielsweise durch die Fusionen einiger südholländischer Versteigerungen zur riesigen 'Versteigerung Holland' erreicht werden konnte.

Dieser Entwicklung wird ein weiteres Kapitel hinzugefügt. Beim Gewächshaus der Zukunft, das die Land- und Gartenbauorganisationen der Niederlande vorstellen, handelt es sich auf den ersten Blick um ein konventionelles Gewächshaus. Auf Substrat gezüchtete Gerbera und Tomaten bringen uns nicht mehr zum Staunen; Lehmboden wird schon seit Jahren nicht mehr verwendet. Dem konventionellen Gewächshaus wurden zwei Gewächshäuser hinzugefügt, die eine völlig andere Präsentation der Gartenbauzucht zeigen: eine aus Kunststoffglas und eine aus gehärtetem

Kas van de toekomst
La Serre de l'Avenir
Gewächshaus der Zukunft
The Glasshouse of the Future

Het oppervlak van gehard glas is beter bestand tegen een hagelbui. Maar de belangrijkste innovatie is zo goed als onzichtbaar. Het is de regulering van de luchtvochtigheid in de kas. Het vocht dat verdampt, wordt opgeslagen in de grond, zodat de tuinder in de winter zijn tekort aan warmte kan aanvullen. Deze gesloten kas vergt minder energiegebruik en fourneert meer CO_2. Verschillende gewassen worden volgens dit nieuwe systeem gepresenteerd zoals tomaten, paprika's, komkommers, rozen, fresia's, chrysanten, gerbera's, en potplanten. Ze gedijen niet door het gebruik van chemische bestrijdingsmiddelen maar door het effectief inzetten van insecten. En het blijft niet bij het presenteren van de nieuwe kweekmethode: in het bijbehorende restaurant laten we de zo gekweekte gewassen over de tong gaan. Waarmee inherent een boodschap wordt afgegeven dat de consument ook nadrukkelijker wil weten waar de wortels van zijn maaltijd liggen. Duurzaamheid is een issue, zeker, maar eerlijkheid eveneens.

Tienduizend hectare wordt in Nederland in beslag genomen door kassen, met grote concentraties in het Westland, bij Aalsmeer, en recentelijk ook in Zuidoost-Drente of Noord-Limburg. De kas is niet meer weg te denken in het landschap. Maar steeds vaker klinkt de roep om het areaal te beperken of anderszins te verfraaien. De integratie van wonen, werken in een natuurlijke omgeving gaat ook aan de tuinbouw niet voorbij. Deze kas wil door zijn uiterlijk geen vreemde eend in de bijt zijn, maar een bestanddeel van het landschap. Om te illustreren dat we in de toekomst niet zonder deze gewasvoorziening kunnen. Het belang van planten, zo wil het Bloemenbureau Holland onderstrepen door verschillende presentaties op de Floriade, heeft niet alleen een economische, werkgelegenheidstechnische basis. Het pro-

qui se déplace mais le produit qui est convoyé par un système automatisé, si bien que la récolte se fait dans un coin de la serre. Le verre trempé craint moins les averses de grêle. Mais la plus importante des innovations est presque imperceptible à la vue puisqu'il s'agit de la régulation de l'humidité ambiante dans la serre. L'humidité qui s'évapore dans la serre est stockée dans le sol, la chaleur est récupérée pour qu'en hiver l'horticulteur puisse combler un manque. Cette serre en circuit fermé consomme moins d'énergie et fournit plus de CO_2. Diverses cultures y sont présentées: tomates, poivrons, concombres, roses, freesias, chrysanthèmes, gerberas et plantes en pots. Les cultures poussent sainement, non pas à coups de produits phytosanitaires mais protégées par l'action programmée et effective de prédateurs. Et nous n'en restons pas à la présentation d'une nouvelle méthode culturale car les végétaux ainsi cultivés se dégustent aussi dans le restaurant attenant. Le message: le consommateur tient fermement à remonter aux racines de son alimentation. Si la durabilité est d'actualité, la transparence ne l'est pas moins. Les serres couvrent aux Pays-Bas une superficie de dix mille hectares, avec de grosses concentrations dans le Westland, du côté d'Aalsmeer et récemment aussi dans le Sud-Ouest de la Drenthe et dans le Nord du Limbourg. Les serres font désormais vraiment partie du paysage bien que des voix s'élèvent de plus en plus souvent pour réduire la surface de serriculture ou pour agrémenter autrement le paysage. L'intégration de l'habitat et de la vie active dans un entourage naturel n'est pas sans impact sur l'horticulture. Cette serre veut justement par son aspect mieux s'intégrer au paysage et en devenir un élément essentiel, illustrant ainsi qu'à l'avenir nous serons dépendants de ce type d'abri pour les cultures. Comme le souligne l'Office hollandais des Fleurs à la Floriade par

damage. The greatest innovation is an invisible one, however. It is the humidity control in the closed system of the glasshouse interior. Water that evaporates from the plants is condensed and stored underground in tanks, which also form a store of heat for the winter. The concentration of CO_2 in the air is also maintained at a controlled level. The Floriade presents a variety of crops which can be cultivated in this new system, such as tomatoes, peppers, cucumbers, roses, freesias, chrysanthemums, gerberas and potted plants. They system enables a more organic approach to cultivation – for example, the use of insects to eliminate crop pests instead of chemical pesticides. In the nearby restaurant, we can taste the excellent fruit and vegetables cultivated by this new method. This brings home the point is that we want to have a better idea of where our food comes from. Organic food is not just about protecting the environment, but also about honesty in food production.

Ten thousand hectares of the Dutch countryside are occupied by glasshouses. There are major concentrations in Westland and near Aalsmeer, and more recently in South-East Drenthe and North Limburg. It is hard to imagine how these landscapes looked before the arrival of the glass horticulturalists. Increasingly, however, voices are being raised to restrict the area of land covered by these structures, or at least to improve their appearance in some way. The integration of housing, employment and the natural environment has had quite an impact on glasshouse horticulture. The designers of this glasshouse have made a conscious attempt at changing it from an eyesore into an integral part of the landscape. After all, glasshouses still will be a necessary evil in the Dutch countryside for a long time to come. The usefulness of plants, as Bloemenbureau Holland aims to convince us by its presentations at the Floriade, is not merely a

Glas. Wesentlich ist zum Beispiel die zweckmäßige Nutzung des Raums, was zur Folge hatte, dass die Laufgänge zwischen den Kästen mit den Gewächsen abgeschafft wurden. Nicht der Züchter bewegt sich, sondern dank eines motorisierten Systems das Gezüchtete, so dass das Pflücken in einer Ecke des Gewächshauses stattfinden kann.

Sogar eine Hagelschauer macht der Oberfläche aus gehärtetem Glas nichts aus. Aber die wichtigste Innovation ist so gut wie unsichtbar. Es ist die Regulierung der Luftfeuchtigkeit im Gewächshaus. Die Feuchtigkeit, die verdampft, wird im Boden gespeichert, so dass der Gärtner im Winter seinen Mangel an Wärme ausgleichen kann. Dieses geschlossene Gewächshaus ist sparsamer im Energieverbrauch und sorgt für mehr CO_2. Mit diesem neuen System werden verschiedene Gewächse wie Tomaten, Paprika, Gurken, Rosen, Freesien, Chrysanthemen, Gerbara und Topfpflanzen gezüchtet. Sie gedeihen nicht durch die Verwendung von chemischen Schädlingsbekämpfungsmitteln, sondern durch den wirkungsvollen Einsatz von Insekten. Und es bleibt nicht bloß bei der Präsentation der neuen Züchtungsmethode: in dem dazugehörigem Restaurant kann man die so gezüchteten Gewächse selbst kosten. Damit wird deutlich gemacht, dass immer mehr Konsumenten wissen wollen, woher die Produkte, die sie verzehren, stammen. Haltbarkeit ist sicher ein Thema, aber Ehrlichkeit genauso.

In den Niederlanden werden zehntausend Hektar von Gewächshäusern in Beschlag genommen, wobei die größte Konzentrationen im Westland bei Aalsmeer und seit kurzem auch in Südost-Drente oder Nord-Limburg liegt. Man kann sich die Landschaft ohne die Gewächshäuser schon gar nicht mehr vorstellen. Aber immer häufiger werden Stimmen laut, die das Areal begrenzen oder auf irgendeine Weise verschönern wollen. Die Integration von wohnen und arbeiten in einer natürlichen Umgebung macht auch vor

Bij het Dak
Près de la Coupole
Am Dach
Near the Roof

ject *Plants for People*, te zien op een van de eilanden in de Groene Stad, toont aan dat potplanten in kantoren er niet alleen hoeven te staan als decoratief object of als alternatieve asbak. Uit onderzoeken is gebleken dat planten (en ook snijbloemen) toxische stoffen uit het binnenmilieu kunnen wegfilteren, waardoor het welzijn van het personeel opknapt. Irritaties van de luchtwegen vanwege een droge lucht zouden met een gerichte vegetatie op kantoor verleden tijd kunnen zijn. Waarmee 'feel the art of nature' ook binnen betekenis zou kunnen krijgen.

diverses présentations, l'importance des plantes n'a pas pour seule assise l'économie ou le marché de l'emploi. Le projet *Les Plantes et les Hommes* (*Plants for People*), situé sur l'une des îles de la Ville Verte, montre que les plantes en pots dans les bureaux peuvent être plus qu'un simple élément décoratif ou un cendrier de secours. En effet, il ressort d'études que les plantes (et les fleurs coupées) filtrent des substances toxiques du milieu ambiant et sont donc bénéfiques au bien-être du personnel. Les irritations des voies respiratoires dues à la sécheresse ambiante pourraient être révolues en agrémentant les bureaux d'une végétation appropriée. 'Vivre l'art de la nature' pourrait donc également s'appliquer à l'intérieur des locaux.

matter of profit or of employment opportunities. The project 'Plants for People', which we can see on one of the Islands in the Green City, reminds us that potted plants in office interiors are more than just decorative elements (or alternative ashtrays, if you insist). Research has shown that plants and cut flowers are capable of filtering harmful components from the internal atmosphere, thereby benefiting the well-being of the employees. Well-deployed vegetation could make respiratory irritations caused by dry air a thing of the past. 'Feel the art of nature' could be a good principle to apply to building interiors.

dem Gartenbau nicht halt. Das Gewächshaus will durch sein Äußeres kein Fremdkörper sein, sondern ein Bestandteil der Landschaft. Um zu illustrieren, dass wir auch in der Zukunft nicht auf diese Einrichtung für Gewächse verzichten können. Die Bedeutung von Pflanzen, wie das Blumenbüro Holland durch verschiedene Präsentationen auf der Floriade betont, besteht nicht nur aus einer wirtschaftlichen Basis zur Arbeitsbeschaffung. Das Projekt *'Plants for People'*, das auf einer der Inseln in der Grünen Stadt zu sehen ist, weist nach, dass sowohl Topfpflanzen als auch Schnittblumen toxische Stoffe aus Räumen wegfiltern können, wodurch sich das Wohlbefinden des Personals verbessert. Mit einer gezielten Vegetation im Büro könnten Irritationen der Luftwege wegen einer trockenen Luft zur Vergangenheit gehören. Womit 'feel the art of nature' auch im Innenraum eine wichtige Rolle spielen kann.

Bomen

Sinds mensenheugenis zijn bomen de gidsen in het landschap geweest. Machtige eikebomen, robuuste dennen, slanke cypressen en vele andere soorten bomen hebben duizenden jaren lang de weg gewezen aan hele volksstammen op reis. In een wereld waarin bomen vaak het hoogste punt in het landschap vormden waren zij als herkenningspunt van onschatbare waarde en daarvan is heel lang dankbaar gebruik gemaakt.

Op deze Floriade komen alle functies die bomen door de eeuwen heen vervuld hebben samen: bomen zijn de pijlers waarop de leukste tuin van Nederland gebouwd is.

In dit poldergebied zijn het natuurlijk de landschappelijke bomen die het minste opvallen omdat zij van nature in deze streek thuishoren en ook op allerlei andere plekken in de wijde omgeving voorkomen. Toch vormen zij een belangrijk onderdeel van het groene raamwerk van deze Floriade en begeleiden zij de bezoekers op hun wandeling door de diverse deelgebieden.

Populieren, elzen en wilgen in diverse verschijningsvormen wisselen elkaar af en maken op markante punten ruimte voor exoten, bomen die van origine niet in dit gebied thuishoren. Juist door die plotselinge aanwezigheid van een afwijkend type boom wordt de aandacht op zo'n plek gevestigd, zoals dat ook altijd gebeurd is in de ontwikkeling van het Nederlandse landschap. Niet voor niets werd in het rivierengebied of op de hoge zandgronden bij rijke hereboeren een rode beuk of een paardenkastanje in de voortuin geplant als blikvanger in een verder door populieren of eiken gedomineerd gebied.

Hier op de Floriade wordt die traditie voortgezet. Waar in het deelgebied 'bij het Dak' de basis van het bomenbestand gevormd wordt door Salix alba 'Barlo' (schietwilg), Populus tremula (ratelpopulier), Alnus cordata (Italiaanse els)

Trees

Trees have been our guides in the landscape from time immemorial. Mighty oaks, sturdy pine trees, slender cypresses and countless other trees have served as landmarks for whole tribes of travellers over thousands of years. Trees were particularly valuable in a region like the Low Countries, where they were generally the tallest things to be seen, and people long made grateful use of them to find their way.

At this Floriade, all the functions that trees have served through the ages come together. Trees are the pillars on which Holland's Most Gorgeous Garden is founded. The kinds of trees which flourish naturally in the polder conditions – poplar, ash and willow – understandably do not attract much attention here; after all, you can see them almost anywhere in this region. Nonetheless, they form an important part of the green framework of this Floriade, and they guide us on our walk from one part of the park to another.

Poplars, ash trees and willows alternate in countless different variants. At prominent points, they make way for exotics. It is the sudden presence of a tree of a kind that does not normally appear in this region that makes a particular place stick in your memory – as was always true in Holland in the days before signposts. That is why wealthy farmers in the river plains and low sandy hills of the Netherlands used to plant copper beeches or horse chestnuts before their farmstead. You could spot these trees miles away in an area otherwise dominated by poplar and oak.

This ancient tradition has been given a new lease of life in the Floriade. The basic stock of trees near the Roof consists of Salix alba 'Barlo' (White Willow), Populus tremula (Aspen), Alnus cordata (Italian

Les arbres

Depuis toujours, les arbres ont joué le rôle de guides dans le paysage. Des chênes imposants, de robustes sapins, de sveltes cyprès et beaucoup d'autres encore indiquaient pendant des milliers d'années la route à de nombreux peuples itinérants. Dans un site où les arbres étaient souvent les plus hauts points du paysage, ils constituaient des repères inestimables dont il a été fait usage très longtemps.

Cette Floriade réunit toutes les fonctions qu'ont remplies les arbres au fil des temps: les arbres sont les piliers autour desquels a été réalisé le jardin le plus passionnant des Pays-Bas.

Les arbres à caractère paysager sont bien sûr ceux qui se remarquent le moins dans cette région de polders puisque c'est leur habitat naturel et qu'ils peuplent aussi les alentours. Ils constituent pourtant un élément important du canevas vert de cette Floriade et conduisent les visiteurs dans leur promenade à travers les diverses parties du parc.

Les peupliers, les aulnes et les saules s'alternent dans des formes diverses et aux endroits les plus marquants, font place aux exotiques, c'est-à-dire aux arbres qui d'origine ne sont pas de la région. La présence soudaine d'un arbre de type différent attire justement l'attention sur l'endroit en question comme c'était toujours le cas dans l'évolution du paysage néerlandais. Ce n'est pas pour rien si, dans la région des rivières ou sur les hauteurs sablonneuses, les riches gentlemen-farmers plantaient et tape-à-l'œil devant leur maison un hêtre pourpre ou un marronnier d'Inde quand seuls des peupliers ou des chênes poussaient dans les alentours.

Cette tradition est perpétuée à la Floriade. Dans la partie du parc 'Près de la Coupole' où la végétation d'arbres se compose à la base de Salix alba 'Barlo' (saule blanc), de Populus tremula (tremble), d'Alnus cordata

Bäume

Seit Menschengedenken sind Bäume die Führer in der Landschaft gewesen. Mächtige Eichen, robuste Tannen, schlanke Zypressen und viele andere Baumarten haben ganzen Völkern jahrtausendelang den Weg gewiesen. In einer Welt, in der Bäume oft den höchsten Punkt in der Landschaft bildeten, waren sie als Erkennungspunkt von unschätzbarem Wert und davon wurde lange dankbar Gebrauch gemacht.

Auf dieser Floriade kommen alle Funktionen, die Bäume durch die Jahrhunderte hindurch erfüllt haben, zusammen: Bäume sind die Pfeiler, auf denen der schönste Garten der Niederlande errichtet worden ist. In diesem Poldergebiet sind es natürlich die landschaftlichen Bäume, die am wenigsten auffallen, weil sie von Natur aus in dieses Gebiet gehören und auch an allerlei anderen Stellen in der weiten Umgebung vorkommen. Dennoch bilden sie einen wichtigen Bestandteil des grünen Gerüsts von dieser Floriade und begleiten die Besucher auf ihrem Spaziergang durch die diversen Teilgebiete.

Pappeln, Erlen und Weiden in verschiedenen Erscheinungsformen wechseln sich gegenseitig ab und machen an markanten Punkten Platz für Exoten – Bäume, die ihrer Herkunft nach nicht in diesem Gebiet zuhause sind. Gerade durch diese plötzliche Anwesenheit eines abweichenden Baumtyps wird die Aufmerksamkeit auf einen solchen Ort gelenkt, so wie das auch immer in der Entwicklung der niederländischen Landschaft geschehen ist. Nicht umsonst wurde im Flussgebiet oder auf den hohen Sandböden bei reichen Herrenbauern eine Rotbuche oder eine Rosskastanie im Vorgarten als Blickfang in einem des weiteren von Pappeln oder Eichen dominiertem Gebiet gepflanzt.

Hier auf der Floriade wird diese Tradition fortgesetzt. Wo im Teilgebiet 'am Dach' die Basis des Baumbestandes von Salix alba 'Barlo' (Silberweide),

Schijnhazelaar
Corylopsis
Scheinhasel
Witch Hazel

Populieren
Peupliers
Pappeln
Poplars

Sierappel
Pommier d'ornement
Zierapfel
Ornamental Apple Tree

Den
Pin
Kiefer
Pine

Lijsterbes
Sorbier
Eberesche
Rowan

en Salix sepulcralis 'Tristis' (gele treurwilg) zijn het toch vooral de exoten die erop wijzen dat op deze plek heel veel bijzonders te verwachten valt.

Blikvangers aan de linkerzijde van het dak zijn Gleditsia triacanthos (Valse Christusdoorn) en Hippophae salicifolia 'Robert', een slanke boomvorm van de alom bekende duindoorn. En aan de hoofdroute links van de grote waterpartij zijn het flinke platanen (Platanus acerifolia) die de bezoeker op zijn wandeling begeleiden.
Specifieke aandacht verdient de beplanting onder het dak. Hier is in de beschutting van de overkapping een glooiend landschap geschapen waarin de Oostenrijkse den (Pinus nigra nigra) een hoofdrol vervult. Door flinke bosschages van deze indrukwekkende conifeer af te wisselen met soortgenoten als Abies grandis (Reuzenzilverspar), Pinus koraiensis, Pinus nigra 'Austriaca Fastigiata' en Chamaecyparis lawsoniana 'Imbricata Pendula' ontstaat een basis voor een mediterraan berglandschap. En dat landschap komt daadwerkelijk tot leven door toevoeging van soorten met een elegant zuidelijk voorkomen die het in een koude Hollandse winter niet gemakkelijk zouden hebben, maar zich in deze beschermde omgeving prima handhaven. Het meest winterhard zijn Sophora japonica (honingboom), Koelreuteria paniculata (lampionboom) en Pterostyrax hispida. Sierlijke bomen die in Nederland, dank zij het mildere klimaat van de laatste jaren, steeds vaker aangeplant worden in tuinen en parken. Albizzia julibrissin en Lagerstroemia indica gedijen alleen in de warmte van het Middellandse Zeeklimaat. Hier zijn ze als meerstammige heesters aangeplant, maar ze kunnen in hun eigen omgeving gemakkelijk tot boom uitgroeien.
De coupure in de Geniedijk vormt de poort tot het tweede parkdeel van de Floriade, 'naast de Berg'. Onder de hoge treurwilgen (Salix sepulcralis

(aulne) et de Salix sepulcralis 'Tristis' (saule pleureur jaune), tandis que les exotiques sont les signes précurseurs de l'insolite qui nous y attend.

Sur la gauche de la Coupole, ce sont le Gleditsia triacanthos (Fausse Epine du Christ) et l'Hippophae salicifolia 'Robert', une forme élancée de l'argousier bien connu, qui attirent d'abord les regards alors que sur l'allée principale à gauche du grand plan d'eau, le visiteur est guidé dans sa promenade par de gros platanes (Platanus acerifolia).
La végétation sous la Coupole mérite une attention particulière. A l'abri de la verrière, a été créé un paysage vallonné où le pin noir d'Autriche (Pinus nigra nigra) joue le rôle principal. L'essentiel d'un paysage montagneux méditerranéen a été réalisé en alternant de gros groupes de ces conifères impressionnants avec des congénères comme l'Abies grandis (Sapin de Vancouver), le Pinus koraiensis, le Pinus nigra 'Austriaca Fastigiata' et le Chamaecyparis lawsoniana 'Imbricata Pendula'. Le dynamisme est apporté par des espèces à l'élégance méridionale qui auraient normalement bien du mal à surmonter la rigueur de l'hiver hollandais mais qui se plaisent parfaitement dans ce cadre protégé. Les plus rustiques sont le Sophora japonica (arbre à miel), le Koelreuteria paniculata (savonnier) et le Pterostyrax hispida; le climat plus clément de ces dernières années permet de les planter de plus en plus souvent dans les jardins et les parcs des Pays-Bas. L'Albizzia julibrissin (arbre de soie) et le Lagerstroemia indica (lilas des Indes) se plaisent uniquement sous le doux climat méditerranéen. Ils ont été plantés ici en arbustes à plusieurs troncs mais peuvent facilement devenir de grands arbres dans leur milieu d'origine.
La coupure dans la Geniedijk donne accès à la deuxième partie du parc de

---

Alder) and Salix sepulcralis 'Tristis' (Weeping Willow). But it is the exotics among them that mark out the places where something special awaits us.
The eye-catchers at the left-hand side of the Roof are Gleditsia triacanthos (Honey Locust) and Hippophae salicifolia 'Robert', a slender tree-form of the Sea Buckthorn, which is common in the sand dunes along the Dutch coast. Alongside the main route to the left of the maze of pools and ditches, the handsome strangers who guide us on our way are rugged Plane trees (Platanus acerifolia).
The plant life under the Roof merits our special attention. Here, under the shelter of the canopy, we find a rolling landscape in which the dominant note is set by the Austrian Pine (Pinus nigra nigra). Alternating clumps of these impressive conifers with their cousins such as Abies grandis (Giant Fir), Pinus koraiensis, Pinus nigra 'Austriaca Fastigiata' and Chamaecyparis lawsonia 'Imbricata Pendula' forms the basis for a Mediterranean upland landscape. And this landscape really springs to life owing to species with an elegant southerly aspect, which would have a hard time of it in a cold Dutch winter but do just fine in this sheltered environment. The hardiest of these are Sophora japonica (Honey Tree), Koelreutaria paniculata (Lantern Tree) and Pterostyrax hispida. These are ornamental trees that have become increasingly common in Dutch gardens and parks, having survived in the relatively warm weather of recent years. Albizzia julibrissin and Lagerstroemia indica flourish only in a true Mediterranean climate. Here, they have been planted as bushy shrubs although they can easily reach tree size in their home conditions.
The gap in the Geniedijk forms the entrance to the second part of the

---

Populus tremula (Zitterpappel), Alnus cordata (Italienische Erle) und Salix sepulcralis 'Tristis' (Trauerweide) gebildet wird, sind es doch vor allem die Exoten, die andeuten, dass man an dieser Stelle etwas ganz Besonderes erwarten kann.
Blickfänger auf der linken Seite sind Gleditsia triacanthos (Lederhülsenbaum) und Hippophae salicifolia 'Robert', eine schlanke Baumform des allerorts bekannten Sanddorn. Und an der Hauptroute links von der großen Wasserpartie sind es kräftige Platanen (Platanus acerifolia), die den Besucher auf seinem Spaziergang begleiten.
Besondere Aufmerksamkeit verdient die Bepflanzung unter dem Dach. Hier wurde im Schutz der Überdachung eine Hügellandschaft geschaffen, in der die Schwarzkiefer (Pinus nigra nigra) eine Hauptrolle spielt. Indem man kräftige Baumgruppen dieser beeindruckenden Konifere mit Artgenossen wie Abies grandis (Abies-Tannen), Pinus koraiensis, Pinus nigra 'Austriaca Fastigiata' und Chamaecyparis lawsonia 'elmbricata Penduala' variiert, entsteht die Grundlage für eine mediterrane Berglandschaft. Diese Landschaft wird tatsächlich zum Leben erweckt durch Hinzufügung von Arten mit einem eleganten südlichen Äußeren, die es zwar in einem kalten holländischen Winter schwer hätten, sich in dieser geschützten Umgebung jedoch ausgezeichnet behaupten. Am meisten winterfest sind Sophora japonica (Japanischer Schnurbaum), Koelreuteria paniculata (Rispiger Blasenbaum) und Pterostyrax hispida, zierliche Bäume, die in den Niederlanden dank des milderen Klimas der letzten Jahre immer häufiger in Gärten und Parks angepflanzt werden. Albizzia julibrissin und Lagerstroemia indica gedeihen nur in der Wärme des Mittelmeerklimas. Hier werden sie als mehrstämmige Sträucher gesetzt, in ihrer eigenen Umgebung können sie jedoch problemlos zum Baum anwachsen.
Der Durchbruch im Geniedijk bildet das Tor zum zweiten Parkteil der

37

Sierkersen

Cerisier

Zierkirsche

Flowering Cherry

'Tristis') is het lastig om een keuze voor het vervolg van de wandeling te maken: van hieruit gaat de hoofdroute rechtsom over de promenade en is helemaal tot aan het derde deelgebied zichtbaar door een begeleidende aanplant van Alnus cordata (Italiaanse els). Links, op het dorpsplein van de Groene Stad, lonkt een grote, meerstammige plataan: een baken dat aangeeft dat daar opnieuw iets bijzonders aan de hand is. En nog verder naar links doemt een heus bos van zwarte dennen (Pinus nigra) op, dat allerlei geheimen lijkt te herbergen.

De vierkante vorm van de eilanden wordt behalve door hagen van wilg ook benadrukt door zogenaamde 'singels' van es (Fraxinus excelsior) en zwarte els (Alnus glutinosa). Hier hebben zij een puur representatieve functie, maar in het vroegere Nederlandse landschap werden zij vooral aangeplant vanwege de gebruikswaarde van het hout. Deze bomen kregen nooit de kans om volwassen te worden, maar sleten hun leven in hakhoutsingels waarin regelmatig gesnoeid en gezaagd werd. De es heeft bijzonder hard, elastisch hout en is buitengewoon geschikt voor de vervaardiging van handvaten en stelen van gereedschappen zoals spades en bijlen. In vroeger tijden werden bovendien de jonge twijgen gebruikt als wintervoedsel voor het vee. Het hout van de zwarte els is goed bestand tegen water en daarom worden klompen meestal van elzenhout gemaakt.
In het derde parkdeel van de Floriade wordt de sfeer bepaald door een meer dan 30 jaar oud populierenbos dat voornamelijk bestaat uit Populus x euramericana (Canadapopulier), af en toe onderbroken door groepen Salix alba (schietwilg) en Acer pseudoplatanus (gewone esdoorn).
Deze machtige bomen vormen het frame waarbinnen andere soorten bomen de kans krijgen om op redelijk beschutte plekken op te groeien. Het allervroegst in

la Floriade: 'A côté de la Colline'. Sous les hauts saules pleureurs (**Salix sepulcralis 'Tristis'**), il est difficile de décider par où poursuivre son chemin: l'allée principale continue à droite vers la promenade, bordée d'**Alnus cordata** (aulne à feuilles en cœur), elle se profile jusqu'à la troisième partie du parc. A gauche, sur la place centrale de la Ville Verte, un gros platane à plusieurs troncs nous salue: signe que l'insolite nous attend là aussi. Et encore plus à gauche se dresse une vraie forêt de pins noirs (**Pinus nigra**) semblant héberger toutes sortes de secrets.

La forme carrée des îles est accentuée non seulement par les haies de saules mais aussi par les bordures (singels) de frênes (**Fraxinus excelsior**) et d'aulnes communs (**Alnus glutinosa**). Ces arbres n'ont ici qu'une fonction purement décorative alors que d'antan, ils étaient surtout plantés pour en tirer du bois. Ils n'avaient jamais le temps de devenir adultes mais passaient leur vie dans les **singels** de bois de coupe où ils étaient fréquemment taillés ou sciés. Le bois du frêne particulièrement dur et extensible servait à fabriquer des poignées et des manches d'outils tels que les pelles et les haches. En plus, les jeunes pousses étaient autrefois données en fourrage hivernal au bétail. Le bois de l'aulne commun est très résistant à l'eau, aussi les sabots sont-ils souvent taillés dans ce type de bois.
L'ambiance de la troisième partie de la Floriade est définie par un bois de peupliers de plus de 30 ans d'âge comptant principalement des **Populus x euramericana** (peuplier du Canada), avec ici et là des groupes de **Salix alba** (saule blanc) et d'**Acer pseudoplatanus** (érable sycomore).
Ces superbes arbres forment une sorte de voûte sous laquelle d'autres essences peuvent se développer relativement à l'abri. Les plus précoces à se présenter dans la saison sont plusieurs cerisiers à fleurs, dont le **Prunus**

Floriade park, by the Hill. Pausing beneath the tall Weeping Willows (**Salix sepulcralis 'tristis'**), it is hard choose which way to take next. The main footpath turns right across the promenade and remains visible all the way up to the third part of the park, accompanied by a plantation of **Almus cordata** (Italian Alder). To the left, on the village green of the Green City, a large multi-stemmed Plane tree catches our eye. It is a beacon that tells us something special is going on that way. A dark coppice of Corsican Pine (**Pinus nigra**) holds out the promise of mysterious discoveries there.

The square shape of the Islands is emphasized by fringes of Willow and also by rows of Ash (**Fraxinus excelsior**) and Alder (**Alnus glutinosa**). Here their function is purely symbolic, but they used to be planted in the Dutch countryside for their wood. These trees never had the chance to reach adult size, but awaited their fate in coppices which were regularly pruned and felled. The Ash has a particularly hard, elastic wood which makes it excellent for the handles of tools such as spades and axes.
The young twigs of the Ash were also used as winter fodder for cattle.
The wood of the Alder is highly water resistant and has therefore always been the favourite material for Dutch clogs.
The mood of the third part of the Floriade park is set by a Poplar wood that has been there for over thirty years. It consists mainly of **Populus x euramericana** (Canadian Poplar) which are broken here and there by groups of **Salix alba** (White Willow) and **Acer pseudoplatanus** (Sycamore). These mighty trees make up a sheltering structure within which other species of tree can find spots to take root. The very first to make an showing in the season are a number of flowering cherries, includ-

Floriade: 'Neben dem Berg'. Unter den hohen Trauerweiden (Salix sepulcralis 'Tristis') fällt es schwer, eine Wahl für die Fortsetzung des Spaziergangs zu treffen; von hier aus verläuft die Hauptroute rechts über die Promenade und ist durch eine begleitende Anpflanzung von Alnus cordata (Italienische Erle) bis zum dritten Teilgebiet ganz sichtbar. Links auf dem Dorfplatz der Grünen Stadt prunkt eine große, mehrstämmige Platane: ein Zeichen dafür, dass es dort erneut etwas Besonderes gibt. Geht man weiter nach links, taucht ein echter Wald voller Schwarzkiefern (Pinus nigra) auf, der allerlei Geheimnisse zu bergen scheint.

Die viereckige Form der Inseln wird neben Weidehecken auch durch Reihen aus Gemeiner Esche (Fraxinus excelsior) und Schwarzerle (Alnus glutinosa) betont. Hier haben sie eine rein repräsentative Funktion, aber in früheren Zeiten pflanzte man sie in der niederländischen Landschaft vor allem wegen des Gebrauchswerts des Holzes an. Diese Bäume erhielten nie eine Chance zum Erwachsenwerden, sondern fristeten ihr Leben in Unterholzschneisen, in denen regelmäßig geschnitten und gesägt wurde. Die Esche hat ein besonders hartes, elastisches Holz und eignet sich hervorragend für die Anfertigung von Handgriffen und Stielen von Werkzeugen wie Spaten und Beilen. Früher wurden die jungen Zweige außerdem als Winterfutter für das Vieh verwendet. Das Holz der Schwarzerle ist sehr wasserfest, aus dem Grund werden Holzschuhe meistens aus Erlenholz hergestellt.
Im dritten Parkteil der Floriade wird die Atmosphäre von einem mehr als 30 Jahre alten Pappelwald bestimmt, der hauptsächlich aus Populus x euamericana (Kanadische Pappel) besteht, hier und da unterbrochen von Gruppen Salix alba (Silberweide) und Acer pseudoplatanus (Bergahorn). Diese mächtigen Bäume bilden das Gerüst, in dem andere Arten die Gelegenheit erhalten, an

Viburnum

Schijnhazelaar

Corylopsis

Scheinhasel

Witch Hazel

Populieren
Peupliers
Pappeln
Poplars

het seizoen presenteert zich een aantal sierkersen, waaronder Prunus sargentii, Prunus avium *(zoete kriek)* en Prunus 'Accolade'. *Met hun roze en
witte bloesem vormen zij een feestelijk lint langs de Europese landentuinen
aan de zuidkant van het meer.*
De tuinen van het Verre Oosten zouden zich geen betere blikvanger gewenst
kunnen hebben dan Metasequoia glyptostroboides *(watercypres)* en Taxodium distichum *(moerascipres). Beiden zijn het bladverliezende coniferen met
zo'n lange geschiedenis dat het bijna levende fossielen genoemd mogen worden.*

*Wie zijn weg via de pontonbrug vervolgt naar de andere kant van het water
komt aan in een heel ander soort wereld: die van de Nederlandse natuurgebie-
den. Een samenspel van vennetjes, stroompjes en drassige gronden waar naast
de oorspronkelijke wilgen en populieren ook de knotvormen voorkomen die zo
typerend zijn voor het Hollandse landschap. In deze omgeving is* Alnus spaethii 'Spaeth' *een opvallende verschijning. Een markante, snelgroeiende boom
die behoort tot de familie der elzen, maar hogere ogen gooit dan de anderen vanwege de vroege, talrijke katjes en de paarsrode herfstkleur van het blad.
Bij berken zijn het meestal juist de stammen die het meest opvallend zijn.
En dat die stammen nergens beter tonen dan tegen de geheimzinnige achter-
grond van een verwilderend bos is ook hier weer heel goed te zien. Langs de
randen van de natuurtuinen duikt de witte bast van* Betula utilis *en* Betula
jacquemontii *regelmatig op, als levend lichtpunt langs de route.*

De vleugelnoot (Pterocarya fraxinifolia) *is in ons land relatief onbekend.
En dat is misschien maar goed ook, want zo blijft de verrassing, wanneer je
ze weer eens ergens ziet staan, des te groter. In het deelgebied 'aan het Meer'
staan* Pterocarya's *op het hoogste punt van het bos, aan weerszijden van*

---

ing Prunus sargentii, Prunus avium *(Wild Cherry)* and Prunus
'Accolade'. *Their pink and white blossoms form a festive ribbon along
the gardens of the Countries of Europe on the south shore of the Lake.
The Gardens of the Far East could not wish for better eye-catchers than
the* Metasequoia glyptostroboides *(Dawn Redwood)* and Taxodium
distichum *(Swamp Cypress). Both of these deciduous conifers are of such
antiquity that we may practically call them living fossils.
Following the route over the pontoon bridge to the other side of the water
takes us into a totally different world. It is a nationally recognized nature
reserve and contains a complex of little peat bogs, brooks and marshes.
Besides the original Willows and Poplars, many of these trees are present
in a pollarded form, so typical of the landscape of Holland.* Alnus
spaethii 'Spaeth' *is a notable resident here. This striking, fast-growing
tree is a member of the widespread Alder family but betrays pretensions of
grandeur with its early abundance of catkins and its purplish-red leaves in
the autumn.
In the case of Birch trees it is the trunks which capture our attention. And
nowhere do these trunks look better than against the murky background of
an overgrown wood, as is clearly demonstrated here. The white bark of*
Betula utilis *and* Betula jacquemonti *shine out at intervals along the
route like living strips of light.*

The Wingnut (Pterocarya fraxinifolia) *is relatively unfamiliar in the
Netherlands – luckily, perhaps, because the surprise when you do see one
is all the greater.* Pterocaryas *can be seen in the 'on the Lake' area at the
highest point of the wood, on either side of the main route. They are trees
with broad, spreading crowns and female catkins which can reach 40 cm.*

---

sargentii, *le* Prunus avium *(merisier des oiseaux) et le* Prunus 'Accolade'. *Leurs fleurs roses et blanches déploient un joyeux ruban le long des
jardins européens au sud du lac.*
*Les jardins d'Extrême-Orient n'auraient pu souhaiter de meilleures
enseignes que le* Metasequoia glyptostroboides *(cyprès aquatique) et le*
Taxodium distichum *(cyprès chauve). Tous deux sont des conifères à
feuillage caduc et remontent si loin dans l'histoire que l'on pourrait
presque les qualifier de fossiles vivants.*

*Le promeneur qui poursuit son chemin vers l'autre rive et empruntant le
ponton se retrouve dans un tout autre monde: celui des aires naturelles des
Pays-Bas. C'est un ensemble de petits étangs, de minuscules cours d'eau
et de marais où les saules et peupliers aborigènes sont de temps en temps
côtoyés par des spécimens taillés en têtards si caractéristiques du paysage
hollandais. Dans cet entourage, l'* Alnus spaethii 'Spaeth' *n'est pas
sans passer inaperçu. Cet arbre à croissance rapide fait partie de la famille
des aulnes mais connaît plus de succès que ses congénères du fait de l'apparition précoce d'innombrables chatons et de son feuillage rouge violacé à
l'automne. Chez les bouleaux par contre, ce sont en général les troncs qui
sont les plus spectaculaires. Et nulle part ailleurs, semble-t-il, ces troncs
pourraient mieux se profiler que sur l'arrière-plan quelque peu mystérieux
d'un bois à l'état sauvage. L'écorce blanche du* Betula utilis *(bouleau de
l'Himalaya) et du* Betula jacquemontii *apparaît régulièrement le long
des jardins naturels comme un véritable repère lumineux au fil du chemin.*

Le Pterocarya fraxinifolia *(Pterocarya du Caucase) n'est pas vraiment
connu dans notre pays. Ce n'est peut-être pas plus mal d'ailleurs puisque*

---

leidlich beschützten Stellen aufzuwachsen. *Ganz früh in der Saison präsentieren
sich einige Zierkirschen, darunter* Prunus sargentii, Prunus avium *(Süßkir-
sche) und* Prunus 'Accolade'. *Mit ihren rosa und weißen Blüten bilden sie ein
festliches Band entlang der europäischen Ländergärten an der Südseite des Sees.
Die Gärten des Fernen Ostens hätten sich keinen besseren Blickfang wünschen
können als* Metasequoia glyptostroboides *(Chinesischer Rotholzbaum) und*
Taxodium distichum *(Sumpfzypresse). Bei beiden handelt es sich um Koniferen mit einer dermaßen langen Geschichte, dass man sie fast als lebende Fossilien
bezeichnen kann.*
*Wer seinen Weg über die Pontonbrücke auf der anderen Seite fortsetzt, kommt
in einer völlig anderen Welt an: die der niederländischen Naturgebiete. Ein
Zusammenspiel von Moorgebieten, Flüssen und sumpfiger Erde, wo neben den
ursprünglichen Weiden und Pappeln auch die für die niederländische Landschaft
so charakteristischen Kopfweiden vorkommen. In dieser Umgebung ist* Alnus
spaethii 'Spaeth' *eine auffällige Erscheinung. Ein markanter, schnellwachsen-
der Baum, der zur Familie der Erlen gehört, aber wegen der frühen, zahlreichen
Kätzchen und der violettroten Herbstfarbe des Blatts größere Aufmerksamkeit
auf sich zieht.*
*Bei Birken sind es meistens gerade die Stämme, die am auffallendsten sind.
Und dass diese Stämme nirgendwo besser zur Wirkung kommen als vor dem
geheimnisvollen Hintergrund eines verwilderten Waldes, kann man auch hier
wieder sehr gut beobachten. Entlang der Ränder der Naturgebiete taucht die
weiße Borke von* Betula utilis *und* Betula jacquemontii *regelmäßig als leben-
der Lichtpunkt entlang der Route auf.*

Die Flügelnuss (Pterocarya fraxinifolia) *ist in unserem Land relativ unbe-
kannt. Vielleicht ist das auch gut so, denn so ist die Überraschung, wenn man*

Bomen werden vooral in vroeger eeuwen vaak aangeplant als herkenningspunt. Een zware beplanting met bomen in overigens kale uiterwaarden duidde vaak op de aanwezigheid van een veerhuis. En wie in het Brabantse landschap, waar van nature eiken groeien, in de verte drie linden ontwaarde, kon er zeker van zijn dat daar een kapel stond. De drie linden stonden symbool voor de drie-eenheid van de Vader, de Zoon en de Heilige Geest en daarmee was voor de vermoeide reiziger redding in zicht.

Knotbomen zijn karakteristiek voor het Hollandse landschap. Een knotboom is geen apart soort boom, maar een boom die aangepast is aan het gebruik dat ervan gemaakt wordt. Toen men lang geleden ontdekte dat het hout van wilg, populier, els en es voor vele doeleinden gebruikt kon worden, werden jonge bomen op een gemakkelijk te bereiken hoogte afgezaagd, zo hoog dat het vee de jonge uitlopers niet kon opeten. Door de boom om de 3 tot 5 jaar steeds op dezelfde hoogte te knotten ontstaat daar een dikke knoest waarop steeds weer nieuwe uitlopers verschijnen.

Trees were often planted in former centuries to serve as landmarks. A dense clump of trees in the otherwise bare river washlands usually marked the location of a ferry house. The landscape of North Brabant is naturally rich in oak trees, but anyone who spotted a distant group of three Linden trees knew there must be a chapel nearby. The three Lindens were a symbol for the Holy Trinity and thus promised sanctuary for the weary traveller.

Pollarded trees are a typical feature of the landscape in Holland. A pollarded tree is not any particular species, but any tree that is regularly cut back in a certain way. People discovered long ago that the wood and twigs of Willow, Poplar, Alder and Ash had many different uses. So they sawed off the top of the tree at a height that was easy to reach but just too high for cattle to nibble at the young shoots. Trimming the tree to this height every 3-5 years produced a short trunk with the characteristic thickening at the top, and with new twigs sprouting continually from the club-shaped trunk.

En général, les arbres étaient fréquemment plantés dans les siècles précédents pour servir de points de repères. Ainsi, une concentration d'arbres au milieu d'un espace à découvert indiquait-elle souvent la présence de chauve-souris. Et quand on discernait au loin trois tilleuls dans la campagne du Brabant, domaine naturel des chênes, on pouvait en déduire à coup sûr l'existence d'une chapelle. Les trois tilleuls étaient symboles de la Trinité: le Père, le Fils et le Saint-Esprit; le voyageur fatigué savait alors que le repos était proche.

Les arbres taillés en têtards sont des formes typiques du paysage hollandais. Il ne s'agit pas d'une espèce spéciale mais d'un arbre adapté à l'usage dont on veut en faire. Lorsqu'on découvrit, il y a bien longtemps, que le bois du saule, du peuplier, de l'aulne et du frêne pouvait être utilisé de maintes façons, on décida de couper les jeunes arbres à une hauteur facilement accessible et juste assez élevée pour que le bétail ne puisse manger les jeunes pousses. En écimant l'arbre tous les 3 à 5 ans toujours à la même hauteur, se formait une grosse excroissance où naissaient à chaque fois de nouvelles pousses.

In der Vergangenheit hat man Bäume oft als Erkennungspunkt angepflanzt. Eine kompakte Bepflanzung mit Bäumen in ansonsten kahlen überschwemmungsgebieten deutete oft auf die Anwesenheit eines Fährhauses hin. Und wer in der Brabanter Landschaft, wo von Natur aus Eichen wachsen, in der Ferne drei Linden gewahr wurde, konnte sicher sein, dass dort eine Kapelle stand. Die drei Linden standen als Symbol für die Dreifaltigkeit des Vaters, des Sohnes und des Heiligen Geistes, und damit war für den müden Reisenden Rettung in Sicht.

Kopfbäume sind charakteristisch für die holländische Landschaft. Bei einem Kopfbaum handelt es sich nicht um eine Baumart, sondern um einen Baum, der dem Gebrauch, der von ihm gemacht wird, angepasst wurde. Als man vor langer Zeit entdeckte, dass man das Holz von Weide, Pappel, Erle und Esche für viele Zwecke verwenden konnte, wurden junge Bäume auf einer einfach zu erreichenden Höhe abgesägt, so hoch, dass das Vieh die jungen Ausläufer nicht auffressen konnte. Indem man den Baum alle 3 bis 5 Jahre immer auf derselben Höhe zurückstutzt, entsteht an der Stelle ein dicker Knorren, an dem immer wieder neue Ausläufer erscheinen.

Wilg
Saule
Weide
Willow

de hoofdroute. Bomen die, met hun brede, spreidende kroon en tot 40 cm lange vruchtkatjes, uitermate geschikt zijn voor parken en pleinen. Hier, op deze plek met uitzicht op de bloemenvallei en het water, had geen betere keus gemaakt kunnen worden.

De doorbraak (Coupure)

De futuristische architectuur, in de vorm van een organisch ruimteschip, is de bijdrage van de provincie Noord-Holland (titel: Het Web). Dit onvergelijkbaar 'promotievoertuig' steekt scherp af met een relict uit het verleden, de Geniedijk, het militaire verdedigingswerk dat dwars door de Floriade snijdt. De Geniedijk maakt deel uit van de Stelling van Amsterdam die is geplaatst op de Werelderfgoedlijst van Unesco. Na anderhalve eeuw is de dijk voor de tentoonstelling doorsneden om een overgang af te dwingen tussen het 'Dak' en 'de Berg', de overgang ook van de groente, fruit- en sierteelt naar een archipel met bebouwing en kunst. Nog steeds geeft het park zich niet in zijn volle omvang prijs, omdat de parkdelen zo van elkaar verschillen, qua karakter en presentatie. Onzichtbaar is ook de opzet en organisatie van de Floriade, die is opgebouwd uit partnership en 'de concepting'. Toen na 1994 bekend werd dat de Haarlemmermeer was uitverkoren als vestigingsplaats van de Floriade, besloot de gemeente de organisatie en het financieel risico uit handen te geven. Drie partijen namen het initiatief en kwamen met een onorthodoxe formule.

De partijen zijn landschapsarchitect Niek Roozen, het ingenieursbureau Arcadis en de aannemersorganisatie Dura Vermeer.

Concepting is vernieuwende gedachte die zijn wortels heeft in de opvatting dat de kritische en verwende consument een thema verlangt

44

la surprise reste ainsi d'autant plus grande quand on a la chance de le voir. Les Pterocaryas se trouvent dans la partie 'Au bord du Lac', au plus haut point du bois et de chaque côté de l'allée principale. Avec leur couronne étalée et leurs chatons pouvant atteindre 40 cm de longueur, ce sont de merveilleux sujets dans les parcs et sur les places. Cet endroit où la vue s'étend sur la vallée de fleurs et sur l'eau n'aurait pu être mieux choisi.

La Coupure

L'architecture futuriste de Kas Oosterhuis qu'incarne un vaisseau spatial organique, concrétise la participation de la province de la Hollande septentrionale (titre: La Toile). Ce 'véhicule publicitaire' sans pareil est en contraste flagrant avec une relique du passé: la Geniedijk, ancien ouvrage militaire de défense stratégique, qui coupe la Floriade en deux. La Geniedijk fait partie du Stelling d'Amsterdam classé sur la liste du Patrimoine Mondial de l'Unesco. Après un siècle et demi, la digue a été coupée pour l'exposition afin de créer une percée entre la 'Coupole' et la 'Colline' et de faire aussi la transition entre la culture fruitière, maraîchère et ornementale et un archipel de constructions et d'art. Le parc ne divulgue toujours pas toute son ampleur tant les secteurs sont distincts les uns des autres par leur caractère et leur présentation; de même que restent imperceptibles la structuration et l'organisation de la Floriade qui a été édifiée sur la base du partenariat et de 'l'idéation'. En 1994, quand l'Haarlemmermeer fut officiellement choisi pour y implanter la Floriade, la municipalité décida de confier à des tiers le soin de l'organiser et de la financer. Trois parties prirent alors les initiatives et venant avec une formule non conformiste: l'architecte paysagiste Niek Roozen, le bureau d'ingénieurs Arcadis et le groupe de construction Dura Vermeer.

---

and they are ideal for parks and public squares. At this spot, with its view of the Valley of Flowers and the Lake, a better choice of tree could not have been made.

The Gap

The futuristic architecture of Kas Oosterhuis, a building shaped like an organic space ship, is the contribution of the Province of North Holland (titled 'The Web'). It forms a sharp contrast with the historic Geniedijk fortification, which cuts right across the Floriade Park. The Genidijk is part of a much larger structure called the Stelling van Amsterdam which is on Unesco's list of World Heritage Sites. A hundred and fifty years after it was built, a gap has been made through the dyke for the occasion of the Floriade. The gap forms the transition from near the Roof to by the Hill. It is also the point of transition from the area of vegetables, fruit and ornamental cultivation, to an archipelago with buildings and art. The park has not yet revealed its true size to us, because the individual parts are so different in character and presentation. Another thing that remains hidden from the eye is the structure and organization of the Floriade, which is made up of partnerships and the 'concepting'. When it was announced that the Haarlemmermeer had been selected as the location for Floriade 2002, the municipality decided to hive off the organization and the financial risk of the project. Three parties took the initiative and devised an unorthodox formula. The players were the landscape architect Niek Roozen, the consulting engineers Arcadis and the construction group Dura Vermeer. 'Concepting' is an new marketing approach based on the idea that to sell something, you have to curry favour with the critical, spoilt consumer by offering a 'concept' – something which goes beyond a mere slogan. As

sie wieder einmal irgendwo sieht, umso größer. Im Teilgebiet 'am See' stehen Pterocarya auf der höchsten Stelle des Waldes, an beiden Seiten der Hauptroute. Bäume, die sich – mit ihrer ausgebreiteten Krone und den bis zu 40 cm langen Fruchtkätzchen – äußerst gut für Parks und Plätze eignen. An dieser Stelle, mit Aussicht auf das Blumental und das Wasser, hätte man keine bessere Wahl treffen können.

Der Durchbruch (Coupure)

Die futuristische Architektur von Kas Oosterhuis in der Form eines organischen Raumschiffs, ist der Beitrag der Provinz Nordholland (Titel: das Netz). Dieses unvergleichliche 'Beförderungsfahrzeug' hebt sich stark ab von einem Relikt der Vergangenheit, dem Geniedijk, der militärischen Verteidigungsanlage, die quer durch die Floriade verläuft. Der Geniedijk gehört zur Festung von Amsterdam, die von der Unesco zum Weltkulturerbe erklärt worden ist. Nach hundertfünfzig Jahren wurde der Deich für die Ausstellung durchschnitten, um einen Übergang zu schaffen zwischen dem 'Dach' und dem 'Berg', auch der Übergang vom Gemüse-, Obst- und Zierpflanzenanbau zu einem Archipel mit Bebauung und Kunst. Noch immer gibt sich der Park nicht in seinem ganzen Umfang preis, weil sich die Parkteile – was Charakter und Präsentation betrifft – so voneinander unterscheiden. Unsichtbar sind auch die Absicht und die Organisation der Floriade, die sich aus Partnerschaft und dem 'Concepting' zusammensetzen. Als nach 1994 bekannt wurde, dass die Wahl auf das Haarlemmermeer als Standort der Floriade gefallen war, beschloss die Gemeinde, die Organisation und das finanzielle Risiko aus den Händen zu geben. Drei Parteien, der Landschaftsarchitekt Niek Roozen, das Ingenieurbüro Arcadis und die Bauunternehmerorganisation Dura Vermeer,

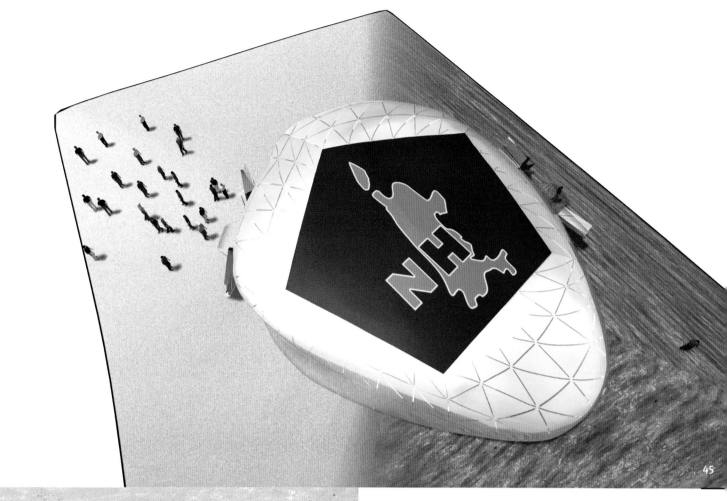

Kas Oosterhuis, 'Het Web',
bijdrage van de provincie Noord-
Holland
Kas Oosterhuis, 'La Toile',
participation de la province de
la Hollande
Kas Oosterhuis, 'das Netz', der
Beitrag der Provinz Nordholland
Kas Oosterhuis, 'The Web',
contribution of the Province of
North Holland

dat hem verleidt. Feel the art of nature, toen dat thema was bedacht, viel alles op zijn plaats. Want het omvat de componenten rijkdom aan kleur, beleving, water en internationaliteit. Een thema als verbindend element geeft steun aan de drie gedeeltes waaruit het park bestaat. Bovendien stoelt het op de gedachte dat de gast krijgt wat hij verlangt; Floriade 2002 legt het gewicht bij de vraag, niet bij het aanbod. Dat thema moet ook gedurende zes maanden waargemaakt kunnen worden. Nooit een tegenvaller, en nooit een verregende dag waardoor de bloemen hun kelken sluiten. De beleving staat voorop, nergens mag het saai zijn, een aspect dat tot in de details is uitgewerkt. Een eet-studio in de Kas van de Toekomst waar men de producten kan veror-beren die ter plekke geteeld worden, de voorlichting die en passant wordt gegeven in de Arcadië-vallei, de restaurants en cafés die de gas-ten even tot rust brengen, de kinderspeelplaatsen die variëren van geregeld tot ongeordend (het spannendste dat een kind meemaakt is toch uit afvalhout zijn eigen hut te bouwen) of de Groene Stad waarin je kunt verdwalen: alle zintuigen moeten worden beroerd. Elke gene-ratie wil op zijn manier aangesproken voelen.
Die wisselende ervaring wordt bevorderd door de drie segmenten waaruit het park is opgebouwd, rondom het Dak waar vooral de Neder-landse tuinbouw is neergestreken in het gezelschap van Mediterrane inzendingen. Dan ligt er achter de Geniedijk aan de voet van de Berg de Groene Stad met een beeld van de woningtypologieën in 2010, aan-gevuld met presentaties van de Universiteit van Wageningen, de Waterschappen en de verzamelde Glastuinbouw, de Boomkwekerij- en Bloembollensector met hun *Tuinbouw Experience,* dat reclame maakt voor een baan in een florerende bedrijfstak. Terra Futura, een initiatief

L'idéation s'entend ici dans le sens de pensée innovatrice partant du prin-cipe que le consommateur critique et exigeant a besoin d'un thème qui le séduit. Avec l'idée du thème 'Vivre l'art de la nature', tout le problème était résolu. Le thème aurait pour composantes la richesse des couleurs, l'expérience vécue, l'eau et la mondialisation. Un seul thème coordinateur sert donc de soubassement aux trois secteurs qui composent le parc. A la base, réside en plus l'idée de satisfaire les expectatives du visiteur; la Floriade 2002 pose ainsi l'accent sur la demande et non sur l'offre. Le thème doit par ailleurs pouvoir être concrétisé pendant six mois, en éliminant les risques de contretemps décevants ou de jours pluvieux pen-dant lesquels les fleurs se dissimulent. L'expérience vécue est primor-diale, rien ne doit être monotone; un aspect qui a été étudié jusque dans les détails. Tous les sens doivent être éveillés: un studio de dégustation dans la Serre de l'Avenir permet au public de savourer les produits culti-vés sur place; une documentation est fournie en passant dans la vallée Arcadië; des restaurants et cafés accueillent les visiteurs désireux de se reposer un instant; des aires de jeux réjouissent les enfants, les unes bien ordonnées et les autres laissant cours à l'imagination (quoi de plus pas-sionnant pour un enfant que de construire sa propre hutte avec des restes de bois); une Ville Verte fait office de jeu de piste ... Chaque génération veut vivre sa propre aventure. Et cette aventure intermittente est accen-tuée au fur et à mesure des trois secteurs du parc, d'abord autour de la Coupole où l'horticulture néerlandaise s'est principalement installée en compagnie des présentations méditerranéennes. Ensuite, derrière la Geniedijk, au pied de la Colline, s'étend la Ville Verte avec une image futuriste des types d'habitations de 2010 complétée par des présentations de l'Université de Wageningen, des *Waterschappen* (administrations des

soon as someone came up with the theme 'Feel the Art of Nature', the Floriade organizers knew that was what they were looking for. It carries all the connotations of colour, experience, water and internationality. The theme provides a link between the three sections into which the park is divided. It also implies that visitors will find they are looking for here: Floriade 2002 has shifted the emphasis from the supply to the demand. Now the Floriade will have to live up to its message for a full six months. Disappointments – on a rainy day, perhaps, when the flowers refuse to open – must not be allowed to happen. The visitor experience is upper-most, and the show must never be dull; this is an aspect that the Floriade has worked out down to the last detail – for example, the restaurant in the Greenhouse of the Future where we can taste the produce on the spot. The Arcadië Valley is full of interesting information for the passing visitor. There is a choice of restaurants and bars where visitors can take a break. There are children's playgrounds in styles that range from well-organized to practically wild (what could be more fun than building your own hut out of scrap timber?) There is the Green City to explore, full of ideas about greenery and the urban environment.
All the senses must be stimulated. Every generation has its own expecta-tions and demands. The wide variety of experiences is boosted by the three sections of the park. Near the Roof is the main area for Dutch horti-cultural entries, side-by-side with the Mediterranean contributions. The zone behind the Geniedijk, by the Hill, contains the Green City with its concept house for 2010. This is accompanied by exhibitions presented by the University of Wageningen, by the Water Boards, and by the glasshouse, tree nursery and flower bulb sector organizations whose 'Horticultural Experience' promotes employment in their flourishing field.

ergriffen die Initiative und einigten sich auf ein unorthodoxes Konzept. 'Concepting' ist der innovative Gedanke, dem die Auffassung zugrunde liegt, dass der kritische und verwöhnte Konsument nach einem Thema ver-langt, das ihn verführt. 'Feel the Art of Nature' – als man sich erst einmal auf dieses Thema geeinigt hatte, ergab sich der Rest von alleine. Denn es vereint die Komponenten Reichtum an Farbe, Erlebnis, Wasser und Interna-tionalität. Ein Thema als verbindendes Element unterstützt die drei Teile, aus denen der Park besteht. Außerdem basiert es auf dem Gedanken, dass der Gast bekommt, was er verlangt; die Floriade 2002 legt den Akzent auf die Nachfrage, nicht auf das Angebot.
Dieses Thema soll auch während der sechs Monate verwirklicht werden. Es soll keine Enttäuschung und keinen verregneten Tag geben, wodurch die Blumen ihre Kelche schließen könnten. Das Erleben steht an erster Stelle, nirgendwo darf sich der Besucher langweilen – ein Aspekt, der bis in alle Einzelheiten ausgearbeitet wurde. Ein Essstudio im Gewächshaus der Zukunft, wo man die an Ort und Stelle angebauten Produkte verzehren kann, die Information, die man im Arcadië-Tal erhält, die Restaurants und Cafés, wo die Gäste zur Ruhe kommen können, die Kinderspielplätze, die von geregelt zu unordentlich (das Spannendste, was ein Kind erlebt, ist doch, wenn es sich aus Abfall seine eigene Hütte baut) variieren oder die 'Grüne Stadt', in der man sich verirren kann: alle Sinne sollen aktiviert wer-den. Jede Generation will sich auf ihre eigene Art angesprochen fühlen. Diese wechselnde Erfahrung wird durch drei Segmente gefördert, aus denen das Terrain aufgebaut ist, rund um das Dach herum, wo sich hauptsächlich der niederländische Gartenbau in der Nachbarschaft von mediterranen Einsendungen niedergelassen hat. Dann liegt hinter dem Geniedijk am Fuße des Berges die 'Grüne Stadt' mit einem Bild der Wohn-

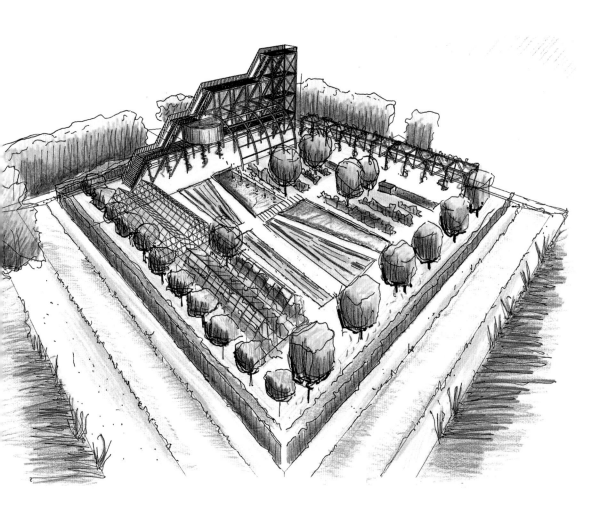

van de Nationale Postcodeloterij en de Stichting Doen, trekt op een van de eilanden de aandacht door de ongebruikelijke samenwerking in een paviljoen tussen de traditionele en de biologische tuinbouw. Zo is er na jaren van afstand een brug geslagen in de sierteelt tussen de commerciële en ecologische partijen.

Tenslotte is er het Meer, met veel buitenlandse inzendingen, twintig in getal, waaronder Duitsland, Oostenrijk, België en ook een groot Aziatisch segment aan de oever van het meer. Een theehuis aan het water, een Oosterse Markt. Even kijkt Bangkok om de hoek. Hier dient de aanwezige natuur als een vanzelfsprekend decor voor allerlei stemmingen die de flora kan oproepen, van bezinning tot uitgelatenheid, van harmonie tot contrast.
Wie de plattegrond, ontworpen door Niek Roozen, overziet, ontdekt dat de tegenstellingen zijn aangezet, vanuit de gedachte dat de rechte weg de meest slaapverwekkende is. Formeel is de opzet van 'Naast de Berg', informeel juist 'Aan het Meer', terwijl 'Bij het Dak' een collage laat zien van landschappen, als puzzelstukken tegen elkaar aangezet. Twee ingangen geven toegang tot die driedelige puzzel, zodat voor iedereen de tocht anders kan zijn. Maar die dubbele entree heeft ook nog een belangrijke logistieke verklaring. Zo kan de bezoekersstroom zich gemakkelijker verspreiden tot in alle hoeken en uithoeken van het park en wordt voorkomen dan men in gelid vanaf een ingang langs de attracties trekt.

One of the Islands is home to 'Terra Futura', a joint initiative by the National Postcode Lottery and Stichting Doen (a Dutch organization which supports green institutions in developing countries). This pavilion presents a surprising collaboration between traditional horticulture and organic horticulture. After years of reserve, ornamental plant cultivation has become a bridge between the commercial and ecological growers.

Finally there is the area on the Lake, with many contributions from abroad. Horticulturalists from 20 different countries, including Germany, Austria and Belgium, are represented at the lakeside. There is also a large Asian area on the shore of the lake, with a teahouse at the waterside and an Oriental Market. Suddenly we catch a whiff of Bangkok. The existing natural vegetation acts as a neutral backdrop for the countless moods that flowers and plants can evoke, ranging from reflection to elation, or from harmony to contrast.
When we examine the layout of the park designed by Niek Roozen, we discover that the contrasts are deliberate. The underlying idea is that a straight path is a boring one. The Hill is formal in its design, the Lake is informal and the Roof has a patchwork of landscapes like a jigsaw puzzle. With two different entrances to the park, every visitor can go on a different journey. The double entrance also has a pragmatic purpose – it helps spread the visitors efficiently throughout the park, and prevents the feeling that you are part of a long crocodile of visitors threading its way past the attractions.

eaux) et du groupe sectoriel réunissant la Serriculture, l'Arboriculture et la Bulbiculture avec leur projet *Tuinbouw Experience* soulignant l'attrait d'une carrière dans une branche florissante. Terra Futura, une initiative de la loterie 'Nationale Postcodeloterij' et de l'association 'Stichting Doen', attire l'attention sur l'une des îles en abritant sous un seul et même pavillon le mariage insolite de l'horticulture traditionnelle et biologique. Ainsi, un pont a-t-il été jeté au-dessus de l'abîme qui séparait pendant des années les intérêts commerciaux des aspirations écologiques dans le monde de l'horticulture ornementale.

Enfin, le Lac accueille sur ses rives maintes présentations de l'étranger: 20 pays au total parmi lesquels l'Allemagne, l'Autriche, la Belgique et une grande délégation asiatique. Un pavillon de thé au bord de l'eau, un Marché Oriental. Bangkok est au détour du chemin. La nature est ici le décor logique de tous les états d'esprit inspirés par la flore: de la réflexion à l'exubérance, de l'harmonie au paradoxe.
Quiconque regarde le plan du parc réalisé par Niek Roozen, découvre que les paradoxes sont délibérés, sachant que la ligne droite est aussi la plus monotone. 'La Colline' témoigne d'une certaine formalité, 'Le Lac' justement pas, alors que 'La Coupole' propose un collage de divers paysages qui se juxtaposent comme des morceaux de puzzle. Deux entrées permettent d'accéder à ce puzzle en trio, si bien que la promenade peut y être différente pour chacun. Mais cette double entrée a en plus une fonction logistique non négligeable puisque le flux de visiteurs peut ainsi se disperser plus facilement vers tous les angles du parc, évitant que le public parte d'un seul et même point pour défiler en queue devant les attractions.

typologien im Jahr 2010, ergänzt mit Präsentationen der Universität von Wageningen, den Wasserbehörden und der versammelten Gewächshauskultur, dem Baumschulen- und Blumensektor mit ihrer Gartenbau Experience, das Werbung für eine Arbeitsstelle in einem blühenden Betriebszweig macht. Terra Futura, eine Initiative der Nationalen Postleitzahlenlotterie und der Stiftung Doen, zieht auf einer der Inseln die Aufmerksamkeit auf sich durch die ungewöhnliche Zusammenarbeit in einem Pavillon zwischen dem traditionellen und dem biologischen Gartenbau. So wurde nach Jahren der unterschiedlichen Auffassungen im Zierpflanzenanbau eine Brücke zwischen den kommerziellen und den ökologischen Parteien geschlagen.
Schließlich gibt es den See, mit insgesamt zwanzig ausländischen Einsendungen, darunter Deutschland, Österreich, Belgien und auch ein großes asiatisches Segment am Ufer des Sees. Ein Teehaus am Wasser, ein orientalischer Markt. Für einen Moment fühlt man sich nach Bangkok versetzt. Hier dient die vorhandene Natur als eine selbstverständliche Dekoration für allerlei Stimmungen, die die Flora hervorrufen kann, von Besinnung zu Ausgelassenheit, von Harmonie zu Kontrast. Schaut man sich den von Niek Roozen entworfenen Plan an, wird einem bewusst, dass die Gegensätze aus dem Gedanken heraus konzipiert wurden, dass der gerade Weg der langweiligste ist. Formell ist das Konzept 'vom Berg', informell gerade 'der See', während 'das Dach' eine Collage von Landschaften zeigt, die wie Teile eines Puzzles gegeneinander gesetzt wurden. Über zwei Eingänge gelangt man zu diesem dreiteiligen Puzzle, so dass die Tour für jeden anders sein kann. Aber dieser doppelte Eintritt hat auch noch einen wichtigen logistischen Grund. Der Besucherstrom kann sich dadurch einfacher bis in alle Ecken und entlegene Winkel des Parks verteilen und es wird vermieden, dass man von einem Eingang an in Reihen an den Attraktionen vorbeizieht.

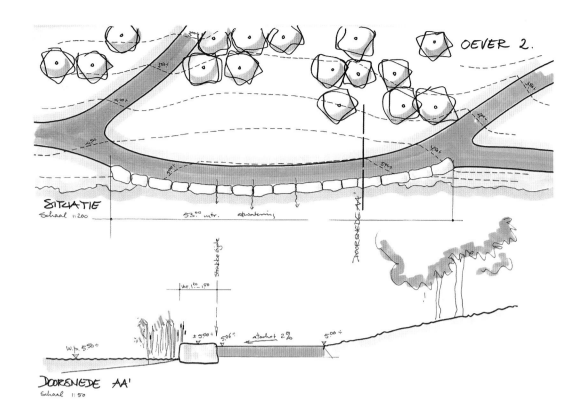

OEVER 2.

SITUATIE
Schaal 1:200

53.00 mtr. afwatering

DOORSNEDE AA'
Schaal 1:50

W.p. 5.50÷

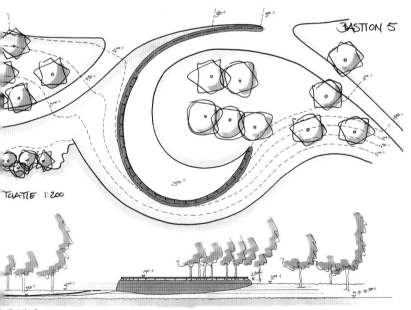

BASTION 5

SITUATIE 1:200

ZICHT 1:200

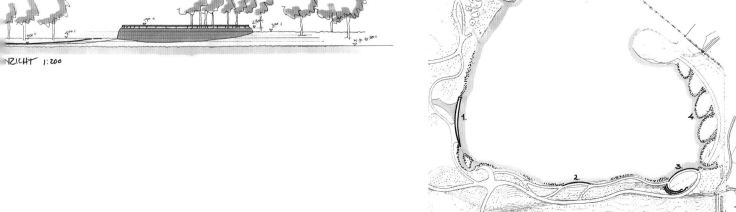

DIVERSE OEVERS'

Naast de Berg

By the Hill

À côté de la Colline

Am Hügel

Het onwaarschijnlijke tot waarschijnlijkheid verheffen, namelijk dat je niet in Nederland en al helemaal niet in de Haarlemmermeer een piramide verwacht aan te treffen, dat is het bijzondere van Big Spotters' Hill met op de top een kunstwerk van Auke de Vries. De Vries excelleert in reusachtige beeldhouwwerken, langs het perron bij Station Hollands Spoor in Den Haag en in de vijver bij het Nederlands Architectuurinstituut in Rotterdam, maar deze 'heuvelbekroning' spant de kroon. Het bouwsel heeft hetzelfde effect als de Eiffeltoren: van verre gezien is het een 'landmark' dat zich opdringt in het landschap, eenmaal in of op de piramide beleef je dat niet meer als zodanig. Het perspectief is gewisseld. Bovenop Big Spotters' Hill, en dat is ongeveer 30 meter boven NAP, ontvouwt zich het panorama, niet alleen van de Floriade, maar van de platte pannenkoek van een polder inclusief het

Rendre l'invraisemblable vraisemblable, autrement dit ne pas s'attendre à trouver une pyramide aux Pays-Bas et a fortiori dans l'Haarlemmermeer, c'est là tout l'insolite de Big Spotters' Hill avec à son sommet une œuvre d'art d'Auke de Vries. De Vries excelle dans les sculptures gigantesques, comme celles sur le quai de la gare Hollands Spoor à La Haye et dans l'étang de l'Institut néerlandais pour l'Architecture à Rotterdam, mais ce 'couronnement de la colline' bat tous les records. La construction a le même effet que la Tour Eiffel: de loin, c'est un 'emblème national' qui s'impose dans le paysage; une fois dans la pyramide ou à son sommet, ce n'est plus la même chose. La perspective a changé. En haut de Big Spotter's Hill, c'est-à-dire à environ 30 mètres au-dessus du niveau de la mer, se déploie le panorama, non seulement de la Floriade mais aussi du plat pays des polders y compris l'aéroport de Schiphol toujours en pleine acti-

Elevating the improbable to the undeniable – a pyramid is not something we expect to find in Holland, let alone in Haarlemmermeer. But Big Spotters' Hill is here all the same, and it has a work of art by Auke de Vries on top. De Vries excels in making gigantic sculpture. His work can be seen on the platform in Hollands Spoor railway station in The Hague, and in the pool at the Netherlands Architecture Institute in Rotterdam. But this hilltop construction takes the cake. Its effect is rather like that of the Eiffel tower – seen from a distance it is a landmark that dominates the surroundings, but once we are inside or on the pyramid, it loses this power. The perspective has changed. From the top of Big Spotters' Hill, the panorama unfolds – not only all of the Floriade, but the whole pancake-flat polder including busy Schiphol, Amsterdam on the horizon, and Kennemerland out to the west, with the rows of sand dunes behind it.

Das Unwahrscheinliche zur Wahrscheinlichkeit erheben, nämlich, dass man in den Niederlanden, und schon gar nicht im Haarlemmermeer, nicht erwarten würde, auf eine Pyramide zu stoßen – das ist das Besondere von Big Spotters' Hill, auf dessen Spitze sich ein Kunstwerk von Auke de Vries befindet. De Vries brilliert mit riesigen Skulpturen, die zum Beispiel auf dem Bahnsteig bei der Haltestelle Hollands Spoor in Den Haag und im Teich beim Nederlands Architectuurinstituut in Rotterdam stehen, aber diese Hügelbekrönung übertrifft alles. Das Gebilde hat den gleichen Effekt wie der Eiffelturm: von weitem gesehen ist er ein 'Landmark', das sich der Landschaft aufdringt, ist man jedoch einmal in oder auf der Pyramide, stellt sich ein anderes Gefühl ein. Die Perspektive hat sich verschoben. Oben auf Big Spotters' Hill – das sind ungefähr 30 Meter über dem Amsterdamer Pegel – entfaltet sich das ganze Panorama, nicht nur von der Floriade, sondern auch

53

the art of

bezige Schiphol, Amsterdam aan de horizon, en in het westen Kennemerland met een glimp van de duinenrij erachter.

Big Spotters' Hill is het scharnierpunt in de assen van de Floriade, het is het eindpunt van de as vanaf de noordingang maar tegelijk ook het baken gezien vanaf het bos. Roozen tekende dit markeerpunt al in een vroeg stadium, het is gebleven en het is versterkt. Het is het zwenkwiel geworden van de Floriade dat de bezoekers geleidt.

Ook in dit geval is het onzichtbare het cruciale onderdeel van Big Spotters' Hill, het is het fundament onder de piramide die voorkomt dat de berg als een tompouce in de modder wegzakt. Er is gekozen voor een zorgvuldig tempo van ophoging, de zandlagen zijn in fasen aangebracht. Met enig ceremonieel vertoon is bij de fundering van de piramide een bunker met tekstrollen in de grond geplaatst die vele generaties verder het geheim zal kunnen prijsgeven waarom hier een heuvel werd aangelegd in het jaar 2002. Daarmee reikt deze piramide de hand naar de oude in Egypte die ook een verborgen schat of schatkamer kende.

De ruimte is immens, stelde De Vries vast voordat hij ging schetsen, en dus moest er een enorm beeld komen. Een beeld dat de gasten oriëntatie verleent bij het rondwandelen, zoals ook beelden in de stad kunnen helpen om de weg te bepalen. Bovendien moet het kunstwerk zo'n sensatie losmaken dat je ernaar toe wil, het is de magie die de Lorelei op de schippers in de Rijn uitoefende.

Die sensatie blijft niet beperkt tot een visuele attractie. Je bent binnen en op het beeld, je vergroeit ermee. Je voelt de wind om je hoofd, er drupt regen door het grote canvas doek: dat is de ervaring die je lijfelijk ondergaat zodra je het platform betreedt, nadat de spanning van wat er

vité, Amsterdam à l'horizon, et à l'ouest: le Kennemerland avec un aperçu des dunes par derrière.

Big Spotters' Hill est le point d'articulation des axes de la Floriade, c'est l'extrémité de l'axe partant de l'entrée nord mais c'est en même temps une balise vue du bois. Roozen avait noté ce point à un stade très précoce, il a été retenu et même renforcé. C'est devenu le pivot de la Floriade qui guide les visiteurs.

Là aussi, l'élément crucial de Big Spotter's Hill est invisible: il s'agit des fondations sous la pyramide qui empêchent que la colline s'affaisse dans le sol humide comme un bloc de béton posé sur un matelas de plumes. L'amoncellement a été fait à un rythme soigneusement choisi, les couches de sable ont été superposées par phases. Lors de la pose des fondations et avec le rituel de circonstance, a été déposée dans le sol une casemate avec des textes sur rouleaux qui divulgueront à de lointaines générations derrière nous la raison pour laquelle cette colline fut construite en l'an 2002. Ainsi cette pyramide se conforme-t-elle à sa vieille consœur en Egypte puisqu'elle aussi cachait un trésor.

L'espace est immense, affirma De Vries avant de se mettre à dessiner; il fallait donc créer un ouvrage énorme. Une création qui aiderait les visiteurs à s'orienter au cours de leur promenade, comme les œuvres d'art nous aident à nous repérer dans la ville. En plus, l'ouvrage d'art devait provoquer une sensation et inciter le public à aller le voir de plus près, tout comme la Lorelei attirait magiquement les bateliers du Rhin.

Cette sensation ne se limite pas à l'attrait visuel. On entre dans l'œuvre d'art, on l'escalade, on s'y assimile. Le visage est caressé par le vent, les gouttes de pluie traversent la grande toile en canevas: ce sont les sensations physiques éprouvées dès que la plate-forme est franchie, après

Big Spotters' Hill is the focal point in the lines of the Floriade. It terminates the axis leading from the north entrance, but it is also a beacon visible from the woods. Roozen drew this focal point in his design at an early stage, and it has remained there since and grown stronger. It has become a kind of swivel that sends visitors to the Floriade off in one direction or another.

A crucial aspect of Big Spotter's Hill is something we cannot see – the foundations under the pyramid, which stop the hill from sinking into the mud like a failed soufflé. The engineers decided to build it up gradually, adding the sand in a series of layers. With a certain amount of pomp and circumstance, they built a concrete bunker in the base of the pyramid. It contains scrolls of text which are meant to explain to the archaeologists of some distant future just why people decided to erect an artificial hill here in 2002. This too is nod towards the pyramids of ancient Egypt, with their secret chambers and hidden treasures.

The sense of space around the hill is vast, De Vries decided before he started sketching his ideas. So the sculpture would have to be of immense size to match it. The object would have to give the visitors something to orient themselves by as they explored the park, like a statue in the city. It also had to create a sensation that would make us want to climb the hill to see it from close up – the same kind of magic as the Lorelei ruin on the Rhine always had for people sailing on that river.

That sensation is not only a visual one. When we are at the top of the hill, we are inside and on the object; we become part of it. We feel the wind on our faces, and rain drips through the huge tarpaulin. It is a sensation that we experience physically as soon as we step onto the platform, following the tense expectation we feel in the dark, enclosed space beneath it.

vom flachen Pfannekuchen eines Polders einschließlich des geschäftigen Flughafens Schiphol, am Horizont Amsterdam und im Westen das Kennemerland mit einem Blick von der dahinter liegenden Dünenreihe.

Big Spotters' Hill ist der Dreh- und Angelpunkt in den Achsen der Floriade; er ist der Endpunkt der Achse ab dem Nordeingang, aber gleichzeitig auch das Orientierungszeichen vom Wald aus gesehen. Roozen hat diesen Markierungspunkt schon in einem frühen Stadium gezeichnet, er ist geblieben und wurde verstärkt. Er ist zum Wahrzeichen der Floriade geworden, das die Besucher begleitet.

Auch in diesem Fall ist das Unsichtbare der wesentliche Bestandteil von Spotters' Hill, es ist das Fundament unter der Pyramide, das verhindert, dass der Berg wie eine Cremetorte im Schlamm wegsackt. Man hat sich für ein moderates Tempo der Erhöhung entschieden, wobei die Sandschichten in Phasen aufgeschüttet wurden. Mit einem gewissen zeremoniellen Aufwand wurde bei der Fundierung der Pyramide eine Kammer mit Textrollen in die Erde eingebaut, die nachfolgenden Generationen das Geheimnis verraten wird, warum man hier im Jahre 2002 einen Hügel angelegt hat. Damit erinnert diese Pyramide an die ägyptische, die auch einen verborgenen Schatz oder eine Schatzkammer besaß. Da der Raum immens ist, musste de Vries zufolge auch eine riesige Skulptur geschaffen werden. Eine Skulptur, die den Besuchern als Orientierung beim Herumspazieren dient, wie auch Skulpturen in der Stadt dabei helfen können, den Weg zu finden. Außerdem soll das Kunstwerk solches Aufsehen erregen, dass jeder es unbedingt sehen will; es ist wie der Zauber, den die Lorelei auf die Rheinschiffer ausübte.

Die Empfindung bleibt jedoch nicht auf eine visuelle Attraktion beschränkt. Man ist in und auf dem Kunstwerk, man verwächst mit ihm. Man fühlt den Wind im Gesicht, durch die große Leinwand tröpfelt Regen: das ist die

komen gaat eerst is opgebouwd in de duistere gesloten ruimte eronder. Ik heb nooit ideeën, vertelt De Vries over zijn werk, want die lopen je maar voor je voeten. 'Het begint in zichzelf. De vraag die je jezelf stelt, is niet zo duidelijk, en dus komt het antwoord ook langzaam.' Toch bleef er een associatie tijdens de voorstudies haken, het idee van de Ark van Noach. Dat was genoeg als start. Zo vreemd is de vergelijking met het bijbelse schip niet. We bevinden ons per slot van rekening op een terp in een landschap dat bij een dijkdoorbraak moeiteloos kan volstromen, we steken ver boven het maaiveld uit op een platform in een zee van kleur en water. De associatie met de Ark gaat nog verder: je bent op het plateau met een menigte lotgenoten, die 'de vlucht naar boven' hebben gewaagd. Dat is een compromis. De sensatie van ruimtelijkheid beleef je sterker in je eentje op de verhoging met alleen dat wapperende canvas doek boven je hoofd als beschutting.

De Vries ziet het plateau als een kamer met een baldakijn erboven waar een hengel doorheen schiet met een hoedje aan het uiteinde. De assemblage van dergelijke ingrediënten voorkomt dat de ruimte zelf onduidelijk, onbegrensd blijft. Door er een element aan toe te voegen, een doek of een gat, krijgt de ruimte maat, waardoor de bezoeker zich niet ontheemd voelt. Dat aan het canvas een oranje kleur is toegevoegd, is ook al een bewuste keuze. Die kleur steekt vanuit de verte gezien af bij de Hollandse hemel, die altijd weifelt tussen grijs en blauw. 'Oranje heeft iets etherisch.'

Het is een forum van 22 meter omtrek, uitdrukkelijk geen belvédère, omdat een klimtocht naar een uitkijkpost als te banaal werd beschouwd. De Vries: 'Hoogte is *au fond* niet interessant.' Wat wordt beoogd is juist de sensatie van het er zijn, op een berg die referenties

avoir ressenti un suspense en crescendo dans l'espace sombre et fermé du dessous. 'Je n'ai jamais d'idées au préalable parce qu'elles deviennent des barrières', dit De Vries en parlant de son travail. 'Cela vient tout seul et la question que je me pose n'étant jamais très nette, la réponse met un certain temps à venir'. Pourtant une association de pensée ne l'a pas quitté au cours des études préliminaires: l'idée de l'Arche de Noé. C'était déjà un départ. D'ailleurs la comparaison avec le navire biblique n'est pas si étrange que ça. Finalement, nous nous trouvons sur un tertre au milieu de terres qui seraient vite inondées en cas de rupture d'une digue, bien au-dessus du sol, sur une plate-forme surplombant une étendue de couleurs et d'eau. L'association à l'Arche va même plus loin: on est sur le plateau avec une foule d'autres personnes qui, elles aussi, ont osé faire 'l'ascension du sommet': c'est une forme de compromis. La sensation d'espace se perçoit mieux quand on est seul sur la butte avec le battement de la toile au-dessus de la tête comme protection.

De Vries voit le plateau comme une chambre avec pour plafond un baldaquin transpercé par une gaule coiffée d'un chapeau et son extrémité. L'assemblage de tels ingrédients évite que l'espace, imprécis en soi, reste illimité. En y ajoutant un élément, une toile ou un orifice, l'espace devient dimensionné et le visiteur ne se sent pas dépaysé. La couleur orange du canevas a été délibérément choisie, elle aussi. De loin, elle se détache bien sur le ciel hollandais toujours hésitant entre le gris et le bleu. 'L'orange a quelque chose de volatil'.

C'est un forum de 22 m. de diamètre, et expressément pas un belvédère car une ascension vers un poste d'observation est considérée trop banale. De Vries commente: 'La hauteur, au fond, n'est pas importante'. Ce qui est recherché, c'est justement la sensation éprouvée en étant là-haut, sur une

'I never have sudden ideas', De Vries explained about his sculpture, 'because they just get in the way. It starts at its own pace. The question you set yourself isn't all that clear, so the answer comes gradually.' But there was one association that kept coming back in his early studies for the sculpture, that of Noah's Ark. It was enough to start with. The comparison was not all that strange, for we find ourselves on an isolated hill in a plain that could easily fill with flood water if the dykes were ever breached again. We stand well above ground level, surrounded by a sea of colour and glittering waterways. The association with the Ark goes further, though. We share the platform with hundreds of fellow creatures who have all sought their refuge at the top of the hill. Of course, it is a bit of a compromise. The sense of the space is much greater when you are alone there, with only the flapping tarpaulin between you and the sky.

De Vries describes the platform as a chamber topped by a canopy with a pole thrust through it, supporting a little hat at its tip. An assembly of components like this stops the space from being unclear or boundless. Adding a component like the canopy or the hole sets a measure for the space so that we are not left feeling completely out of our element. The orange colour of the tarpaulin is a well-considered choice. It forms the ideal contrast with the Dutch skies which always dither between blue and grey. 'Orange has something ethereal,' De Vries claims.

The platform has a circumference of 22 metres. Climbing a hill to a lookout point is nice but it's nothing new. It's not the height that matters, says De Vries, but the sensation of being there, on a hill that carries suggestions of other mystical places, such as the mastabas of Egypt, the terraced pyramids of the Aztecs or the temples of the ancient Greeks. The work of art, with its flexible tarpaulin roof restrained by sturdy hawsers, is meant

physische Erfahrung, sobald man die Plattform betritt, nachdem die Spannung darüber, was wohl kommen mag, erst in dem dunklen, geschlossenen Raum darunter aufgebaut worden ist.

Ich habe nie Ideen, erzählt de Vries über sein Werk, denn die legen einem nur Steine in den Weg. Es beginnt in sich selbst. 'Die Frage, die man sich stellt, ist nicht so deutlich und also kommt auch die Antwort langsam.' Dennoch blieb eine Assoziation während der Vorstudien hängen, und zwar der Gedanke an die Arche Noah. Das reichte für den Anfang. So merkwürdig ist der Vergleich mit dem biblischen Schiff gar nicht. Wir befinden uns schließlich auf einer Warf in einer Landschaft, die bei einem Deichbruch mühelos vollströmen kann. Die Assoziation mit der Arche geht sogar noch weiter: man ist mit einer Menge Gleichgesinnter auf dem Plateau, die 'die Flucht nach oben' gewagt haben. Das ist ein Kompromiss. Die Empfindung des Raums erlebt man alleine stärker auf der Erhöhung, nur mit die flatternde Leinwand als Schutz über dem Kopf.

De Vries sieht das Plateau als ein Zimmer mit einem Baldachin, durch den eine Angel mit einem Hut an der Spitze schießt. Die Assemblage von solchen Ingredienzen verhindert, dass der Raum selbst undeutlich, unbegrenzt bleibt. Indem man ein Element hinzufügt, eine Leinwand oder ein Loch, erhält der Raum ein bestimmtes Maß, wodurch sich der Besucher nicht desorientiert fühlt. Dass die Leinwand eine orangene Farbe erhalten hat, ist ebenfalls ganz bewusst geschehen. Aus der Ferne hebt sich diese Farbe gegen den holländischen Himmel ab, der immer zwischen grau und blau zu schwanken scheint. 'Orange hat etwas ätherisches.'

Es ist ein Forum von 22 Metern Umfang, dabei ausdrücklich kein Belvedere, weil man eine Kletterpartie zu einem Aussichtsposten für zu banal gehalten hat. De Vries: 'Höhe ist im Grunde nicht interessant.' Was hin-

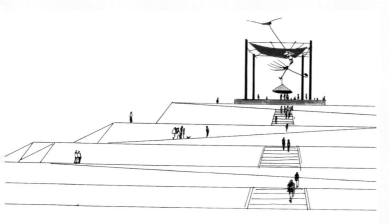

Belangrijk ORIENTATIE punt op Floriade terrein.
→ Verheven - expressief.
→ Verbinding tussen de lucht en de aarde.

oproept naar andere mystieke plekken zoals de mastaba's, de getrapte heuvels van de Aztecen of de Griekse tempels. Het kunstwerk met zijn bewegende dak dat met stevige kabels in bedwang wordt gehouden, moet vragen oproepen waarvan je het antwoord misschien pas weet als je de Floriade allang hebt verlaten. En soms zul je het antwoord nooit weten, en blijft het zoals het is.

Zo poëtisch als de ervaring op Big Spotters' Hill is, zo prozaïsch is de Groene Stad die aan de voet van de heuvel ligt. Eigenlijk zijn het geen eilanden, maar tochten met stukken land ertussen. We dwalen door de Groene Stad, bestaande uit het weide-eiland, het cultuureiland, het bos- en het watereiland en passeren een honderd jaar oude plataan die uit Noord-Brabant naar de Haarlemmermeer is overgeplant en deze operatie wonderwel heeft doorstaan. Trots staat hij daar in het middelpunt van een stadspleintje. Op het Cultuureiland zijn verschillende hoveniers en groenvoorzieners aanwezig, in dit geval om aanschouwelijk te maken hoe je ook op een klein oppervlak een 'gevoelvolle' tuin kunt opbouwen. De waterbeheerders, met de waterschappen als Nederlands oudste bestuurslichaam, zijn op een van de Eilanden neergestreken met een paviljoen dat in het teken staat van de duurzaamheid. Met duurzaamheid wordt niet alleen de kwaliteit van het oppervlaktewater aan de orde gesteld, maar ook de functie van water in ons landschap:

colline faisant référence à d'autres endroits mystiques comme les mastabas, les collines et terrasses des Astèques ou les temples grecs. L'œuvre d'art avec son toit flottant retenu par de robustes câbles, doit soulever des questions auxquelles on ne pourra peut-être répondre qu'après avoir quitté la Floriade depuis longtemps. Et parfois, on ne trouvera jamais la réponse, tout reste alors dans l'état.

Si la sensation est poétique sur la Big Spotters' Hill, la Ville Verte au pied de la colline, elle, est prosaïque. En fait, il ne s'agit pas vraiment d'îles mais plutôt de voies d'eau entrecoupées de lopins de terre. Nous errons à travers la Ville Verte constituée par l'île prairie, l'île de la culture, l'île boisée et l'île aquatique et passons devant un platane centenaire qui a été transplanté du Brabant septentrional à l'Haarlemmermeer et a miraculeusement survécu à cette opération. Il se dresse fièrement au milieu d'une petite place dans la ville. Les arboriculteurs et les horticulteurs sont de nouveau présents sur l'île de la culture, cette fois pour démontrer comment même une toute petite surface peut héberger un jardin 'très chaleureux'. Les administrations des eaux, avec les *waterschappen* qui sont les organes de gestion les plus anciens des Pays-Bas, se sont installées sur l'une des îles dans un pavillon placé sous le signe de la durabilité. La durabilité ne sous-entend pas uniquement la qualité des eaux de surface mais aussi la fonction de l'eau dans notre paysage: en tant que réserve,

to raise questions. The answers may only occur to us long after we have left the Floriade, and sometimes we will never know. Maybe there is no answer.

The experience on Big Spotters' Hill may be a poetic one, but that of the Green City that lies at its foot is much more down to earth. We have called it a group of islands, but to be accurate they are not true islands. The 'city' really consists of water channels with stretches of land between them. Each of these almost-islands has a different character; there is a meadow island, an inhabited island, a woodland island and a water island. The pride of the inhabited island is a hundred-year old plane tree which has been transplanted to Haarlemmermeer over a distance of more than 100 km. (and somehow survived). It stands at the centre of a 'city square'. The inhabited island offers room to a number of tree and cut-flower nurserymen, here demonstrating how we can lay out a garden with flair in a densely built-up area.

The Water Boards of Holland are the country's oldest local organizations still in existence. The modern managers of the Dutch water table have descended on one of the islands and erected a pavilion to sustainability. Sustainability is not only a matter of water quality but also the functions of water in the Dutch landscape – as storage, as open space in a crowded country, as a link in the ecological chain and as a recreational attraction.

gegen angestrebt wird, ist gerade das Gefühl des dort Seins, auf einem Berg, der auf andere mystische Orte wie die Mastabas, die treppenförmigen Hügel der Azteken oder die griechischen Tempel verweist. Das Kunstwerk mit seinem beweglichen Dach, das mit starken Kabeln in Schach gehalten wird, soll Fragen aufwerfen, von denen man die Antwort vielleicht erst weiß, wenn man die Floriade schon lange verlassen hat. Und manchmal wird man die Antwort nie finden und bleibt alles, wie es ist.

So poetisch die Erfahrung auf Spotters' Hill ist, so prosaisch ist die Grüne Stadt, die am Fuße des Hügels liegt. Eigentlich sind es keine Inseln, sondern Wassergräben mit Stücken Land dazwischen. Wir streifen durch die Grüne Stadt, die aus der Weideinsel, der Kulturinsel, der Wald- und Wasserinsel besteht und gehen an einer hundert Jahre alten Platane vorbei, die aus Nord-Brabant stammt und ins Haarlemmermeer gepflanzt wurde und diese Operation ausgezeichnet überstanden hat. Stolz steht sie jetzt im Mittelpunkt eines Stadtplatzes. Auf der Kulturinsel sind auch wieder die Bäume und Baumzüchter präsent, in diesem Fall um zu illustrieren, wie man auch auf einer kleinen Oberfläche einen 'gefühlvollen' Garten anlegen kann. Die Wasserverwalter, mit den Wasserbehörden als ältestem Verwaltungsorgan der Niederlande, haben sich auf einer der Inseln in einem Pavillon niedergelassen, der im Zeichen der Dauerhaftigkeit steht. Mit Dauerhaftigkeit wird nicht nur die Qualität des Oberflächenwassers zur Diskussion gestellt,

De Groene Stad
La Ville Verte
Der Grünen Stadt
The 'Green City'

als berging, als ruimtescheppend element in een vol land, als schakel in de milieuketen en als recreatieve attractie. Water als bedreigende factor in een land dat onder de zeespiegel ligt, is inmiddels een achterhaalde visie. Water wordt nu juist gezien als een element dat structuur brengt in stad en land, omdat het scheidt en verbindt, en in het volle Nederland vooral de horizon breekt.

Toch kunnen we er niet aan voorbijgaan dat de ligging van deze Floriade uniek is, en ongetwijfeld indruk maakt op de buitenlandse gasten die zijn aangevlogen op een luchthaven die vijf meter onder de zeespiegel ligt. Honderdvijftig jaar geleden was dit nog een van de grootste binnenmeren van Nederland, waar het kon spoken en stormen. Om dat te illustreren laten de waterschappen ons in een tijdreis door middel van een simulator zien hoe het er toen op deze plek uitzag, een onstuimige en verraderlijke binnenzee met scheepswrakken op de bodem. Vervolgens verplaatst de periscoop zich boven de waterspiegel en registreert hoe het meer polder werd en hoe we honderdvijftig jaar later worstelen met nieuwe problemen, zoals de klimaatwijziging waardoor de lozing van het water steeds ingewikkelder wordt. Is de toekomst aan het aanleggen van drijvende wijken, zoals gebeurt in de nieuwste uitleg van Amsterdam, IJburg? Maken we van polders weer water? Het zou geen verwondering hoeven te wekken in een land dat te boek staat als het meest kunstmatige en geordende ter wereld, een land dat door mensenhanden is opgebouwd.

en tant que génératrice d'espace dans un pays qui en manque, en tant que maillon de la filière environnementale et en tant qu'attraction récréative. L'eau vue comme un facteur menaçant par un pays situé en dessous du niveau de la mer est une idée maintenant dépassée; elle est désormais justement considérée comme un élément qui confère une structure à la ville et au pays, car l'eau sépare et unit à la fois, et apporte surtout une brèche dans l'horizon surpeuplé des Pays-Bas.

Nul ne saurait nier toutefois que l'emplacement de la Floriade est unique en son genre et impressionnera sans aucun doute les visiteurs étrangers qui auront atterri à l'aéroport de Schiphol situé à cinq mètres au-dessous du niveau de la mer. Il y a cent cinquante ans, se trouvait à cet endroit la plus grande mer intérieure des Pays-Bas où de violentes tempêtes pouvaient sévir. A titre d'illustration, un documentaire des *waterschappen* nous montre, au cours d'un voyage dans le temps que nous fait vivre un simulateur, l'aspect de ce lieu à l'époque: une mer intérieure houleuse et traîtresse avec des carcasses de navires échoués. Le périscope remonte ensuite à la surface de l'eau et divulgue comment cette mer intérieure est devenue polder, ensuite nous sont expliqués les nouveaux problèmes auxquels il faut faire face cent cinquante ans plus tard tel le changement de climat qui rend l'évacuation de l'eau de plus en plus difficile à réaliser. L'avenir nous amènera-t-il à réaliser des quartiers flottants, tel IJburg, le tout dernier élargissement d'Amsterdam ou tel l'exemple présenté sur une île de la Ville Verte? Ou devrons-nous redonner les polders à l'eau? Ceci ne surprendrait pas forcément dans un pays réputé pour être le plus artificiel et le plus ordonné du monde, un pays construit à mains d'hommes.

We have long ceased to worry about water as a threat to our land below sea level. Now we welcome it as a structuring element in our landscapes and townscapes. In the crowded cities of the Netherlands, canals and rivers are cherished for the open space they create.

We must not forget that the location of this Floriade is unique. It is bound to make quite an impression on foreign visitors who have just landed at an airport which is five metres below sea level. One hundred and fifty years ago, this was still one of Holland's biggest inland seas where storms could ravage and rage. The Water Boards take us on a trip through time to show us how this place used to look with shipwrecks dotted around the sea bed. The periscope then rises above the surface to show us how the region was drained bit by bit, and how, 150 years later, we are now struggling with problems such as global warming which make water management more complicated than ever. Does the future lie in floating towns, like the new Amsterdam district of IJburg or a floating house on the inhabited island in the Green City? Or should we be converting the polders back into lakes? Nobody would be surprised at that in country that is famed as the most artificial and orderly in the world – a man-made land.

sondern auch die Funktion des Wassers in unserer Landschaft: als Abstellraum, als Raum schaffendes Element in einem vollen Land, als Glied in der Umweltkette und als erholsame Attraktion. Wasser als bedrohender Faktor in einem Land, das unter dem Meeresspiegel liegt, ist inzwischen ein überholter Gedanke, Wasser wird jetzt gerade als ein Element betrachtet, das Struktur in Stadt und Land bringt, weil es trennt und verbindet und in den vollen Niederlanden vor allem den Horizonz bricht.

Dennoch kann man nicht ignorieren, dass die Lage dieser Floriade einzigartig ist und ohne Zweifel Eindruck auf die ausländischen Gäste macht, die auf einem Flughafen angekommen sind, der fünf Meter unter dem Meeresspiegel liegt. Vor hundertfünfzig Jahren war dies noch einer der größten Binnenseen der Niederlande, wo es stürmisch hergehen konnte. Um das zu illustrieren, zeigt der Film der Wasserbehörden uns in einer Zeitreise mit Hilfe eines Simulators, wie es damals an diesem Ort aussah: ein stürmischer und tückischer Binnensee mit Schiffswracks auf dem Boden. Danach bewegt sich das Periskop über den Wasserspiegel und registriert, wie der See zum Polder wurde und wie wir hundertfünfzig Jahre später mit neuen Problemen wie beispielsweise der Klimaveränderung kämpfen, wodurch die Abführung des Wassers immer komplizierter wird. Liegt die Zukunft im Bauen von schwimmenden Stadtvierteln, wie es in dem neuesten Wohngebiet von Amsterdam, in IJburg, geschieht? Machen wir aus Poldern wieder Wasser? Es würde keinen wundern in einem Land, das den Ruf hat, das künstlichste und geordnetste der ganzen Welt zu sein – ein Land, das von Menschenhänden geschaffen wurde.

De Groene Stad
La Ville Verte
Der Grünen Stadt
The 'Green City'

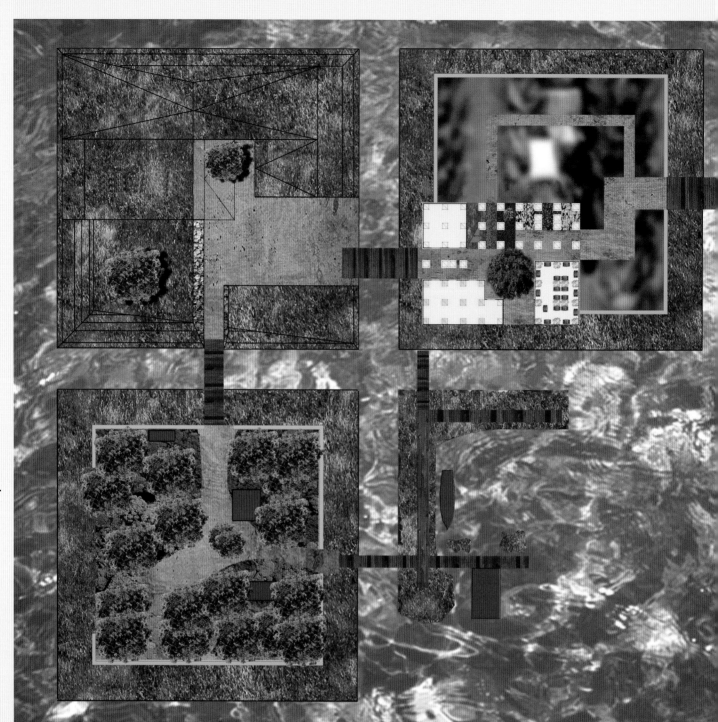

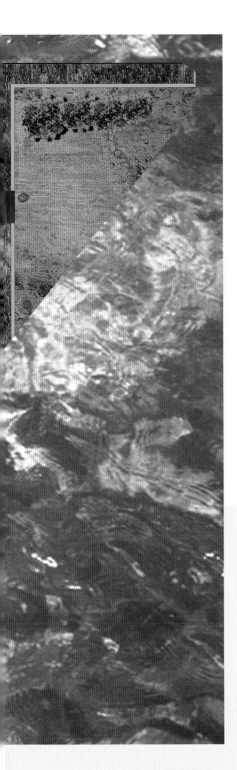

De Groene Stad, bestaande uit het
weide-eiland, het cultuureiland,
het bos- en het watereiland
**La Ville Verte, constituée par l'île
prairie, l'île de la culture, l'île boisée et l'île aquatique**
Der Grünen Stadt, die aus der
Weideinsel, der Kulturinsel, der
Wald- und Wasserinsel besteht
**The 'Green City': a meadow island,
an inhabited island, a woodland
island and a water island**

Water

'Denkend aan Holland zie ik brede rivieren traag door oneindig laagland gaan'. Beter had de dichter Marsman ons land niet kunnen typeren. Holland waterland. Dat waterrijke karakter is op Floriade 2002 volop vertegenwoordigd: in een bron, in beekjes, vijverpartijen, een vaart, slootjes en een heus meer. Water fascineert. Het is altijd in beweging, weerspiegelt de wisselende luchten en herbergt een eigen wereld van dieren en… planten.

Wie herinnert zich niet dat hij als kind op zijn knieën langs een slootje lag, turend naar schrijvertjes en libellen? Wat je toen op die leeftijd niet zo in de gaten had is dat het plantenleven op de grens van water en land ongelooflijk gevarieerd is. Die rijkdom toont zich op deze Floriade in al zijn schoonheid langs de slootjes die het eilandenrijk naast de Berg doorsnijden. Vroeg in het voorjaar zijn het de gele linten van dotterbloemen (Caltha palustris) die je blik vangen en meevoeren langs de randen van het water. Daar staan in april ook allerlei narcissen in bloei.
Absolute heerser over deze verlandingsstroken is de imposante moeraswolfsmelk (Euphorbia palustris) die minzaam toeziet hoe in de loop van de volgende maanden buren als kattestaart (Lythrum salicaria), moerasspiraea (Filipendula vulgaris), koninginnekruid (Eupatorium cannabinum) en duizendknoop (Persicaria amplexicaulis) tot bloei komen, in de rug gesteund door grote wolken van smele (Deschampsia cespitosa). Hollandser kan een slootkant niet zijn.

L'eau

'Pensant à la Hollande, je vois de larges rivières couler lentement à travers un plat pays interminable'. Le poète Marsman n'aurait pu mieux décrire notre pays. Les Pays-Bas, pays des eaux. Cette omniprésence de l'eau est parfaitement illustrée à la Floriade 2002: par une source, par des ruisselets, par des étangs, par un canal, par des cours d'eau et par un véritable lac. L'eau est fascinante. Elle est toujours en mouvement, reflète les alternances du ciel et abrite un monde animal et … végétal qui lui est propre.

Qui ne se revoit pas enfant agenouillé au bord d'un cours d'eau pour observer les petits insectes glissant à la surface et les libellules? Ce que l'enfant ne remarquait peut-être pas vraiment à cet âge, c'est l'incroyable diversité de la flore là où la terre et l'eau se côtoient. Cette richesse nous est présentée dans toute sa beauté à la Floriade, le long des canaux qui entrecoupent le royaume des îles Près de la Colline. Tôt dans la saison, le regard est attiré par le cordon jaune des soucis d'eau (Caltha palustris) qui nous guide le long des rives. En avril y fleurissent aussi toutes sortes de narcisses et jonquilles. Le maître absolu de ces rivages est l'imposant euphorbe aquatique (Euphorbia palustris) qui attend courtoisement que ses voisines fleurissent dans les mois suivants: la salicaire (Lythrum salicaria), la spirée (Filipendula vulgaris), l'eupatoire (Eupatorium cannabinum) ou la renouée (Persicaria amplexicaulis), adossées contre de gros nuages de canche (Deschampsia cespitosa).
La rive d'un canal ne pourrait être plus hollandaise.

64

Water

'Dreaming of Holland, I see broad rivers winding lazily through an endless lowland.' It would be hard to improve on this description by the poet Marsman. Holland is a land of water. This aspect is fully represented at Floriade 2002, with a spring, brooks, pools, a navigable watercourse, countless ditches and of course the Lake. Water has its fascination. It is always in motion, it reflects the changing skies and it is home to a unique realm of creatures – and of course plants.

Who cannot remember kneeling as a child on the banks of stream, peering at whirligig beetles at dragon flies? Something we may not realize at that age is that the plant life on the border between water and dry land is incredibly diverse. This wealth reveals itself by the narrow watercourses that pervade the Islands, by the Hill. Early in spring, it is the yellow ribbons of Marsh Marigolds (Caltha palustris) that draw our gaze along the waterways. Later, in April, there will be countless varieties of daffodil in bloom here.
The lord and master of these strips of marshy land is the imposing Bog Spurge (Euphorbia palustris), which looks benignly on as month by month such neighbours as Purple Loosestrife (Lythrum salicaria), Dropwort (Filipendula vulgaris), Hemp Agrimony (Eupatorium cannabinum) and Knotweed (Persicaria amplexicaulis) come into flower, backed up by great clouds of Tufted Hair Grass (Deschampsia cespitosa). Now this is what we call Holland!

Wasser

'Denke ich an Holland, sehe ich breite Flüsse sich träge durch unendliches Flachland ziehen.' Besser hätte der Dichter Marsman unser Land nicht charakterisieren können. Dieser wasserreiche Charakter ist auf der Floriade 2002 in Hülle und Fülle vertreten: in einer Quelle, in Bächen, Teichpartien, einem Kanal, einem Wassergraben und einem großen See. Wasser fasziniert. Es ist immer in Bewegung, reflektiert den wechselnden Wolkenhimmel und beherbergt eine eigene Tier- und Pflanzenwelt.

Wer erinnert sich nicht daran, wie er als Kind auf den Knien an einem Wassergraben lag und nach Taumelkäfern und Libellen Ausschau gehalten hat? Damals war es einem natürlich noch nicht so bewusst, dass die Flora und Fauna auf der Grenze von Wasser und Land unglaublich abwechslungsreich ist. Auf der Floriade zeigt sich dieser Reichtum in seiner ganzen Schönheit entlang der Wassergräben, die das Inselreich neben dem Berg durchschneiden. Zum Frühlingsanfang sind es die gelben Blüten der Sumpfdotterblume (Caltha palustris), die die Aufmerksamkeit auf sich ziehen und den Besucher an die Wasserränder mitnehmen. Dort stehen im April auch allerlei Narzissen in Blüte.
Absoluter Herrscher über diese Verlandungsstreifen ist die imposante Sumpf-Wolfsmilch (Euphorbia palustris), die huldvoll zusieht, wie im Lauf der nächsten Monate Nachbarn wie Blutweiderich (Lythrum salicaria), Mädesüß (Filipendula vulgaris), Kunigundenkraut (Eupatorium cannabinum) und Knöterich (Persicaria amplexicaulis) erblühen werden, im Rücken von großen Wolken Bronzeschleier (Deschampsia cespitosa) gestützt.
Holländischer kann ein Grabenrand nicht mehr sein.

65

In het derde deel van de Floriade, 'aan het Meer', is voor het water een hoofdrol weggelegd, zoals de naam al doet vermoeden. En ook nu weer is het niet alleen het water op zich, maar vooral ook het samenspel tussen water en beplanting dat bepaalde onderdelen van dit gebied zo bijzonder maakt.
Zo zijn er de oevers langs het meer, waar de al eerder aanwezige beplanting van riet en lisdodde op sommige plekken gehandhaafd is. Deze vitrage langs de rand van de plas is hier en daar aangevuld met gele lis, kattestaart en koningsvarens en verzacht de overgang van water naar land. Daar krijg je als bezoeker een heel ander gevoel dan bij de 'harde' overgang van water naar rotsblokken en het is juist die tegenstelling die een wandelings langs het water zo interessant maakt.
Tot de hoogtepunten behoort een inzending van 200 verschillende soorten waterlelies, de grootste collectie die ooit getoond is.
Deze collectie is bijeen gebracht in een zijarm van het meer en is onderdeel van een gecombineerde inzending van vaste planten en waterplanten. Het thema van deze inzending is 'het ritme van de dag', gebaseerd op de gedachte dat bij het vroege ochtendlicht vooral lichte tinten zoals wit en geel tot hun recht komen en dat, naarmate de dag vordert, het kleurenschema verschuift naar schakeringen in roze, rood, oranje en lila om in de avonduren te eindigen bij purper en donkerrood.
In het water en in schalen op de metalen vlonders presenteren zich de waterlelies in een kleurenschema dat afgestemd is op het ritme van de dag en dat gelijk op gaat met de kleuren van de vaste planten langs de oevers.
Witte, gele, roze, rode en zelfs blauwe waterlelies afkomstig uit Amerika, Engeland, Duitsland, Thailand, Japan, Bangladesh en natuurlijk ook Nederland verenigen zich hier in één groot kleurenfeest.
Daarnaast hebben deze waterlelies nog iets extra's in petto: het wonderlijke

Dans la troisième partie du parc de la Floriade, Au bord du Lac, l'eau joue, comme le nom le laisse supposer, un rôle principal. Et de nouveau, ce n'est pas non plus l'eau à elle seule mais c'est plutôt et surtout le jeu de l'eau et de la végétation qui donne à certaines des composantes de ce domaine un caractère si particulier. Prenons les rives par exemple, où la végétation déjà existante de roseaux et de massettes a été maintenue à certains endroits. Par contre, ce cordon du rivage a été garni ici et là de lys jaunes, de salicaires et d'osmondes royales comme pour amortir la transition entre la terre et l'eau. L'effet ainsi produit est tout à fait différent de ce que ressent le visiteur lorsque l'eau se heurte à la barrière stérile de rochers, et c'est justement ce contraste qui rend la promenade au fil de l'eau si intéressante.
L'un des points culminants est une présentation de 200 variétés de nénuphars, la plus grande collection qui ait été exposée.
Cette collection se niche dans un bras latéral du lac et fait partie d'une présentation mixte de plantes vivaces et aquatiques. La présentation a pour thème 'le rythme de la journée', partant du fait que les tons clairs comme le blanc et le jaune sont particulièrement mis en valeur par la pâle lumière de l'aube et que la palette des couleurs évolue avec le jour qui avance vers des nuances de rose, de rouge, d'orange et de mauve pour donner libre cours au pourpre et au rouge foncé aux heures plus tardives du soir.
Dans l'eau et dans les coupes sur les passerelles métalliques, les nénuphars ouvrent leur éventail de couleurs en harmonie avec le rythme de la journée et avec les couleurs des plantes vivaces sur les rives. Des nénuphars blancs, jaunes, roses, rouges et même bleus, venant d'Amérique, d'Angleterre, d'Allemagne, de Thaïlande, du Japon, du Bangladesh et bien sûr des Pays-Bas, se rassemblent ici pour nous offrir une grande fête des couleurs.

In the third section of Floriade, 'on the Lake', water has the starring role as the name suggests. However, it is not just the water itself but the combined effect of water and vegetation that makes certain parts of this area so special. An example is the lake shore where the existing flora of Reeds and Bulrushes has been preserved. This lacy curtain on the lake margin is enlivened here and there with Yellow Flag, Loosestrife and Royal Fern, and softens the transition between land and water. It gives us quite a different feeling to the 'hard' boundary between the water and rocks, and it is this contrast that makes it so interesting to walk along the shore.
One of the highlights of the Floriade is the entry of 200 different kinds of Water Lily. It is the greatest collection of these plants that has ever been shown. The water lilies occupy a side arm of the Lake and form part of a combined entry of perennials and water plants. The theme of this entry is 'the rhythm of the day'. It is based on the principle that lighter colours such as white and yellow come out best in the early morning light, and as the day progresses, the colour scheme gradually shifts from pink, to red, to orange, to violet and finally at dusk toe purple and deep red.
In the water and in shallow basins on the metal platforms, the Water Lilies are arrayed in a scheme of colours which is attuned to the rhythm of the day and which parallels the colours of the perennials on the shore.
White, yellow, red and even blue Water Lilies, originating from America, Britain, Germany, Thailand, Japan, Bangladesh and of course the Netherlands, unite to create a feast of colour.
What is more, these Water Lilies have something else in store for us: the astonishing but true fact that each species has a unique built-in biological clock. The alarm is set to a different time for each kind. The flower of the familiar White Water Lily (Nymphaea alba) spends an hour from

Im dritten Teil der Floriade, 'am See', ist dem Wasser – wie der Name schon suggeriert – eine Hauptrolle vorbehalten. Und auch dieses Mal geht es nicht ausschließlich um das Wasser an sich, sondern ist es hauptsächlich das Zusammenspiel zwischen Wasser und Bepflanzung, das bestimmte Teile dieses Gebiets so außergewöhnlich macht. So gibt es die Ufer am See, wo die schon früher vorhandene Bepflanzung aus Riet und Rohrkolben an manchen Stellen beibehalten wurde. Diese Gardine entlang des Seerandes wird hier und da mit Sumpf-Schwertlilien, Blutweiderich und Königsfarn ergänzt und mildert den Übergang vom Waser zum Land. Als Besucher überkommt einen ein völlig anderes Gefühl als beim 'harten' Übergang vom Wasser zu den Felsbrocken, und es ist gerade dieser Kontrast, der einen Spaziergang am Wasser so interessant macht.
Zu den Höhepunkten gehört eine Einsendung von 200 verschiedenen Seerosenarten, wobei es sich um die größte Kollektion handelt, die je gezeigt wurde.
Diese Kollektion wurde in einem Seitenarm des Sees zusammengebracht und ist Teil einer kombinierten Einsendung von Dauer- und Wasserpflanzen.
Das Thema dieser Einsendung ist 'der Rhythmus des Tages' und basiert auf dem Gedanken, dass im frühen Morgenlicht vor allem helle Töne wie weiß und gelb zu ihrem Recht kommen und dass, in dem Maße, wie der Tag vortschreitet, sich die Farbskala zu rosa, rot, orange und lila bewegt, um in den Abendstunden bei violett und dunkelrot zu enden.
Die Seerosen präsentieren sich im Wasser und in Schalen auf den Metallstegen in einer Farbpalette, die auf den Tagesrhythmus abgestimmt ist und gleichzeitig mit den Farben der Dauerpflanzen entlang der Ufer harmoniert. Weiße, gelbe, rosa, rote und sogar blaue Seerosen aus Amerika, England, Deutschland: ein einziges großes Fest der Farben.
Außerdem können diese Seerosen mit einer weiteren überraschung aufwarten: der sonderbare, aber bewiesene Umstand, dass jede Gattung eine eingebaute Uhr

Naast de Berg
À côté de la Colline
Am Hügel
By the Hill

Dotterbloem
Soucis d'eau
Sumpfdotterblume
Marsh Marigolds

Moeraswolfsmelk
Euphorbe aquatique
Sumpf-Wolfsmilch
Bog Spurge

maar ware gegeven dat iedere soort een ingebouwde klok in zich heeft.
Per soort werkt die klok op andere tijden: de gewone witte boerenwaterlelie
(Nymphaea alba) gaat iedere dag open tussen 9.00 en 10.00 uur en sluit haar
bloembladen weer tussen 17.00 en 18.00 uur. Veel stipter zijn Nymphaea
'Escarboucle' en Nymphaea laydekeri 'Purpurata', beiden rode schoonhe-
den die eveneens om 9.00 uur hun eerste bloembladen openvouwen, maar al
om 9.05 uur hun stralende hart laten zien. Weer andere soorten gaan eerder of
later open en sluiten ook weer op andere tijdstippen.
En dat is nog niet alles, want een tweede bijzondere eigenschap is dat iedere
waterreliebloem drie volle dagen bloeit, waarna de volgende knop zich presenteert. Zo kan het voorkomen dat een volwassen plant in een warme zomer
meer dan 60 bloemen produceert.

Ces nénuphars nous réservent une autre surprise: aussi étrange que cela
puisse paraître, chaque variété a sa propre programmation quant à ses
'heures d'ouverture'. L'heure d'épanouissement n'est pas la même d'une
variété à l'autre: le grand nénuphar commun (Nymphaea alba) s'ouvre
chaque jour entre 9.00 et 10.00 h. et referme ses pétales entre 17.00 et
18.00 h. Le Nymphaea 'Escarboucle' et le Nymphaea laydekeri
'Purpurata', tous deux de splendides variétés rouges, sont plus ponctuels
puisqu'ils déploient leurs premiers pétales à 9.00 h. et ouvrent leurs cœurs
rayonnants dès 9 h 05. D'autres variétés s'épanouissent plus tôt ou plus
tard et se referment aussi à d'autres moments. Et ce n'est pas tout, les
nénuphars ont une deuxième particularité, à savoir que chaque bouton
fleurit trois jours avant que se présente le bouton suivant. Il peut donc arriver qu'une plante adulte produise plus de 60 fleurs au cours d'un été chaud.

9 a.m. and 10 a.m opening its petals, and another from 5 p.m. and 6 p.m.
closing them again. The two red-flowering beauties Nymphaea 'Escarboucle' and Nymphaea laydekeri 'Purpurata' are much prompter:
they similarly begin opening at 9 a.m., but by 9.05 their glowing flower
hearts are already exposed. Other species open earlier or later, and close at
other times too.
And that is not the end of the story, for Water Lilies have another unique
trait. The Water Lily flower lives for exactly three days, after which
another bud appears to replace it. An adult plant can produce over 60
blooms in a warm summer.

besitzt. Bei jeder Sorte arbeitet die Uhr zu anderen Zeiten: die weiße Seerose
(Nymphaea alba) geht jeden Tag zwischen 9.00 und 10.00 Uhr auf und
schließt ihre Blütenblätter wieder zwischen 17.00 und 18.00 Uhr. Viel exakter
sind Nymphaea 'Escarboucle' und Nymphaea laydekeri 'Purpurata',
beides rote Schönheiten, die ebenfalls um Punkt 9.00 Uhr ihre ersten Blütenblätter auseinanderfalten und schon um 9.05 Uhr ihr leuchtendes Herz zeigen.
Wieder andere Arten gehen früher oder später auf und schließen auch wieder zu
anderen Zeiten.
Und das ist noch nicht alles, denn eine weitere, besondere Eigenschaft der Seerose
liegt darin, dass jede Seerose drei volle Tage blüht, wonach sich die nächste
Knospe präsentiert. So kann es vorkommen, dass eine erwachsene Pflanze in
einem Sommer über 60 Blüten produziert.

Waterlelies zijn planten met karakter. Daarom is het niet zo verwonderlijk dat iedereen die een vijver in zijn tuin heeft, daarin ook graag een waterlelie wil hebben. Helaas gaat het dan nogal eens mis omdat de onwetende tuinliefhebber de waterlelie laat verdrinken. Hoe dat kan? Waterlelies ademen door hun blad. Wanneer de nieuwe waterlelie direkt na aankoop op de diepte gezet wordt waarop hij moet gaan groeien, verdwijnt het jonge blad onder water. Op dat moment kan de plant geen adem meer halen en stikt tenslotte. Daarom moeten waterlelies altijd in een aantal stappen naar het uiteindelijke dieptniveau gebracht worden, net zo vaak totdat de stengels van het blad lang genoeg zijn om aan de oppervlakte te komen.

Een waterlelie kan ook verdrinken wanneer hij te dicht bij een sproeier of fontein geplaatst wordt. Het op het blad neervallende water heeft op den duur eveneens een verstikkend effect.

Les nénuphars ayant un caractère particulier, il n'est donc pas étonnant que tout celui qui possède un étang dans son jardin veuille aussi y mettre un nénuphar. Hélas, le succès n'est pas toujours garanti car l'amateur mal informé peut noyer le nénuphar. Comment cela? Et bien, sachez que ces plantes respirent par leurs feuilles et que si le nénuphar tout juste acheté est directement mis à la profondeur définitive, les jeunes feuilles se trouvent sous l'eau, la plante ne peut plus respirer et finit par être asphyxiée. Aussi les nénuphars doivent-ils être mis par étapes à des profondeurs successives jusqu'à ce que les feuilles aient des tiges assez longues pour flotter.

Un nénuphar ne supporte pas non plus d'être à directe proximité d'un gicleur ou d'une fontaine. L'eau qui tombe sur les feuilles peut aussi l'asphyxier à la longue.

Water Lilies are plants with a character. So it's not surprising that everyone who owns a garden pond likes to have a Water Lily plant flowering in it. Sometimes things go wrong because the Water Lily can be drowned by an inexperienced gardening enthusiast. How can that happen? Water Lilies breathe through their leaves. The optimistic pool-owner comes home from the garden centre clutching the Water Lily and immediately plants it in deep water, from where he expects it to grow to the surface. But that means the young leaves will be under the water. The plant cannot breathe and it dies. The correct way is to move the Water Lily progressively into deeper water as it grows, always making sure that the leaf stems are long enough to reach the surface.

A Water Lily can also drown if you plant it too close to a sprinkler or a fountain. Water continually falling on the leaves can eventually suffocate the plant.

Seerosen sind Pflanzen mit Charakter. Deshalb wundert es einen nicht, dass jeder, der einen Teich im Garten hat, auch gerne Seerosen haben möchte. Leider geht das schon mal schief, weil der unwissende Gartenliebhaber die Seerose ertrinken läßt. Wie ist das möglich? (Seerosen atmen durch ihr Blatt. Wenn die neue Seerose direkt nach dem Kauf in der Tiefe gesetzt wird, aus der sie wachsen soll, verschwindet das junge Blatt unter Wasser. In diesem Moment kann die Pflanze nicht mehr atmen und erstickt schließlich. Darum müssen Seerosen immer in einigen Schritten auf das letztendliche Tiefenniveau gebracht werden, und zwar so oft, bis die Blattstängel lang genug sind, um an die Oberfläche zu kommen.

Eine Seerose kann auch ertrinken, wenn sie zu nahe an einem Sprinkler oder einen Brunnen gesetzt wird. Das auf das Blatt fallende Wasser hat auf die Dauer ebenfalls eine erstickende Wirkung.

Kattestaart

Salicaire

Blutweiderich

Purple Loosestrife

Moeraswolfsmelk

Euphorbe aquatique

Sumpf-Wolfsmilch

Bog Spurge

Moerasspiraea

Spirée

Mädesüß

Dropwort

De kunst om grond uit water te winnen staat gelijk met overlevings-kunst. De volgende stap is hoe daar vorm aan te geven in de manier van wonen, de brug te slaan van noodzaak naar comfort. En van comfort naar innovatie en variatie. Via terpen en het bouwen van huizen op palen en woonschepen zijn we aangeland bij het drijvend wonen, op een ponton of piepschuim. Landschap en milieu laten zich in Nederland nu eenmaal niet los zien van bebouwing, vandaar de keus om in de Eilanden aan de voet van de Berg de intense verstrengeling van natuur en stedenbouw te presenteren. Niet alleen: *how low can we live* maar ook *how close can we live*. Toen het verzelfstandigde Woningbedrijf Amsterdam enkele jaren geleden zijn territorium uitbreidde naar de Haarlemmermeer, lag het voor de hand de Floriade te gebruiken als podium voor nieuwe visies op het wonen in de toekomst. Hoewel het geen proeftuin is geworden in de strikte betekenis van het woord, tasten we op een oppervlakte van twintig bij twintig meter de grenzen van de leefbaarheid af in een compacte stedelijke omgeving.

We praten hier, met andere woorden, over een huwelijk tussen blauw, rood en groen, in de kern de opgave voor de Nederlandse stedenbouwers voor de komende jaren. De Gelaagde Stad, zo is dit 'experiment' gedoopt. We lopen over een entree-eiland de Gelaagde Stad binnen,

L'art de gagner du terrain sur l'eau équivaut à l'art de survivre. Ceci dit, il faut ensuite savoir quelle forme donner à ce gain de terrain dans le mode de l'habitat, franchir le pas de la nécessité au confort, du confort à l'innovation et à la variation. En passant par les tertres, la construction de maisons sur pilotis et les bateaux-logements, nous en arrivons aux maisons flottantes sur un ponton ou sur du polystyrène. Et ce, parce qu'aux Pays-Bas le paysage et l'environnement doivent toujours être envisagés dans le contexte de l'urbanisation. Raison pour laquelle l'intense intégration de la nature et de l'urbanisation est visualisée dans les Iles au pied de la Colline. La question n'est pas seulement de savoir: *jusqu'à quelle profondeur peut-on vivre* (how low can we live), mais aussi: *jusqu'à quelle proximité peut-on vivre* (how close can we live). Lorsque l'organisme de logement privatisé Woningbedrijf Amsterdam décida, il y a quelques années, d'élargir son champ d'action à l'Haarlemmermeer, il s'avéra logique de faire de la Floriade le podium de nouvelles optiques sur l'avenir de l'habitat. Bien que ce ne soit pas devenu un jardin expérimental au sens strict, nous tâtons sur un espace de 20 m. sur 20 les limites de la qualité de la vie dans la compacité d'un cadre urbanisé.

Autrement dit, il s'agit ici d'un mariage entre le bleu, le rouge et le vert, arrivant ainsi à l'essentiel du problème posé aux urbanistes néerlandais

De Gelaagde Stad
La Ville Superposée
Die Geschichtete Stadt
the 'Layered City'

The technique of reclaiming land from the sea is practically a matter of survival in the Netherlands. Once reclamation has been carried out, the question arises how design the reclaimed land so that people can use it and live on it – to make the transition from necessity to comfort. And that is followed by progress from mere comfort to innovation and variety. The alternatives used to be to build houses on artificial mounds or on stilts, or to live in houseboats. Now there is another possibility – floating houses. New houses can be built on floating foundations of steel pontoons or plastic foam. It is impossible to consider the Dutch landscape and natural environment separately from the question of housing and building. That is why it was decided to use the Islands by the Hill to demonstrate the intense interdependence of nature and urban development. Some years ago, the newly privatized Amsterdam Housing Corporation extended its territory to Haarlemmermeer. It made sense to take advantage of the Floriade as a platform for presenting some of their ideas about houses of the future. In a mere twenty square metres, we get a taste of what life could be like in the compact city environment of the near future.

This 'experiment' has been titled the 'Layered City'. In town planners' terms, it is a three-way marriage between red, green and blue – in other words, between built up areas, parks and countryside, and water.

Die Kunst, Boden aus Wasser zu gewinnen, ist gleichbedeutend mit Überlebenskunst. Der nächste Schritt liegt darin, wie man diese in der Art zu wohnen gestaltet und eine Brücke zwischen Notwendigkeit zu Komfort schägt. Und von Komfort zu Innovation und Variation. Über Warfen und dem Bau von Häusern auf Pfählen und Hausbooten sind wir jetzt beim Wohnen auf dem Wasser angelangt, entweder auf einem Ponton oder auf Styropur. In den Niederlanden können die Landschaft und die Umwelt nun einmal nicht von der Bebauung losgelöst betrachtet werden. Aus dem Grund hat man sich entschieden, auf den Inseln am Fuße des Berges die intensive Verflechtung von Natur und Städtebau zu präsentieren. Nicht nur: *how low can we live*, sondern auch *how close can we live*. Als sich die Wohnungsbaugesellschaft Amsterdam vor einigen Jahren verselbständigte und ihr Territorium ins Haarlemmermeer ausbreitete, lag es auf der Hand, die Floriade als Podium für neue Ideen in Bezug auf das Wohnen der Zukunft zu gebrauchen. Obwohl es kein Versuchsfeld in der strengen Bedeutung des Wortes geworden ist, tasten wir auf einer Oberfläche von zwanzig mal zwanzig Metern die Grenzen der Lebensqualität in einer kompakten urbanen Umgebung ab.

Wir reden hier mit anderen Worten von einer Verbindung zwischen blau, rot und grün, im Wesentlichen die Aufgabe für die niederländischen Stadt-

waar we die oude plataan aantreffen, residu van het verleden in de woonomgeving van de toekomst. Ze symboliseert het estafettestokje dat de huidige Nederlanders doorgeven aan de volgende generatie. De Gelaagde Stad staat in verbinding met weide-eiland, boseiland en watereiland met een drijvende woning als vingerwijzing naar toekomstige woningbouw. Het parcours dat we volgen – over bruggen met rode spijlen, het signaal in dit onderdeel – maakt aanschouwelijk dat steden vol en intens kunnen zijn, maar dat er wel degelijk ruimte is voor groen. Door de huizen op te tillen, wordt het maaiveld opengegooid, door af te zien van schuine kappen kunnen we daktuinen maken. Je zou bij het zien van deze miniatuurvesting met niveauverschillen kunnen mijmeren over mediterrane stadjes, die ondanks hun compactheid nooit een claustrofobisch effect oproepen.

Omdat er een concessie gedaan moet worden aan de grote bezoekersstroom zijn de trappen en straten breder dan normaal; het concept daarentegen blijft dat van een kleine citadel die bestaat uit verschillende lagen, ingebed in het groen. De kleur van de zonnepanelen is aangepast aan de binnenstedelijke atmosfeer. Intussen wil die stedelijke samenleving zich op het gebied van energie zelf kunnen bedruipen. Mocht de zon tekort schieten dan is wind het alternatief. Er wordt een miniatuur windmolen ontwikkeld voor stedelijke situaties, waarvan

pour les années à venir. Cette 'expérience' à été baptisée La Ville Superposée. Une île d'accès nous fait entrer dans la Ville Superposée où nous trouvons de vieux platanes, vestiges du passé, au milieu de l'habitat du futur. Elle symbolise le flambeau que les Néerlandais d'aujourd'hui passent aux générations de demain. La Ville Superposée est reliée à l'île prairie, l'île boisée et l'île aquatique avec son logement flottant à titre d'index pointé vers l'avenir. Notre parcours franchissant des passerelles à balustrades rouges, signe de l'insolite à découvrir dans cette partie, nous prouve que même les villes très construites et surpeuplées laissent de la place à la verdure. En soulevant les maisons au-dessus du niveau du sol, celui-ci reste disponible; et en supprimant les toits en pente, des jardins peuvent être aménagés sur les toits en terrasses. Cette forteresse miniature sur plusieurs niveaux nous rappelle un peu les petites villes méditerranéennes qui malgré leur compacité ne donnent jamais une impression de claustrophobie.

Comme il a fallu tenir compte d'un gros flux de visiteurs, les escaliers et les rues sont plus larges que d'habitude tout en conservant l'idée d'une petite citadelle en dénivellation blottie dans la verdure. Les panneaux solaires sont de couleur s'harmonisant avec l'ambiance au cœur de la ville. Car entre-temps, cette forme de cohabitation urbaine se veut en même temps autonome quant à son approvisionnement en énergie.

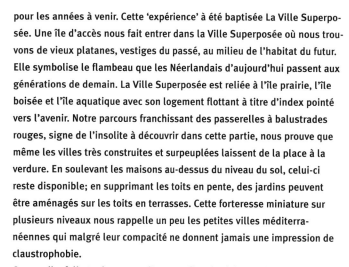

We enter the Layered City via an entrance island and come face to face with that venerable Plane tree – a reminder of the past in the living situation of the future. It symbolizes the heritage passed on from one generation of Dutch inhabitants to the next. The Layered City is linked to the Meadow Island, the Woodland Island and the Water Island. The last of these has floating house, a hint at future possibilities in housing. The route we follow, across bridges with red posts (the identifying colour for this area), provides a tangible demonstration that cities can be crowded and busy but still leave room for greenery. We could raise the houses on piles to leave the ground beneath them free, or give houses flat roofs that can be used for roof gardens. Seeing this mini-city with its multiple levels, we could imagine ourselves in a Mediterranean village, for they are never claustrophobic despite their compactness.

The designers had to make some concessions to the large volumes of visitors expected at the Floriade, so the stairways and streets are wider than normal. But the concept remains clear enough: a miniature citadel, consisting of several layers embedded in greenery. The urban society of the future will have to be self-sufficient in energy to some extent. Among other things, that means relying less on fossil fuel energy. Among other renewable energy sources, the Layered City has solar panels – in a colour modified to suit the city centre. When there is insufficient sunlight, the

planer für die kommenden Jahre. Die Geschichtete Stadt, so wurde dieses Experiment getauft. Über eine Eingangsinsel betreten wir die Geschichtete Stadt, wo wir die alte Platane vorfinden, ein Überbleibsel der Vergangenheit in der Wohnumgebung der Zukunft. Sie symbolisiert den Staffelstab, den die Niederländer von heute der nächsten Generation übergeben. Die Geschichtete Stadt steht in Verbindung mit der Wiesen-, Wald- und Wasserinsel, mit einer schwimmenden Wohnung als Fingerzeig auf den Wohnungsbau der Zukunft. Der Strecke, der wir – über Brücken mit roten Gitterstäben, das Signal in diesem Teil – folgen, veranschaulicht, dass Städte voll und intensiv sein können, es aber durchaus Platz für Grün gibt. Indem die Häuser hochgehoben werden, entsteht eine offene Bodenoberfläche, indem wir auf schräge Dächer verzichten, können wir Dachgärten kreieren. Sobald man diese Miniatursiedlung mit Niveauunterschieden sieht, fallen einem die mediterranen Städte ein, die trotz ihrer Kompaktheit niemals einen klaustrophobischen Effekt haben. Weil man eine Konzession an den großen Besucherstrom machen musste, sind die Treppen und Straßen breiter als gewöhnlich; das Konzept dagegen bleibt das von einer kleinen Zitadelle, die aus verschiedenen Lagen besteht und eingebettet ist ins Grüne. Die Farbe der Solarkollektoren wurde an die innerstädtische Atmosphäre angepasst. Inzwischen will sich diese städtische Gesellschaft auf dem Gebiet der Energie selbst versorgen können. Gibt es zuwenig Sonne, dann

78

een proeve beschikbaar kan zijn op de Floriade. Wie beperkt woont, moet slim met zijn details omspringen. Het hemelwater vloeit niet in een beweging af naar het oppervlaktewater, vandaar het belang van daktuinen en sedum (een assortiment van mossen en vetplanten), en wat wel dreigt door te stromen, kan als grijs water de toiletten spoelen. Op het boseiland, bebouwd met een transparante aanplant – een vorm van *light landscaping* – zien we aan de hand van een uitkijkpost hoe het mogelijk is de bodem vrij te houden en een nieuw perspectief te openen op boomkruinen. In het weide-eiland is het tegenovergestelde het geval: daar verdwijnt het wonen juist voor een deel in de grond. Wat Woningbedrijf Amsterdam als een van de participanten wil aantonen is niet alleen een concept van nieuwe woontypologieën maar ook een nieuwe benadering van de stad. Op grote schaal wordt die filosofie uitgewerkt in de westelijke tuinsteden van Amsterdam. De opzet daarvan luidde in de jaren vijftig: ruim en licht wonen in het groen met aparte winkelvoorzieningen in de buurt. De bewoners werden toen gerekend tot een homogene middenklasse. Vijftig jaar verder luidt de conclusie dat die monofunctionele opzet niet langer voldoet. Tuinstad verandert geleidelijk aan in Parkstad, hetgeen een integrale planologie veronderstelt waarin de aandacht voor bijvoorbeeld bevolkingssamenstelling, infrastructuur en werkgelegenheid gelijk opgaat. In Parkstad wonen verschillende milieus in een gedifferentieerde omgeving. Het groen is geen restruimte maar een wezenlijk bindmiddel. Zo is het milieu evenmin een sluitpost. Integendeel, waterhuishouding en stroomvoorziening zijn geïncorporeerd in de architectuur. Op kleine schaal vormt de Gelaagde Stad een voorbode van de nieuwe menging van rood met groen. Compacte stad ontmoet ruimtelijke

Et si le soleil arrivait à manquer, le vent prendrait la relève. Une éolienne miniature est à l'étude pour les milieux urbains dont un prototype permet de voir les effets à la Floriade. Vivre à l'étroit implique une certaine intelligence des détails. L'eau de pluie ne rejoint pas directement les eaux de surface sans autre forme de profit, d'où l'importance des jardins en terrasses et du sedum (un assortiment de mousses et plantes grasses), alors que les écoulements éventuels sont utilisés comme 'eau grise' pour le rinçage des toilettes.

Sur l'île boisée où la plantation est transparente – une forme de *paysage à clairevoie* (*light landscaping*) – un poste d'observation nous montre une autre façon de gagner du terrain et ouvre de nouvelles perspectives pour les couronnes des arbres. L'île prairie témoigne de l'alternative contraire puisque l'habitat y est partiellement enfoui sous terre.

Woningbedrijf Amsterdam, en tant que l'un des participants, veut ainsi nous sensibiliser non seulement à une nouvelle conception des types de logement mais aussi à une nouvelle approche de la notion de ville. Cette philosophie est concrétisée à grande échelle dans les villes jardins à l'ouest d'Amsterdam. Le principe de base s'est affirmé dans les années cinquante: vivre spacieux, à la lumière et dans la verdure, avec des commerces à proximité; les habitants appartenant à l'époque à une classe moyenne et homogène. La conclusion à en tirer un demi-siècle plus tard est que ce principe monovalent n'est plus suffisant. La Ville Jardin se transforme petit à petit en Ville Parc, ce qui suppose un urbanisme intégral tenant compte à part égale de la composition de la population, de l'infrastructure et du marché de l'emploi par exemple. Dans la Ville Parc, les habitants appartiennent à diverses classes de la société et vivent dans une forme de cohabitation identifiée. La verdure n'est pas un simple amé-

wind offers an alternative. A miniature wind-powered generator had been developed for urban applications, and a test version can be seen at the Floriade. People who live in a restricted amount of space have to be clever when it comes to details. It's wasteful to allow the rainwater to run straight down the drain: roof gardens and green roofs (which are planted with varieties of moss or Stonecrop) can make good use of it. The houses also have a 'grey water' plumbing system which collects rainwater from the roof and uses it for purposes like flushing the toilets. Using grey water is economical in comparison to mains water, which takes energy to purify. On the Woodland Island, planted with a fine, almost translucent leaf canopy – a form of 'light landscaping' – a viewing platform shows us how it is possible to keep the ground free and enjoy a new outlook on the treetops. The opposite situation applies on the Meadow Island. There, the house is sunk partly into the ground.

The aim of the Amsterdam Housing Corporation's participation is to demonstrate, firstly, ideas about new types of house, and secondly, the modern approach to city planning. This approach was first tried out on a large scale in garden suburbs, for example those in western Amsterdam. They were conceived in the 1950s to offer people light and spacious living surroundings, with plenty of urban greenery and shopping amenities in the vicinity. Now, fifty years later, the planners have concluded that the garden suburbs are too monofunctional by present day standards. Garden suburbs are gradually changing into Park Towns, which presupposes an integral urban planning strategy that takes into account factors like population structure, infrastructure and employment opportunities. A Park Town houses a heterogeneous population in a differentiated environment. Greenery is not just a way of filling up leftover space but a functional

ist der Wind eine Alternative. Für städtische Situationen wird eine Miniatur-Windmühle entwickelt, von der eine Probe auf der Floriade verfügbar sein kann. Wer beengt wohnt, muss mit seinen Details klug umgehen. sogar eine experimentelle Windmühle aufgestellt, die speziell für die Stadt entwickelt wurde. Das Regenwasser fließt nicht in einer Bewegung zum Oberflächenwasser ab – deshalb die Bedeutung von Dachgärten und Sedum (ein Sortiment an Moosen und Fettpflanzen) – und was offenbar wohl durchströmt, kann als graues Wasser die Toiletten spülen. Auf der Waldinsel mit ihrer transparenten Anpflanzung – eine Art von 'light landscaping' – sehen wir anhand eines Beobachtungspostens, wie es möglich ist, den Boden frei zu halten und eine neue Perspektive auf Baumkronen zu schaffen. Auf der Wieseninsel ist das Gegenteil eingetreten: dort verschwindet das Wohnen gerade teilweise in der Erde.

Was die Wohnungsbaugesellschaft Amsterdam als einer der Teilnehmer zeigen will, ist nicht nur ein Konzept neuer Wohntypologien, sondern auch eine neue Betrachtungsweise der Stadt. Diese Philosophie wird in großem Umfang in den westlichen Gartenstädten Amsterdams angewendet. Die Parole war in den fünfziger Jahren: geräumig und hell im Grünen wohnen mit extra Einkaufsmöglichkeiten im Viertel. Die Bewohner zählte man damals zu einer homogenen Mittelklasse. Fünfzig Jahre später lautet die Schlussfolgerung, dass dieser monofunktionelle Vorsatz nicht länger ausreicht. Die Gartenstadt verändert sich allmählich in eine Parkstadt, was eine integrale Stadtplanung voraussetzt, in der die Berücksichtigung von beispielsweise Bevölkerungszusammensetzung, Infrastruktur und Arbeitsgelegenheit zu gleichen Teilen aufgeht. In der Parkstadt wohnen verschiedene Milieus in einer differenzierten Umgebung. Das Grün ist kein Restraum, sondern ein wesentliches Bindemittel. Ebenso wenig wird die

Smeerwortel

Consoude

Beinwohl

Comfrey

Het watereiland
L'île aquatique
Der Wasserinsel
The water island

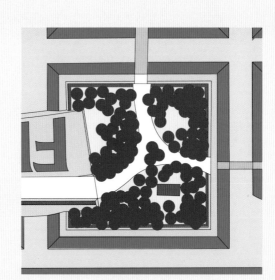

oplossingen, en omgekeerd. Met de introductie van stedelijk groen op de Floriade onderstreept de tentoonstelling dat beplanting geen privilege voor buitenwijk en het platteland is. De Groene Stad is op te vatten als een laboratorium van experimenten van hoe we het groen dichtbij kunnen halen, zonder dat de belevingswaarde tot nul wordt gereduceerd. Immers, maar al te vaak zijn bermen, perken en rotondes de muurbloempjes van het openbaar milieu, gevuld met onderhoudsvrij schaamgroen. In het besef dat Nederland wel eens wordt gezien als een dunbevolkte stad in plaats van een dichtbevolkt land, is de problematiek van de stadslandschappelijke inrichting actueel. En zo is het ook met de inrichting van het ommeland dat door gebrek aan behoorlijke planning in de afgelopen decennia in snel tempo is versnipperd. Nu uitgerekend Staatsbosbeheer de burger weer wil toestaan om vrijuit te struinen buiten de afgebakende paden, wordt het 'dwalen en verdwalen' op de Floriade voorzichtig op de agenda gezet: als instrument voor de beleving van de natuur. Niet langer natuur om op een museale manier naar te kijken, maar als een ervaring. De bedoeling is dat zodra de hekken verwijderd zijn, een grenzeloos natuurgebied in het hart van de Randstad overblijft.

nagement de l'espace restant mais un véritable agent de liaison. L'environnement n'est pas non plus un poste de second plan. Au contraire, l'approvisionnement en eau et en électricité est incorporé à l'architecture. La Ville Superposée est, à échelle réduite, un précurseur du nouvel amalgame du rouge et du vert. La ville compacte s'allie à l'aménagement de l'espace et réciproquement. Avec l'introduction des espaces verts urbains à la Floriade, l'exposition souligne que la végétation n'est pas le privilège des quartiers extérieurs et de la campagne. La Ville Verte fait fonction de laboratoire expérimental sur la façon de mettre la verdure à notre proximité, sans réduire à néant la valeur de la sensation qu'elle nous procure. Trop souvent en effet, les talus, les massifs et les ronds-points sont des espaces verts sans vie et faisant presque honte sous prétexte de ne pas devoir demander beaucoup d'entretien. Sachant que les Pays-Bas sont parfois vus comme une grande ville sous-peuplée au lieu d'un petit pays surpeuplé, la problématique de l'aménagement du paysage est d'actualité. Et c'est la même chose pour l'aménagement du site environnant, qui par faute de planification adéquate, à été morcelé à vive allure au cours des dernières décennies. Justement maintenant que l'administration des Eaux & Forêts veut à nouveau autoriser le promeneur à déambuler librement dans les bois en dehors des allées tracées, le sujet 'l'errance et le fourvoiement' a été prudemment inscrit à l'ordre du jour de la Floriade: à titre d'instrument pour mieux percevoir les effets de la nature, pour ne plus la considérer comme une sorte de musée naturel mais pour en vivre l'expérience. L'objectif est que subsiste, une fois les clôtures enlevées, un parc naturel illimité au cœur de la conurbation de la Randstad.

binding factor. Nor is the environment a mere afterthought. On the contrary, water recycling and sustainable electricity generation are designed into the architecture. On a small scale, the 'Layered City' presents a foretaste of a new mixture of 'red' and 'green'. The compact city meets spatial solutions and vice versa. The introduction of urban greenery to the Floriade emphasizes that planting is not a privilege reserved for the suburbs and countryside. We may regard the Green City as a laboratory for experiments on how we bring plants closer to people without resorting to the monotonous patches of maintenance-free shrubbery that we so often see in town centres, in verges, flower-beds and roundabouts. The realization that the whole of the Netherlands could be described as a thinly populated city instead of a densely populated country brings the problems of laying out the urban landscape to the fore. The countryside suffers from a lack of thoughtful design too. It has been extensively fragmented in the last twenty or thirty years. The Dutch countryside has long been notorious for its 'keep to the path' notices everywhere, but the National Parks Service has recently relented. Planners are starting to realize that people do not want to goggle at nature like something in a museum, but want to have the experience of being part of it. Now the idea of allowing us to wander off the marked paths has been cautiously placed on the Floriade agenda. After the exhibition is over and the fences have been removed, it will leave an unfenced nature reserve in the middle of the Randstad.

Umwelt vernachlässigt – im Gegenteil: der Wasserhaushalt und die Stromversorgung wurden in die Architektur integriert. In gewisser Hinsicht könnte man die Geschichtete Stadt als Vorboten der neuen Mischung aus Rot und Grün bezeichnen. Die kompakte Stadt trifft räumliche Lösungen und umgekehrt. Die Ausstellung betont mit der Einführung des städtischen Grüns auf der Floriade, dass Bepflanzung kein Privileg der Vororte und des Landes ist. Die Grüne Stadt sollte als ein Laboratorium von Experimenten aufgefasst werden, wie wir uns das Grün in unsere Nähe holen können, ohne dass der Erlebniswert auf Null reduziert wird. Doch nur zu oft sind die Grünstreifen, Rabatten und Rotunden die Mauerblümchen in der Öffentlichkeit, gefüllt mit pflegeleichtem Grün. Im Bewusstsein, dass die Niederlande auch schon mal als dünnbevölkerte Stadt anstatt dichtbevölkertes Land gesehen werden, ist die Problematik der städtelandschaftlichen Einrichtung aktuell. Und so ist es auch mit der Einrichtung des Umlands, das durch mangelnde kompetente Planung in den vergangenen Jahrzehnten in hohem Tempo zerstückelt worden ist. Nun, da ausgerechnet die staatliche Behörde für die Forstverwaltung dem Bürger wieder gestatten will, sich außerhalb der abgegrenzten Pfade frei zu bewegen, wird das 'Wandern und Verirren' auf der Floriade vorsichtig auf die Tagesordnung gesetzt: als Instrument für das Erleben der Natur. Nicht länger Natur, die man wie ein Museum betrachtet, sondern wie eine Erfahrung. Die Absicht besteht darin, dass sobald die Zäune entfernt werden, ein grenzenloses Naturgebiet im Herzen der Ballungsgebiete übrig bleibt.

Daslook

Ail d'ornement

Bärlauch

Ramsons

Onderbeplanting

Op iedere Floriade gaat zoveel mogelijk beschikbare oppervlakte naar inzenders die daarmee de kans krijgen de laatste ontwikkelingen op het gebied van groente-, fruit- en sierteelt te laten zien. Maar logischerwijs blijven er dan ook altijd plekken over die géén speciale bestemming hebben.

Die plekken krijgen op deze Floriade een heel bijzondere invulling en vallen onder de noemer 'onderbeplanting'. Een wat vage term die vooral in gemeentelijke groendiensten gebruikt wordt om plekken onder bomen en heesters mee aan te duiden.

En dat is de enige overeenkomst met de onderbeplanting op deze Floriade: ook hier zijn het overgebleven plekken onder bomen en heesters. Het verschil zit hem in de samenstelling van de beplanting; daardoor zijn het zulke blikvangers geworden dat menige gemeente er jaloers op zou zijn.

Underplanting

As much of the area of the Floriade as possible is dedicated to the participating companies to present their latest developments in the cultivation of fruit, vegetables and ornamental plants. Inevitably there will be some spots left over which do not have an specific function. These spots are given a very special application at this Floriade, and they fall under the heading of 'underplanting'. This is a rather vague term which municipal greenery departments like to use for plants in areas under trees and shrubs.

But that is the only similarity to underplanting at this Floriade – here too it refers to leftover areas under trees and shrubs. The difference is in the composition of the plants that are planted in these places. At the Floriade, they are eye-catchers which must surely be the envy of many a local authority.

Végétation intercalaire

Chaque Floriade réserve le plus possible de surface disponible pour les exposants qui ont ainsi la possibilité de montrer les dernières nouveautés en matière de culture maraîchère, fruitière et ornementale. Mais il reste tout de même toujours des endroits n'ayant pas d'utilisation spécifique. Ces endroits ont à la Floriade 2002 une attribution très spéciale et sont classés sous la dénomination 'végétation intercalaire': un terme plutôt vague surtout utilisé par les services municipaux des espaces verts pour désigner les endroits sous les arbres et les arbustes. C'est d'ailleurs le seul point commun avec la végétation intercalaire de cette Floriade puisque ici aussi, il s'agit d'endroits inoccupés sous les arbres et les arbustes. La différence se situe par contre dans la composition des plantations qui en fait de tels tape-à-l'œil qu'elles ne manqueront pas de faire des jaloux.

Unterbepflanzung

Auf jeder Floriade erhalten die Einsender möglichst viel verfügbare Oberfläche und damit die Gelegenheit, die neuesten Entwicklungen auf dem Gebiet des Gemüse- und Obstbaus sowie des Anbaus von Zierpflanzen zu zeigen. Aber natürlich bleiben dann auch immer Stellen übrig, die keine besondere Bestimmung haben. Diese Stellen erhalten auf dieser Floriade eine ganz besondere Interpretation und werden als 'Unterbepflanzung' bezeichnet. Eine etwas vage Bezeichnung, die vor allem in städtischen Ordnungsämtern verwendet wird, um Stellen unter Bäumen und Hecken zu benennen. Das ist die einzige Parallele mit der Unterbepflanzung auf dieser Floriade: auch hier befinden sich die übrig gebliebenen Stellen unter Bäumen und Hecken. Der Unterschied liegt in der Zusammenstellung der Bepflanzung; dadurch sind sie zu einem solchen Blickfang geworden, dass so manche Gemeinde darauf eifersüchtig sein könnte.

Het aardige is dat deze onderbeplantingsstroken ook bedoeld zijn als voorbeeld voor en ter inspiratie van groendiensten die zoeken naar een andere invulling van hun openbaar groen. Wanneer het openbaar groen vooral in visueel opzicht waardevoller wordt, zal er bewuster en met meer eerbied mee omgegaan worden.

Het uitgangspunt is geweest om gewassen toe te passen die aantrekkelijk zijn en niet al te veel onderhoud vergen. Dat wordt bereikt door te werken met:
– evenwichtige combinaties,
– grote oppervlakten van één soort en
– gewassen die goed sluiten.
Ook is aandacht geschonken aan de aantrekkelijkheid van planten gedurende het hele groeiseizoen (ontwikkeling, bladvorm, bloei, mooi na de bloei, wintersilhouet, karakter).
De nieuwe visie op aanpak van het openbaar groen zou gericht moeten zijn op kwaliteit én duurzaamheid.

In het bos rondom het meer ligt een aantal opvallende voorbeelden van deze nieuwe aanpak, waarvan er hier vier genoemd worden:
– de beplantingsstroken die de Europese landentuinen van elkaar scheiden en die als titel 'Van lommer en lover tot krieken en kruiden' hebben meegekregen, verwijzend naar de flinke hoeveelheid schaduw die de hier aanwezige bomen, waaronder sierkersen, over de kruidachtige onderbeplanting uitwerpen. Die onderbeplanting bestaat uit soorten als Anemone aconitifolia, Digitalis lutea, *bosaardbeitjes (*Fragaria vesca), Lamium orvala *en* Geranium macrorrhizum *met een speciaal voorjaarsaccent van* Hyacinthoides hispanica *(boshyacint).*

Les bandes de végétation intercalaire ont donc aussi pour avantage d'être des exemples et des sources d'inspiration pour les services municipaux en quête d'idées originales pour l'aménagement des espaces verts. En effet, si les espaces verts sont valorisés sur le plan visuel, ils seront mieux appréciés et traités avec plus de respect.
Le principe de base a été d'utiliser des végétaux séduisants qui demandent peu d'entretien. La formule consistait à travailler avec:
– Des combinaisons équilibrées,
– Des grandes surfaces d'une seule espèce,
– Des plantes de végétation dense.
Un autre aspect a été pris en considération, à savoir le fait que les plantes doivent être attrayantes pendant toute leur période de croissance (développement, forme des feuilles, inflorescences, beauté après la floraison, silhouette en hiver, caractère). La nouvelle optique en matière d'espaces verts devrait être axée sur la qualité et la durabilité.
Plusieurs exemples typiques de cette nouvelle approche se trouvent dans le bois autour du lac, nous en nommerons quatre:
*– Les bandes de plantations qui séparent les jardins européens et qui ont reçu pour titre: 'Du feuillage et de ses ombrages jusqu'aux cerises et aux aromates', faisant allusion à la profusion d'ombre que les arbres, parmi lesquels des cerisiers à fleurs, profilent sur les plantations d'herbacées. Cette végétation intercalaire se compose d'espèces telles que l'*Anemone aconitifolia *(anémone), la* Digitalis lutea *(digitale), le* Fragaria vesca *(fraisier des quatre saisons), le* Lamium orvala *(lamier) et le* Geranium macrorrhizum *(bec-de-grue), avec pour accent spécialement printanier les* Hyacinthoides hispanica *(jacinthes des bois).*
– Une bande de plantation autour de la mare, à l'ouest du plan d'eau,

These underplanting beds are meant as an example and inspiration to people from municipal greenery departments, who are always on the lookout for new ways to plant their public parks and gardens. When public greenery is visually appealing, the public will treat it with more attention and respect.
The Floriade based its choice of plants for underplanting on the principle that they must be attractive but not require much maintenance. This was achieved by applying:
– balanced combinations of plants
– large areas planted with a single type of plant
– plants which give good ground coverage.
The attractiveness of the plants throughout the growth season (initial development, leaf appearance, flower, post-flowering, winter silhouette, general character). The new approach to public greenery has to focus on quality and durability. The woods around the Lake contain several striking applications of this new underplanting system. Here are four examples:
– The borders separating the European national gardens from one another have been named 'From shade and foliage to cherries and herbs' – a designation which refers to the many shadows cast by the trees, including ornamental cherry trees, on the herbaceous underplanting. The underplanting consists of species like Anemone aconitifolia, *Small Yellow Foxglove (*Digitalis lutea), *Wild Strawberry (*Fragaria Vesca), Lamium orvala, *and a Cranesbill (*Geranium macrorrhizum) – *with the Bluebell* Hyacinthoides hispanica *add a special spring gaity.*
– A border around the pool on the east of the Lake bears the name 'Disarming Violence'. This title refers to the almost rampant spreading of the perennials Anemone tomentosa 'Robustissima' *(Japanese*

Hinzu kommt, dass diese Unterbepflanzungsstreifen auch als Beispiel für und zur Inspiration von Ordnungsämtern beabsichtigt sind, die nach einer anderen Bestimmung des öffentlichen Grüns suchen. Wenn das öffentliche Grün vor allem in visueller Hinsicht wertvoller wird, geht man damit auch bewusster und mit mehr Respekt um.

Der Ausgangspunkt war die Pflanzung von Gewächsen, die attraktiv aussehen und nicht allzu viel Pflege benötigen. Das wird erreicht, indem man arbeitet mit:
– ausgewogenen Kombinationen,
– großen Oberflächen mit einer einzigen Sorte und
– Gewächsen, die gut schließen.
Auch wird der Attraktivität von Pflanzen während der ganzen Wachssaison Aufmerksamkeit gewidmet (Entwicklung, Blattform, Blüte, schön nach der Blüte, Wintersilhouette, Charakter). Die neue Richtlinie, wie man in Zukunft mit öffentlichem Grün umgeht, sollte sich auf Qualität und Dauerhaftigkeit richten. Im Wald um den See liegen einige auffallende Beispiele dieser neuen Vorgehensweise, von denen hier vier genannt werden:
– Die Bepflanzungsstreifen, die die europäischen Ländergärten voneinander trennen und die als Titel 'Von Schatten und Laubwerk zu Herzkirschen und Kräutern' erhalten haben. Sie verweisen auf die große Menge Schatten, den die hier anwesenden Bäume, darunter Zierkirschen, der kräuterartigen Unterbepflanzung spenden. Diese Unterbepflanzung besteht aus Arten wie Anemone aconitifolia, Digitalis lutea, *Walderdbeeren (*Fragaria vesca), Lamium orvala *und* Geranium macrorrhizum *mit einem speziellen Frühlingsakzent der* Hyacinthoides hispanica *(Spanisches Hasenglöckchen).*
– Ein Bepflanzungsstreifen um den Teich an der Ostseite des Wassers erhielt den Namen 'Entwaffnende Gewalt', der auf die beinahe-wuchernden Dauerpflan-

Bosanemonen
Anémone des bois
Waldanemone
Wood Anemone

– Een beplantingsstrook rondom de poel aan de oostkant van het water, die de benaming 'Ontwapenend geweld' meekreeg. Die naam duidt op de bijnawoekerende vaste planten Anemone tomentosa 'Robustissima' *(Japanse anemoon) en* Geranium phaeum 'Album' *die ondersteund worden door heesters met groot blad:* Alangium chinense, Alangium platanifolium *en* Rubus odoratus, *waarvan de laatste eveneens een behoorlijk explosieve groeikracht heeft. Siergrassen zoals* Molinia litoralis 'Transparent' *en* Deschampsia cespitosa 'Goldschleier' *brengen luchtigheid in dit geheel.*

– De 'Beschermde Berm' die voor het grootste deel uit schermbloemige planten bestaat, gelegen aan een zijpad dat vanaf het eind van de promenade naar de bloemenvallei loopt. In de schaduw van grote bomen komt hier een gigantische border tot bloei die van april tot ver in het najaar verrassend is en er ieder jaar weer anders uit zal zien omdat er veel soorten in zitten die zichzelf uitzaaien. Combinaties van Salvia glutinosa, Lunaria rediviva, Orleya grandiflora, Astrantia major 'Shaggy', Anemone hybr. 'Honorine Jobert' *en* Molinia altissima 'Karl Foerster' *zijn hier beeldbepalend.*

– Het meest sober, maar daarom niet minder indrukwekkend is de onderbeplanting aan de oostkant van de emotietuinen. Ook hier weer hoge bomen en in de schaduw daarvan gedijen Geranium macrorrhizum 'Czakor', Euphorbia amygdaloides robbiae *en* Deschampsia cespitosa 'Goldschleier'. *Niet al te opvallende soorten die toch in combinatie met elkaar tot een bijzonder resultaat komen. Vandaar ook de titel: 'Ongekend traditioneel'.*

Het terraduct lokt met het kunstwerk *The bridge of life* van Frank Gude en Wim Langedijk, een met groen gestoffeerde overspanning die verschillende levensfasen van de mens symboliseert. De eerste levensfase krijgt al voor De Brug gestalte, op de kinderspeelplaats *Op de*

*baptisée 'Force désarmante'. Ce nom s'applique à la vigueur des plantes vivaces presque prolifères: l'*Anemone tomentosa 'Robustissima' *(anémone du Japon) et le* Geranium phaeum 'Album', *soutenus par des arbustes à grandes feuilles: l'*Alangium chinense, l'Alangium platanifolium *et le* Rubus odoratus, *ce dernier étant aussi d'une vigueur explosive. Des herbes d'ornement comme la* Molinia litoralis 'Transparent' *et la* Deschampsia cespitosa 'Goldschleier' *(canche) donnent un aspect vaporeux à l'ensemble.*

– La 'Berge protégée' est composée en majeure partie d'ombellifères et située sur une allée latérale rejoignant la fin de la promenade à la vallée des fleurs. A l'ombre des grands arbres, fleurit un énorme massif qui ne cesse d'étonner d'avril à loin dans l'automne. Il sera différent chaque année puisque maintes espèces s'ensemencent d'elles-mêmes. Les mélanges de Salvia glutinosa *(sauge),* Lunaria rediviva *(lunaire),* Orleya grandiflora, Astrantia major 'Shaggy' *(radiaire),* Anemone hybr. 'Honorine Jobert' *et* Molinia altissima 'Karl Foerster' *déterminent l'effet produit.*

– La végétation intercalaire la plus sobre, au demeurant non moins impressionnante, est celle du côté ouest des jardins des émotions. Là aussi, de grands arbres à l'ombre desquels fleurissent le Geranium macrorrhizum 'Czakor', l'Euphorbia amygdaloides robbiae *et la* Deschampsia cespitosa 'Goldschleier'. *Ce sont des espèces peut-être moins originales mais, combinées les unes aux autres, elles donnent un résultat d'une étrange beauté, d'où le nom: 'Révélation traditionnelle'.*

Le 'terraduc' nous cligne de l'œil par l'œuvre d'art *La Passerelle de la vie* **(***The Bridge of Life***) de Frank Gude et Wim Langedijk, un pont drapé de vert**

Anemone) and Geranium phaeum 'Album', *which are backed up by the large-leaved shrubs* Alangium chinense, Alangium platanifolium *and* Rubus odoratus. *The last of these is almost explosively vigorous in its own right. Ornamental grasses such as* Molinia litoralis 'Transparent' *and* Deschampsia cespitosa 'Goldschleier' *lighten the mixture up a little.*

– The 'Protected Verge', which consists mostly of umbelliferous plants, is located on a side path that leads from the end of the promenade to the Valley of Flowers. Here, in the shadow of tall trees, a huge border is coming into flower. It will continue offering surprises from April until late in the year, and it will look different every year because many of the plants are self-propagating. Combinations of Salvia glutinosa, Lunaria rediviva, Orleya grandiflora, Astrantia major 'Shaggy', Anemone hybr. 'Honorine Jobert' *and* Molinia altissima 'Karl Foerster' *dominate the scene here.*

– The most austere but no less impressive example of underplanting is that on the east of the Emotion Gardens. Here too there are tall trees, and Geranium macrorrhizum 'Czakor', Euphorbia amygdaloides robbiae *and* Deschampsia cespitosa 'Goldschleier' *flourish in their shadow. These are not particularly ostentatious plants but, in combination, the result is splendid. Hence the title, 'Unprecedented / Traditional'.*

The terraduct entices us with a work of art by Frank Gude and Wim Langedijk called 'The Bridge of Life', a green cloth stretched over a framework symbolizing the stages of human life. The first 'stage of life' takes shape before The Bridge itself, in the children's playground Op de zeebodem ('On the Seabed'). Child's play is not just a game at the Floriade, for it is in

zen Anemone tomentosa 'Robustissima' *(Sommeranemone) und* Geranium phaeum 'Album' *verweist, die von großblättrigen Sträuchern unterstützt werden:* Alangium chinense, Alangium platanifolium *und* Rubus odoratus, *von denen letzterer ebenfalls eine ziemlich explosive Wachstumsfähigkeit hat. Ziergräser wie* Molinia litoralis 'Transparent' *und* Deschampsia cespitosa 'Goldschleier' *verleihen dem Ganzen eine gewisse Luftigkeit.*

– Der 'Geschützte Grünstreifen', der größtenteils aus Doldengewächsen besteht, liegt an einem Seitenpfad, der vom Ende der Promenade aus zum Blumental verläuft. Im Schatten der großen Bäume erblüht hier eine gigantische Rabatte, die uns von April bis weit in den Herbst überraschungen bietet und jedes Jahr anders aussehen wird, weil sie viele Arten enthält, die sich selber aussähen. Kombinationen aus Salvia glutinosa, Lunaria rediviva, Orleya grandiflora, Astrantia major 'Shaggy', Anemone hybr. 'Honorine Jobert' *und* Molinia altissima 'Karl Foerster' *bestimmen hier das Bild.*

– Am schlichtesten, deshalb jedoch nicht weniger beeindruckend, ist die Unterbepflanzung an der Ostseite der Gärten der Emotionen. Auch hier stehen wieder hohe Bäume, in deren Schatten Geranium macrorrhizum 'Czakor', Euphorbia amygdaloides robbiae *und* Deschampsia cespitosa 'Goldschleier' *gedeihen. Nicht allzu viele auffallende Arten, die zusammen dennoch ein besonderes Resultat ergeben. Deshalb auch der Titel: 'Ungeahnt traditionell'.*

Der Terradukt lockt mit dem Kunstwerk 'The Bridge of Life' von Frank Gude und Wim Langedijk, eine mit Grün gepolsterte Überspannung, die verschiedene Lebensphasen des Menschen symbolisiert. Die erste Lebensphase wird vor der Brücke gestaltet, auf dem Kinderspielplatz 'Auf dem Meeresboden'. Der spielende Mensch wird auf der Floriade keinesfalls stief-

De beschermde berm
La 'Berge protégée'
Der 'Geschützte Grünstreifen'
The 'Protected Verge'

zeebodem. De spelende mens is geen ondergeschoven kind op de Floriade, want juist in het spel komt de mens op een onnadrukkelijke manier in contact met de natuur. 'Op de zeebodem' vertelt het verhaal van de beweging, in speeltoestellen die speciaal voor de expositie zijn ontworpen, zoals balanceerkrokodillen, veerwippen, springplateaus in de vorm van schelpen, maar ook gevaartes die ons bewust maken van de plek waar we ons bevinden, op een voormalige zeebodem. En daar hoort een scheepswrak bij compleet met klimwant.

Het terraduct

Een Floriade bestaat niet alleen uit bloemen en planten, ze bestaat vooral ook uit cijfers. Het aantal toiletten dat berekend is op een mensenmassa. De breedte van de paden (vijf tot acht meter) die per dag maximaal vijftigduizend mensen moeten aankunnen. En dan natuurlijk de hoeveelheid bollen, borden en bomen.

Wie de kaart van de Haarlemmermeer bekijkt, kan vaststellen dat het Floriade-park een snipper is in een rijk geschakeerd, omgeploegd polderlandschap. Een kwart van het terrein bestaat uit het Haarlemmermeersebos, een ander erfstuk is de Stelling van Amsterdam. De rest was stevig akkerland. Een enkele pachter werd uitgekocht. Het bos, met een zandwinningsplas in het midden, was toe aan opwaardering. Omdat Schiphol wilde uitbreiden met een vijfde baan en Hoofddorp in het kader van de Vinex-opgave de taak had enkele duizenden mensen extra te huisvesten, was er, zoals dat heet, een 'strategisch groenproject' nodig. Een perceel bos- en recreatiegebied dat de noordelijke Haarlemmermeer leefbaar houdt, dat doet vergeten dat dit een ongelofelijk knooppunt van infrastructuur is. Ter compensatie van de plannen

symbolisant les diverses étapes de la vie. La première phase de l'existence se concrétise devant Le Pont, sur l'aire de jeux intitulée *Sur les fonds marins*. A la Floriade, l'homme qui s'amuse est plus qu'un grand enfant car c'est justement par le jeu que l'homme entre discrètement en contact avec la nature. L'aire *Sur les fonds marins* raconte l'histoire du mouvement, par des jeux créés spécialement pour l'exposition: des crocodiles balançoires, un tape-cul à ressort, des trampolines en forme de coquillages, et des colosses qui nous font prendre conscience que gisait autrefois ici le fond de la mer, un lieu de circonstance donc pour une complète épave de navire se laissant escalader.

Le 'terraduc'

Une Floriade n'est pas seulement une histoire de fleurs et plantes, c'est aussi une histoire de chiffres et de calculs: le nombre de toilettes à prévoir pour l'affluence, la largeur des allées (de 5 à 8 m.) devant accueillir un maximum de cinquante mille personnes par jour, et bien entendu, l'énorme quantité de bulbes, de massifs et d'arbres.

Il suffit de regarder la carte de l'Haarlemmermeer pour constater que le parc de la Floriade n'occupe qu'une petite partie du damier de polders labourés. Le bois d'Haarlemmermeer couvre un quart du terrain et fait partie, comme le Stelling d'Amsterdam, des biens hérités du passé. Pour le reste, il y a de bonnes terres arables dont quelques-unes ont été rachetées. Comme le bois, avec une carrière de sable au milieu, avait besoin d'être revalorisé, que Schiphol voulait s'élargir pour créer une cinquième piste et qu'Hoofddorp avait pour tâche, dans le cadre du projet Vinex, de créer des logements pour quelques milliers de personnes en plus, un 'programme stratégique d'aménagement de verdure' s'imposait. Une parcelle

playing that we make our first innocent contact with nature. 'On the Seabed' tells the story of movement in play apparatus designed especially for the exhibition: crocodile balancing beams, springy see-saws, trampoline platforms shaped like shells and several other pieces of hardware that remind us that this was once the bottom of the sea – for example a shipwreck complete with a climbing net.

The Terraduct

To its organizers, the Floriade is not just a collection of flowers and plants; it is also a mass of statistics. How about the countless toilets needed for the hordes of visitors; the paths measuring five to eight metres in breadth, wide enough to carry up to fifty thousand pairs of feet per day; and of course an immense number of seats, signposts and shelters? Looking at the map of Haarlemmermeer, we can see that the Floriade Park is a small piece of a rich patchwork of polder countryside, most of which is cultivated. A quarter of the site consists of a wooded area, the Haarlemmermeersebos, and another section is occupied by part of the historic Stelling van Amsterdam. The rest was farmland (a single tenant farmers had to be bought out). The Haarlemmermeersebos, with a former sand quarry in its middle, was sorely in need of revitalization. This, among other things, made the area a good candidate for what urban planners call a strategic greenery project. In other words, it is to become a block of woodlands and green leisure areas that will contribute to making northern Haarlemmermeer a more pleasant place to live. It will soften the feeling that this whole part of the polder is just a maze of motorways and industrial farmland. The new green zone is also intended to make up for a major new housing development of several thousand homes on the edge of the

mütterlich behandelt, denn gerade beim Spiel kommt der Mensch auf eine ungezwungene Weise mit der Natur in Kontakt. 'Auf dem Meeresboden' erzählt die Geschichte der Bewegung anhand von Spielobjekten, die speziell für die Ausstellung entworfen wurden wie Balancekrokodile, Federschaukeln, Sprungplateaus in der Form von Muscheln, aber auch Monstren, die uns ins Bewusstsein rufen, dass wir uns auf dem ehemaligen Meeresboden befinden. Und dazu gehört auch ein Schiffswrack, komplett mit Klettertauwerk.

Der Terradukt

Die Floriade besteht nicht nur aus Blumen und Pflanzen, sondern in der Hauptsache aus Zahlen. Da ist z.B. die Anzahl der Toiletten im Verhältnis zur Besuchermenge, die Breite der Wege (fünf bis acht Meter), die jeden Tag bis zu 50.000 Menschen aufnehmen müssen, und natürlich die Menge der Blumenzwiebeln, Sträucher, Bäume und Schilder.

Auf der Karte der Gemeinde Haarlemmermeer bildet der Floriade-Park einen Klecks in der abwechslungsreichen, gepflügten Polderlandschaft. Ein Viertel des Geländes ist bewaldet (der Haarlemmermeerse Bos), ein anderes überbleibsel aus der Vergangenheit ist die Stelling van Amsterdam, ein aus verschiedenen Anlagen bestehender Befestigungsring. Das übrige Terrain war mit festem Ackerboden bedeckt. Einige Pächter erhielten eine Abfindung. Auch war es an der Zeit, das Waldgebiet, das einen See zur Sandgewinnung einschloss, neu zu gestalten. Da der Flughafen Schiphol Platz für den Bau seiner fünften Startbahn brauchte und die Gemeinde Hoofddorp im Rahmen des Vinex-Wohnungsbauprogramms Wohnraum für ein paar Tausend Menschen schaffen musste, war ein sogenanntes 'strategisches Grünprojekt' erforderlich. Ein Wald- und Erholungsgrundstück sollte entstehen, das die

van Schiphol is afgesproken dat er een groen carré gevormd zou worden rondom de luchthaven. Het vreemde is, hoe nabij Schiphol ook sluipt, dat je de vliegtuigen niet ervaart, omdat de aanvliegroutes anders liggen.

De Floriade maakt deel uit van de groenstrook. Dat houdt de Haarlemmermeer over aan de grote tuinbouwtentoonstelling. Het zal net als de Stelling van Amsterdam een landschappelijk monument worden, dat aansluiting zoekt en vindt bij het Amsterdamse Bos, Spaarnwoude, de nieuwe zone met landgoederen en de Kagerplassen aan de zuidkant van de polder. Er is een fundament gelegd voor een aaneengeschakeld natuurgebied waarmee opnieuw het begrip duurzaamheid is ingevuld. Het feestje van groei en bloei duurt niet zes maanden lang, het straalt veel langer na.

Er waren dromen en feiten. Een droom was om de piramide op te bouwen uit de klei van de vijfde Schipholbaan. Procedures vertraagden de realisatie. De piramide is uit het water gewonnen, hij baadt in meren en sloten, en dat nota bene in een gebied dat al water is geweest. Leg dat een Amerikaan eens uit.

Duurzaamheid en vernieuwing. Dat het park gebed ligt in een kluwen van infrastructuur – zelfs onder de rook van de vijfde Schipholbaan die in de nabije toekomst op luttele kilometer afstand verwijderd ligt – geeft blijk van een nieuwe opvatting over landschappelijke inrichting die de laatste jaren in Nederland op gang is gekomen. Werd er in de jaren zeventig en tachtig door provincies en landschapsarchitecten vooral gekozen voor scheiding en spreiding, anno 2002 is dat niet langer haalbaar. De oppervlakte van Nederland laat het niet toe. Het huidige beleid is vooral gericht op het verbinden van functies, zodat ze

de site forestier et touristique est conservée et sauvegarde de la qualité de la vie dans le nord de l'Haarlemmemeer et fait oublier que cet endroit est un incroyable nœud d'infrastructures. En compensation des projets de Schiphol, il a été convenu de créer un grand carré de verdure autour de l'aéroport. Il est d'ailleurs assez surprenant que les avions ne troublent pas vraiment le cadre malgré le rapprochement progressif de Schiphol, et ce du fait que les trajectoires d'arrivée sont dans un autre axe.

La Floriade fait partie de la dite 'bande verte'; un cadeau que cette grande exposition horticole laisse en héritage à l'Haarlemmermeer qui, à l'instar du Stelling d'Amsterdam, va être classé patrimoine naturel et prolongement des forêts Amsterdamse Bos et Spaarnwoude, des nouveaux biens domaniaux et des étangs Kagerplassen au sud du polder. Une base est posée pour un site naturel ininterrompu, concrétisant une fois de plus la notion de durabilité. La fête des fleurs et des plantes se perpétue bien au-delà des six mois de la Floriade.

Il y a le rêve et la réalité. Le rêve était de construire la pyramide avec l'argile de la cinquième piste de Schiphol. Les procédures en ont retardé la réalisation. En fait, la pyramide émerge de l'eau, elle baigne dans des lacs et des canaux et se dresse, nota bene, dans une région jadis entièrement submergée. Comment expliquer cela à un Américain par exemple?

Il y a la durabilité et l'innovation. Le fait que le parc soit blotti dans un enchevêtrement d'infrastructures – et même aux portes de Schiphol dont la cinquième piste ne sera plus qu'à quelques kilomètres très prochainement – montre qu'une nouvelle optique s'est profilée ces derniers temps aux Pays-Bas en matière d'aménagement du paysage. Si les autorités provinciales et les architectes paysagistes avaient opté pour la séparation et l'étalement au cours des années soixante-dix et quatre-vingt, l'an 2002

nearby town of Hoofddorp, and for an additional runway for Schiphol International Airport. Schiphol is planned to be completely surrounded by a square of green countryside, of which the Floriade Park will form a part. Surprisingly, we aren't continually deafened by planes landing and taking off, because the park is not directly in line with any of the runways.

The Floriade Park will thus eventually turn into part of a green belt. Like the Stelling van Amsterdam, it will become a piece of the Dutch landscape heritage. The park will link up with other nature areas like the Amsterdam Woodland Park, Spaarnwoude, the new zone of country manors and the Kagerplassen lakes to form part of a larger ecological network. A network of this kind is able to sustain a much greater diversity of wild plants and animals than would be possible in a scattering of separate nature reserves. So the Floriade is more than a six month festival of flourishing plant life, and it will have long-term benefits for nature.

There were dreams and there were realities. One of the dreams was to build the pyramid from the clay excavated for the new Schiphol runway. But the runway has fallen foul of interminable planning procedures. Instead, the pyramid is made of sand dredged from the water, and even now it is bathed in lakes and ditches. These facts, and the knowledge that the area was under the sea until not all that long ago, is something that appeals to the Dutch sensibility. Foreigners may be forgiven for not quite understanding. Sustainability and innovation: the fact that the park is embedded in a knot of main roads and railways and will soon lie only a few kilometres from the planned new airport runway, exemplifies a new approach to landscape planning that has made headway in the Netherlands during recent years. During the 1970s and 1980s, the provincial governments and landscape architects generally opted for a system of zoning with traffic, industry and

Lebensqualität im Nordteil von Haarlemmermeer erhöhen und vergessen machen würde, dass es sich hier um einen gewaltigen infrastrukturellen Knotenpunkt handelt. Zur Kompensation der Schiphol-Erweiterungspläne wurde vereinbart, den Flughafen mit einem grünen Karree zu umgeben. Merkwürdigerweise merkt man dort – so nahe bei Schiphol – kaum etwas von den Flugzeugen, weil die Anflugrouten anders verlaufen.

Die Floriade ist Bestandteil der Grünzone, die Haarlemmermeer auch nach der großen Gartenbauausstellung erhalten bleiben wird. Sie wird genau wie die Stelling von Amsterdam ein landschaftliches Monument werden, das Anschluss an den Amsterdamse Bos, an Spaarnwoude, die neue Zone mit Landgütern und die Kagerplassen, kleine Seen am Südrand des Polders, suchen und finden wird. Man hat damit das Fundament für ein Naturgebiet ohne Unterbrechung gelegt, womit wiederum dem Kriterium der Dauerhaftigkeit Genüge getan wird. Das Fest des Wachstums und der Blüte wird nicht nur sechs Monate dauern, sondern viel länger nachwirken.

Es gab Träume und Fakten. Einer der Träume bestand darin, zum Bau der Pyramide den Lehm der fünften Schiphol-Startbahn zu verwenden. Allerlei Verfahren haben die Realisierung verzögert. Nun wurde die Pyramide dem Wasser entnommen, sie badet in Seen und Kanälen, und das nota bene in einem Gebiet, das einst nur Wasser war. Wie soll man das einem Amerikaner erklären?

Dauerhaftigkeit und Innovation. Dass der Park in ein infrastrukturelles Knäuel eingebettet ist – und dass er in naher Zukunft nur wenige Kilometer von der fünften Schipholbahn entfernt liegen wird – ist ein Beweis für das neue Konzept der Landschaftsgestaltung, das sich in den letzten Jahren in den Niederlanden entwickelt hat. Während die Provinzen und Landschaftsarchitekten in den siebziger und achtziger Jahren vor allem vom Prinzip der

elkaar versterken. Verkeer naast recreatie, wonen naast werken. Er is daadwerkelijk uitvoering gegeven aan het rijksbeleid om de ruimte intensief te gebruiken. De opzet van de Floriade vertoont min of meer gelijkenis met de formule van het Hollandse Expo-paviljoen van Hannover, waar de functies gestapeld werden. Hier, op Floriade 2002, liggen de functies messcherp naast elkaar, en soms over elkaar heen. Die confrontaties maken dat je je er niet van bewust bent dat dit een van de drukste stukken van de Randstad is, zo in beslag genomen word je door de indrukken die op je afkomen.

De Floriade als deel van een groter geheel dat een vloeiende overgang maakt naar zijn omgeving, doet recht aan het principe dat het maken van enclaves voor Nederland geen uitkomst brengt. Aaneengesloten groengebieden moeten de burger het gevoel geven dat het land niet is verstikt, dat de natuur wel degelijk een kans krijgt. Dat is de grondslag van de ecologische hoofdstructuur die op verschillende plaatsen in het land wordt aangelegd, die dassen, ringslangen en muizen vrij doorgang moet verlenen.
De zorg om milieu en landschappelijke inrichting spitst zich toe op waterbeheer. Voor het bouwen van Big Spotters' Hill zijn vaarten, tochten en plassen uitgegraven die het waterschap weer kon gebruiken als afwatering. Werk met werk maken, heet dat in waterstaatkundig jargon. Het zand helpt het water, het water helpt het zand. Zo is er een basis onder de Floriade gelegd, waarvan alle inzenders profiteren, van kunstenaars tot tuinders, van groenbeheerders tot ingelanden.
Water is leidend voor alle ontwikkelingen, het is niet alleen het thema van vandaag maar ook van morgen, en daarom wezenlijk op deze

révèle que ce n'est plus réalisable. La superficie des Pays-Bas ne le permet pas. La stratégie actuelle est principalement axée sur la corrélation des diverses fonctions, de façon à ce qu'elles se consolident entre elles. Les transports et les loisirs, le logement et le travail sont à proximité les uns des autres. La politique gouvernementale plaidant pour un usage intensif de l'espace a été réellement écoutée. Le principe de la Floriade montre une analogie avec la formule du Pavillon-Expo hollandais de Hanovre où la polyvalence est à l'affiche. Ici, à la Floriade de 2002, les finalités sont très mitoyennes ou se chevauchent parfois. De tels rapprochements nous font perdre de vue qu'il s'agit d'un des endroits les plus turbulents de la Randstad tellement nous sommes sous l'emprise des impressions suscitées.
La Floriade, en tant que partie d'un grand ensemble faisant une transition fluide avec le cadre environnant, s'aligne sur le principe selon lequel la création d'enclaves ne solutionne pas le problème aux Pays-Bas. De grandes aires de verdure ininterrompue doivent donner à l'habitant l'impression que le pays ne suffoque pas sous l'urbanisation et que la nature y a bel et bien sa place. C'est la base des structures écologiques fondamentales qui sont appliquées dans plusieurs endroits du pays et donnent libre cours aux blaireaux, aux couleuvres et aux souris.
Le souci de l'aménagement du paysage et de l'environnement se focalise sur la gestion des eaux. Pour la construction de Big Spotters' Hill ont été creusés des canaux, des cours d'eau et des bassins que la *waterschap* a pu utiliser pour le drainage des terres. On appelle cela dans le jargon de l'administration des eaux: 'Les travaux qui en accomplissent d'autres'. La terre aide l'eau, l'eau aide la terre. Ainsi la Floriade repose-t-elle sur un fondement dont tous les exposants peuvent tirer profit, des artistes

housing completely separate. But those tactics are no longer feasible in 2002. The Netherlands is simply not big enough. The present strategy is one of linking functions together so that they reinforce one another. Traffic goes alongside recreation and living alongside working. The government policy is not to use the land area of the Netherlands as efficiently and intensively as possible. The setup of the Floriade is not unlike the formula of the Dutch Pavilion at the World Exhibition in Hannover, where different functions were arranged in vertical layers. Here, at Floriade 2002, the functions sometimes lie side-by-side with sharp boundaries but sometimes overlap. The complex structure dulls our awareness that this is one of the busiest parts of the Randstad, because we are so overwhelmed by the impressions that assail us.
Making the Floriade part of a larger entity with a fluid transition into its surroundings does honour to the principle that it is a wrong to keep dividing the Netherlands into enclaves. Green zones need to be connected up to give people the feeling that the country is not suffocating in urban infrastructure. A network of green areas linked by 'ecological corridors' can support a much greater diversity of plants and animals than separate nature reserves. This is the basic principle of the Ecological Main Structure, which will eventually make an appearance in many parts of the country – a network of highways for badgers, grass snakes and mice.
The complexity of the design of the Floriade is best exemplified by the water management Park. Before Big Spotters' Hill was built, waterways and pools were excavated to provide drainage for the surrounding district. Digging out the sand creates a body of water; and draining the water creates an area of sandy land. 'Doing work with work', that's what people call it in Dutch water engineering circles. Thus the Floriade enjoys a basis from

Funktionentrennung ausgingen, ist das anno 2002 nicht mehr möglich. Die in den Niederlanden verfügbare Fläche erlaubt das nicht. Die heutige Strategie zielt vor allem auf die Verbindung von Funktionen ab, damit sich diese gegenseitig verstärken. Verkehr neben Erholung, Wohnung neben Arbeit. Damit wurde die staatliche Politik der intensiven Raumnutzung tatsächlich realisiert. Die Anlage der Floriade ähnelt dem Konzept des holländischen Pavillons auf der Expo in Hannover, in dem die Funktionen gestapelt wurden. Hier, auf der Floriade 2002, liegen die Funktionen haarscharf nebeneinander oder überlagern sich ein wenig. Diese Konfrontationen bewirken, dass man gar nicht wahrnimmt, dass man sich in einer der belebtesten Zonen des Ballungsgebiets befindet, weil man ganz im Banne der vielen Eindrücke ist, die auf einen einstürmen.
Die Floriade als Teil eines größeren Ganzen, der fließend in seine Umgebung übergeht – das entspricht dem Prinzip, wonach das Kreieren von Enklaven für die Niederlande keine Lösung ist. Aneinander gereihte Grüngebiete sollen den Bürgern das Gefühl geben, dass das Land nicht erstickt ist, dass die Natur durchaus noch lebt. Das ist der Grundsatz der ökologischen Hauptstruktur, die an verschiedenen Stellen des Landes angelegt wird und Dachsen, Ringelnattern und Mäusen freies Geleit geben soll.
Die Sorge um die Umwelt und die landschaftliche Einrichtung konzentriert sich auf den Bereich der Wasserwirtschaft. Beim Bau von Big Spotters' Hill wurden kleine Kanäle und Teiche ausgehoben, die auch zur Entwässerung dienen. Arbeit durch Arbeit, sagt man bei der Wasserwirtschaft. Der Sand hilft dem Wasser, das Wasser hilft dem Sand. So hat man der Floriade eine Basis gegeben, von der alle Einsender profitieren, von den Künstlern bis hin zu den Gärtnern, von den Grünverwaltern zu den Deichverbänden.
Das Wasser spielt die führende Rolle bei allen Entwicklungen. Da es nicht

RIVER CRUISES

MS Viking Pride
Oostelykhandelskade
Achter P.T.A

Phone: 0049-174-303 5106

97

'Floriade' en 'feel', gevormd door
struiken en bloembedden
**'Floriade' et 'feel', formées
d'arbustes et de massifs de fleurs**
'Floriade' und 'feel', aus Sträuchern
und Blumenbeeten geformt
**'Floriade'and 'feel', marked out in
shrubs and flowerbeds**

Floriade, die niet toevallig wordt gehouden in de Haarlemmermeer. De ingenieurs gingen er jaren vanuit dat ze het water de baas zouden blijven totdat ze werden verrast door de effecten van de klimaatverandering en de kwaliteit van het water die vooral in laag gelegen gebieden (de polders) onder druk staat. Vooral de polders merken als eerste dat ze het overtollige hemelwater aangevoerd door de rivieren steeds moeizamer krijgen weggepompt, en omdat het niet kan stromen, komt ook de kwaliteit in het geding. Vervuiling dreigt. Overstromingen eveneens. Letterlijk gaat het zo: het water dat in de Haarlemmermeer valt, ligt drie minuten later in het riool en daarna in de sloot. De stijging van het oppervlaktewater gaat pijlsnel. Het oude Cruquius-gemaal dat net als de Haarlemmermeer in 2002 zijn honderdvijftig jarig bestaan viert, staat evenals de andere gemalen voor een vruchteloze taak. De andere uitweg is om de oppervlakte van de boezem te vergroten.

Floriade 2002 is niet alleen de leukste tuin van Nederland, het is vermoedelijk ook de blauwste. Een waterrijke Floriade, met de Tocht der Tochten, een beek die over het terrein klatert, de 'grijze' waterspoeling in de huizen, en een groot meer dat ontstond door zandwinning en nu een tweede leven krijgt, dat alles laat zien hoe er op kleine schaal al over het Nederland van morgen wordt nagedacht en hoe het landschap gebaat is met water op een manier zoals de lage landen er in de 17ᵉ eeuw hebben uitgezien. Leven in de polder zonder dat je voeten nat worden, dat is de opgave waar we voor staan, en dat betekent dat ironisch genoeg de polder voor een deel weer teruggegeven moet worden aan het water.

aux horticulteurs, des responsables des espaces verts aux sédentaires. L'eau est le fil conducteur de toutes les réalisations, le thème non seulement d'aujourd'hui mais aussi de demain, et c'est pourquoi elle constitue un élément essentiel de cette Floriade qui ne se tient pas par hasard dans l'Haarlemmermeer. Les ingénieurs ont pensé pouvoir maîtriser l'eau pendant des années jusqu'à ce qu'ils soient confrontés aux effets du changement de climat et à l'impact sur la qualité de l'eau soumise à des contraintes comme c'est particulièrement le cas dans les régions de basse altitude (les polders). C'est surtout dans les polders que les excédents d'eau de pluie amenés par les rivières s'évacuent difficilement; et comme l'eau stagne, la qualité en est mise en jeu. La pollution est un danger, les inondations aussi. Concrètement, l'eau qui tombe dans l'Haarlemmermeer est trois minutes après dans les égouts et rejoint ensuite les canaux. Le niveau des eaux de surface monte très rapidement. La vieille station de pompage Cruquius, qui à l'instar de l'Haarlemmermeer fête en 2002 son cent cinquantième anniversaire, assure sa tâche en vain, de même que ses consœurs. L'alternative est d'agrandir l'étendue des bassins collecteurs. Si la Floriade 2002 est le jardin le plus passionnant des Pays-Bas, c'est aussi vraisemblablement le plus bleu. L'eau y est omniprésente sous toutes ses formes. La plus Belle Promenade en Bateau, le murmure d'un ruisseau parcourant le terrain, l'eau 'grise' de rinçage dans les maisons, le grand lac qui, après avoir été carrière de sable, connaît comme une deuxième vie; tout nous montre à petite échelle comment les Pays-Bas voient l'avenir et combien l'eau est bénéfique au paysage en référant à l'image de ce plat pays tel qu'il était au 17ᵉᵐᵉ siècle. Vivre dans les polders et garder les pieds au sec, voilà tout l'énoncé du problème qui implique, si ironique que cela puisse paraître, de redonner une partie des polders à l'eau.

which all the contributors can profit, from artists to gardeners and from city plantation departments to local landholders. Water leads the way for all developments; it is the theme not only of today but also of tomorrow, and is therefore essential to this Floriade. The hydrological engineers used to assume they would be able to maintain their mastery over the water. But then they were surprised by the prospect of climate change, and by the growing problems of deteriorating water quality in lower-lying regions, i.e. the polders. The polders are the first areas to notice the disadvantage of increasing precipitation brought in by rivers, because they lie below sea level. It is becoming more and more difficult to pump the excess water away and because it cannot flow away it becomes increasingly polluted. Literally, this is what happens: rainwater that falls in the polder reaches the sewers within three minutes and ends up in the polder ditches soon afterwards. So the groundwater level rises almost immediately, with a danger of flooding. The old Cruquius Pumping Station, which like Haarlemmermeer itself celebrates its 150th anniversary in 2002, is faced with an almost hopeless task, as are the other pumping stations. Floriade 2002 is not only the Netherlands' most gorgeous garden; it may also be the 'bluest'. This Floriade is full of pools and waterways. It has a system of canals, a brook gurgling through the site, the 'grey water' system in the houses, and a former commercial sandpit which is now enjoying a new lease of life as a lake. All this can be viewed as a small-scale model of how people are thinking about the future of water management in the whole of the Netherlands, and the implications of this for landscape management. Living in polder country without getting your feet wet: that is the problem facing the inhabitants of Holland. Ironically, the only solution may be to sacrifice part of the polder by returning it to the waters.

nur ein Thema von heute, sondern auch von morgen ist, hat es für diese Floriade, deren Standort nicht zufällig Haarlemmermeer ist, besondere Bedeutung. Die Ingenieure sind jahrelang davon ausgegangen, dass sie das Wasser beherrschen könnten, bis sie von den Effekten des Klimawandels und von der Abnahme der Wasserqualität in den niedrig gelegenen Gebieten (den Poldern) eingeholt wurden. In den Poldern zeigt sich zuerst, dass das überschüssige Regenwasser, das die Flüsse anführen, immer schwerer abgepumpt werden kann. Da es nicht strömen kann, verschlechtert sich auch die Qualität. Es drohen Verschmutzung und auch Überströmungen. Konkret läuft das folgendermaßen ab: Das Wasser, das in Haarlemmermeer fällt, landet drei Minuten später in der Kanalisation und anschließend im Graben. Das Oberflächenwasser steigt blitzschnell an. Das alte Cruquius-Schöpfwerk, das – wie ganz Haarlemmermeer – im Jahre 2002 seinen hundertfünfzigsten Geburtstag begeht, kann seiner Aufgabe genauso wenig gerecht werden wie die anderen Schöpfwerke. Der andere Ausweg besteht darin, die Oberfläche des Mahlbusens zu vergrößern. Die Floriade 2002 wird nicht nur der schönste, sondern wohl auch der blauste Garten der Niederlande sein. Eine wasserreiche Floriade, die den 'perfekten Graben' besitzt, einen Bach, der über das Gelände plätschert, eine mit Brauchwasser betriebene Wasserspülung in den Häusern und einen See, der durch Sandgewinnung entstand und jetzt ein zweites Leben erhält. Das alles zeigt, wie schon heute in kleinem Maßstab über die Einrichtung der Niederlande von morgen nachgedacht wird und wie der Landschaft mit Wasser geholfen ist in der Art, wie die Niederlande im 17. Jahrhundert ausgesehen haben. Im Polder leben, ohne nasse Füße zu bekommen – so lautet die Aufgabe, vor der wir stehen, und das heißt ironischerweise, dass wir den Polder zum Teil wieder dem Wasser überlassen müssen.

Moeras vergeet-me-nietje
Myosotis des marais
Sumpf-Vergissmeinnicht
Water Forget-me-not

Japanse anemoon
Anémone du Japon
Japanischer Anemone
Japanese Anemone

99

Aan het Meer | Au bord du Lac
On the Lake | Am See

Zo rechtlijnig als het eilandenrijk is bij de Berg, zo romantisch is het parkdeel Het Meer dat we via de brug over de N205 en de Zuidtangent binnenlopen. De sierteelt is neergestreken tussen de oude populieren, de narcis verwelkomt de lente, het herfsttijloos sluit het jaar af met zijn kleuren in de schaduw, en we zien de grootste collectie bloembollen voor ons uitrollen als we de helling afdalen via een stalen trap. Dat bolgewassen als bodembedekkers kunnen fungeren, is een hint aan de plantsoenendiensten die nu nog vaak kiezen voor onderhoudsvrij of -arm groen. En als de bollen zijn uitgebloeid nemen de eenjarigen hun plaats in. De bonte kleuren steken af bij het diepgroen rondom het Meer.

Unlike the severe straight lines of the island group by the Hill, the section of the park 'on the Lake' is dominated by romantic curves. We reach it by crossing the footbridge over the N205 and Zuidtangent. Ornamental plants and shrubs have found a place between the old Poplar trees. Daffodils greet the spring, the Meadow Saffron rounds off the year with its dash of colour in shady spots, and a vast collection of flowering bulbs rolls out before us as we descend the slope via a steel staircase. Using bulbous plants to carpet the ground instead of creepers is an idea that is likely to appeal to public gardens departments, which nowadays usually opt for greenery that requires little or no maintenance. Once the bulbs have finished flowering, the annual plants take over from them. The vivid colours shine out amid the deep green of the foliage on the Lake.

La rigueur des formes dans le royaume des îles Près de la Colline fait place au romantisme dans la partie Au bord du Lac où nous accédons en franchissant le pont au-dessus de la N205 et de la Zuidtangent. Les végétaux d'ornement s'y sont installés entre les vieux peupliers, le narcisse y accueille le printemps, les couleurs du colchique d'automne viennent égayer l'ombre à l'annonce de la fin de l'année, nous y découvrons aussi la plus grande collection de bulbes en descendant la pente par un escalier métallique. Preuve est faite que les plantes à bulbes sont d'excellents couvre-sol: avis aux services des espaces verts qui aujourd'hui encore donnent la préférence à une verdure demandant pas ou peu d'entretien! Une fois la saison des bulbes passée, les plantes annuelles prennent la place et arborent de vives couleurs qui se détachent sur le vert foncé autour du Lac.

So geradlinig, wie das Inselreich am Berg ist, so romantisch ist der Parkbereich am See, in den man auf der Überführung über die N205 und der Südtangente gelangt. Zierpflanzen haben sich zwischen den alten Pappeln ausgebreitet, die Narzisse begrüßt den Frühling, die Herbstzeitlose schließt mit ihren Farben das Jahr im Schatten ab, und wenn wir den Abhang auf der Stahltreppe hinunter steigen, breitet sich vor uns eine riesige Palette von Blumenzwiebeln aus. Dass Zwiebelgewächse als Bodendecker fungieren können, sollten sich die Verantwortlichen für die städtischen Grünanlagen merken, die ja im Allgemeinen den pflegeleichten Grünbewuchs bevorzugen. Wenn die Zwiebeln verblüht sind, treten die einjährigen Pflanzen an ihre Stelle. Die bunten Farben stechen vom intensiven Grünsaum des Sees ab.

Gele lis

Lys jaunes

Sumpf-Schwertlilien

Yellow Flag

nature

Bijzondere Bolgewassenvallei

Tulpen, hyacinten, narcissen en krokussen; iedereen die maar een beetje verstand van planten heeft weet dat het hier gaat over in het voorjaar bloeiende bloembollen. Dat dahlia's en begonia's tot de groep van de in de zomer bloeiende bol- en knolgewassen behoren is al veel minder bekend en zodra namen als Bellevalia, Dracunculus, Ixiolirion en Hymenocallis opduiken zal menigeen het spoor bijster zijn. De bloembollenwereld is zich daarvan bewust en heeft de kans gegrepen om op deze Floriade het voornaamste deel van haar minder bekende sortiment te tonen in één grote inzending: de Bijzondere Bolgewassenvallei. Wat deze inzending uniek maakt is dat de bollen, knollen en wortelstokken hier getoond worden op een manier die zo nog niet eerder te zien is geweest, namelijk in combinatie met verschillende soorten vaste planten.

De reden daarvan is dat de bezoeker zich kan laten inspireren door een groot aantal voorbeelden die hij thuis, in zijn eigen tuin, zo kan inpassen. Een geweldig idee, want niet alleen wordt ieders kennis op het gebied van bloembollen op een veel hoger peil gebracht, maar is tegelijkertijd ook te zien hoe je die kennis dan in praktijk brengt. Vragen als 'wat is de beste plek voor dit type bol' en 'met welke planten kan ik hem combineren' worden ter plaatse opgelost.

La vallée des bulbes insolites

Tout amateur de plantes sait que les tulipes, les jacinthes, les narcisses et les crocus sont des bulbes qui fleurissent au printemps. Moins de personnes déjà savent que les dahlias et les bégonias sont des bulbes ou des tubercules à floraison estivale. Mais rares sont ceux qui ne restent pas bouche bée en entendant les noms de Bellevalia, Dracunculus, Ixiolirion et Hymenocallis. Les professionnels de la bulbiculture en sont conscients et ont saisi l'occasion de la Floriade pour y exposer la majorité des bulbes les moins connus dans la Vallée des Bulbes Insolites. Cette grande présentation est unique en son genre dans la mesure où les plantes à bulbes, à tubercules ou à rhizomes sont exposées pour la première fois et combinaison avec diverses sortes de plantes vivaces.

Ainsi le visiteur peut-il s'inspirer d'une multitude d'exemples pour agrémenter son propre jardin. Une excellente initiative! D'une part, elle permet à chacun d'approfondir ses connaissances en matière de bulbes, d'autre part, elle démontre en même temps comment ces acquis peuvent être mis en application. Il est répondu sur-le-champ aux questions du genre 'quel est le meilleur emplacement pour ce type de bulbe?' ou 'avec quelles plantes ce bulbe fait-il un beau mariage?'.

Valley of Bulb Specials

Tulips, Hyacinths, Narcissi and Crocuses; anyone with a little plant experience will recognize these as spring-flowering bulbs. That Dahlias and Begonias belong to the category of summer-flowering bulbs and tubers is less widely known. And when it comes to names like Bellevalia, Dracunculus, Ixiolirion and Hymenocallis, even many a keen amateur gardener will be at a loss. The world of flowering bulb cultivation is aware of this situation and has seized the chance to combine a substantial part of its lesser known products into one huge contribution: the Valley of Bulb Specials. A unique aspect of this display is that the bulbs, tubers and rhizomes that bloom in the valley have been combined with various perennials.

The idea is that the visitor can draw inspiration form a large number of examples that could be applied in the domestic garden. Not only will everyone come away with a much wider knowledge of bulbous plants, but also full of ideas how to put that knowledge into practice. Questions such as 'what is the best situation for this particular bulb' or 'what plants can I combine it with' are answered on the spot.

Das Tal der seltenen Zwiebelgewächse

Tulpen, Hyazinthen, Narzissen und Krokusse – dass diese Zwiebelblumen im Frühjahr blühen, weiß fast jeder, der sich ein bisschen für Pflanzen interessiert. Dass Dahlien und Begonien zur Gruppe der im Sommer blühenden Zwiebel- und Knollengewächse gehören, ist schon viel weniger bekannt, und sobald Namen wie Bellevalia, Dracunculus, Ixiolirion und Hymenocallis fallen, ist kaum noch jemand im Bilde. Da das der Blumenzwiebelbranche bewusst ist, nutzt sie die Gelegenheit, um auf dieser Floriade den Hauptteil ihres weniger bekannten Sortiments in geballter Form auszustellen, nämlich im Tal der seltenen Zwiebelgewächse. Diese Floriade-Einsendung ist insofern einmalig, als die Zwiebeln, Knollen und Wurzelstöcke hier anders als bisher üblich in Kombination mit verschiedenen Dauerpflanzen gezeigt werden.

Damit soll der Besucher dazu angeregt werden, die vielen Beispiele zu Hause, in seinem eigenen Garten zu übernehmen. Das ist eine großartige Idee, denn so erfährt man nicht nur viel Neues über die Blumenzwiebelkultur, sondern man wird zugleich mit der praktischen Anwendung dieses Wissens konfrontiert. Fragen wie 'Wo gedeiht diese Zwiebel am besten?' oder 'Mit welchen Pflanzen ist sie zu kombinieren?' werden an Ort und Stelle beantwortet.

Zomerklokjes

Nivéole d'été

Sommerknotenblume

Summer Snowflake

Grootschalige bloembollen-
inzending, deelgebied Haarlemmermeersebos
**Grande présentation de bulbes,
partie de l'Haarlemmermeersebos**
Umfangreiche Blumenzwiebel-
einsendung, Teilgebiet Haarlemmermeersebos
**Large flowering bulb exhibit in
Haarlemmermeersebos section**

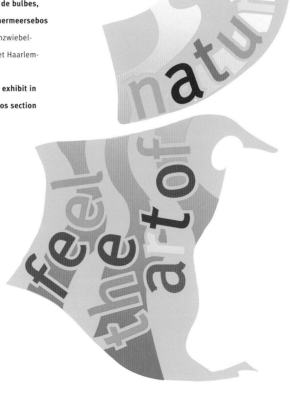

Narcissen, tulpen
en hondstand
**Narcisses, tulipes
et dent de chien**
Narzissen, Tulpen
und Hundszahn
**Daffodil, tulipes and
Dog's Tooth Violet**

Drie voorbeelden van combinaties in de schaduw:
– *Geranium macrorrhizum 'Spessart'* en *Fragaria vesca* met *Allium ursinum* (daslook) en *Hyacinthoides hispanica 'Excelsior'* (boshyacint).
– *Geranium magnificum* (ooievaarsbek) met *Camassia cusickii*
– *Asperula odorata* (lieve-vrouwe-bedstro) met *Anemone blanda 'White Splendour'* (bosanemoontje)

Drie voorbeelden van combinaties in de zon:
– *Ajuga reptans 'Atropurpurea'* en *Ajuga reptans 'Catlins Giant'* met *Oxalis adenophylla* (geluksklavertje) en *Scilla litardierei*.
– *Lysimachia ciliata 'Firecracker'* (roodbladige wederik) met *Allium nigrum* (sierui) en *Eremurus 'Pinokkio'* (woestijnkaars).
– *Phlox subulata 'Emerald Cushion Blue'* (vlambloem) met *Muscari 'Valerie Finnis'* (blauwe druifjes).

Here are three examples of combinations for shaded conditions:
– **Geranium macrorrhizum 'Spessart' and Fragaria vesca with Alllium ursinum (Ramsons) and Hyacinthoides hispanica 'Excelsior' (Spanish Bluebell).**
– **Geranium magnificum (Cranesbill) with Carnassia cusickii.**
– **Asperula odorata (Woodruff) with Anemone blanda 'White Splendour' (Wood Anemone).**

And three examples of combinations that do well in the sun:
– **Ajuga reptans 'Atropurpurea' and Ajuga reptans 'Catlins Giant' with Oxalis adenophylla ('Four-leaved Clover') and Scilla litardierei.**
– **Lysimachia ciliata 'Firecracker' (red-leaved Loosestrife) with Allium nigrum (ornamental Onion) and Eremurus 'Pinokkio' (Desert Candle).**
– **Phlox subulata 'Emerald Cushion Blue' with Muscari 'Valerie Finnis' (Grape Hyacinth).**

Trois exemples de mariages à l'ombre:
– **Le Geranium macrorrhizum 'Spessart' et le Fragaria vesca avec l'Allium ursinum (ail d'ornement) et l'Hyacinthoides hispanica 'Excelsior' (jacinthe des bois).**
– **Le Geranium magnificum (bec-de-grue) et le Camassia cusickii (Quamash).**
– **L'Asperula odorata (petit muguet) et l'Anemone blanda 'White Splendour' (anémone des bois)**

Trois exemples de mariages au soleil:
– **L'Ajuga reptans 'Atropurpurea' et l'Ajuga reptans 'Catlins Giant' (bugle) avec l'Oxalis adenophylla (surelle) et la Scilla litardierei (scille).**
– **Le Lysimachia ciliata 'Firecracker' (lysimaque à feuille rouge) avec l'Allium nigrum (oignon d'ornement) et l'Eremurus 'Pinokkio' (lys du désert).**
– **Le Phlox subulata 'Emerald Cushion Blue' (phlox mousse) et le Muscari 'Valerie Finnis'.**

Drei Beispiele für Kombinationen im Schatten:
– *Geranium macrorrhizum 'Spessart'* und *Fragaria vesca* mit *Allium ursinum* (Bärlauch) und *Hyacinthoides hispanica 'Excelsior'* (Spanisches Hasenglöckchen).
– *Geranium magnificum* (Storchschnabel) mit *Camassia cusickii*
– *Asperula odorata* (Waldmeister) mit *Anemone blanda 'White Splendour'* (Balkan-Windröschen)

Drei Beispiele für Kombinationen in der Sonne:
– *Ajuga reptans 'Atropurpurea'* und *Ajuga reptans 'Catlins Giant'* mit *Oxalis adenophylla* (Sauerklee) und *Scilla litardierei*.
– *Lysimachia ciliata 'Firecracker'* (Purpurfelberich) mit Allium nigrum (Lauch) und *Eremurus 'Pinokkio'* (Steppenkerze).
– *Phlox subulata 'Emerald Cushion Blue'* (Flammenblume) mit *Muscari 'Valerie Finnis'* (Traubenhyazinthe).

Deze Bijzondere Bolgewassenvallei ligt in het deelgebied 'aan het Meer', op een helling aan de oostkant van de hoofdroute en beslaat een oppervlakte van ruim 1500 vierkante meter.

De eigenlijke tuin is opgedeeld in een aantal terrassen die een hoogteverschil van ca. 4 meter overbruggen. Een indrukwekkende stalen trap die deze terrassen doorsnijdt biedt de bezoeker de mogelijkheid om de vallei steeds vanaf een ander niveau te bekijken. Maar de verrassende plantencombinaties van dichtbij bekijken kan ook, want de vallei wordt over de gehele lengte doorsneden door twee wandelpaden. Reeds eerder ter plekke aanwezige bomen en heesters zoals populieren en hazelaars zijn, waar mogelijk, gehandhaafd.

De beide entrees van de tuin worden geaccentueerd door dikke dotten Buxus semperflorens 'Rotundifolia'. In de vallei zelf zijn het groepen of eenlingen van Viburnum lantana, Zelkova serrata en Hydrangea arborescens 'Annabelle' die voor een evenwichtige verdeling van de ruimte zorgen. De bodembedekkende beplanting varieert, afhankelijk van de hoeveelheid licht. Op schaduwrijke plekken groeien Fragaria vesca (bosaardbeitje) en Geranium macrorrhizum 'Spessart' (ooievaarsbek). Op zonnige plekken is een combinatie van twee soorten zenegroen (Ajuga reptans 'Atropurpurea' en Ajuga reptans 'Catlins Giant') aangeplant.

In deze bodembedekkende beplanting zijn plekken open gehouden, kleine tuintjes waarin combinaties van goed bij elkaar passende bollen en vaste planten te zien zijn. De samenstelling van deze combinaties is natuurlijk ook weer gebaseerd op de hoeveelheid licht ter plaatse en zo zijn er ongeveer 15 voorbeelden van tuintjes in de zon en 10 voorbeelden van tuintjes in de schaduw. Genoeg om de geïnteresseerde bezoeker een idee te geven van de vele mogelijkheden die er zijn om bollen met vaste planten te combineren.

La Vallée des Bulbes Insolites s'étend dans la partie 'Au bord du Lac', sur un versant à l'est de l'allée principale et couvre une surface de plus de 1.500 m².

Le versant est travaillé en terrasses pour parer à la dénivellation d'environ 4 m. au total. Un escalier métallique impressionnant traverse les terrasses et permet au visiteur de les surplomber à divers niveaux. Les combinaisons de plantes s'observent de plus près à partir des deux allées coupant la vallée d'un bout à l'autre. Les arbres et arbustes déjà là, tels que les peupliers et les noisetiers, ont été le plus possible épargnés.

Les deux entrées du jardin sont marquées par de grosses touffes de Buxus semperflorens 'Rotundifolia' (buis). Dans la vallée même, le Viburnum lantana (viorne), le Zelkova serrata et l'Hydrangea arborescens 'Annabelle' (hortensia) en groupes ou en sujets solitaires apportent un équilibre à l'ensemble. La végétation couvre-sol varie selon l'intensité de lumière. Le Fragaria vesca (fraisier des quatre saisons) et le Geranium macrorrhizum 'Spessart' (bec-de-grue) poussent dans les endroits ombragés. Aux emplacements plus ensoleillés ont été plantées en combinaison deux sortes de bugles (Ajuga reptans 'Atropurpurea' et Ajuga reptans 'Catlins Giant').

La végétation couvre-sol laisse plusieurs endroits à découvert où se logent des jardinets garnis d'harmonieux mélanges de plantes vivaces et de bulbes. Leur composition dépend de la luminosité, avec pour résultat: environ 15 jardinets ensoleillés et 10 jardinets ombragés; assez en tout cas pour que le visiteur intéressé puisse se faire une idée des nombreux mariages possibles entre les plantes vivaces et les bulbes.

This Valley of Bulb Specials lies in the 'on the Lake' section of the park, on a slope to the east of the main route. It occupies an area of 1,500 square metres. The cultivated part is divided into a number of terraces which span a total height difference of about 4 metres. An impressive steel stairway that cuts through these terraces allows us to view the valley from a succession of different levels. But it is also possible to view the surprising combinations of plants from close up, for the valley is traversed along its full length by two footpaths. Trees and shrubs that were here before the Floriade took the area in hand, such as Poplars and Hazels, have been retained.

The two entrances to the garden are marked by plump tufts of Buxus semperflorens 'Rotundifolia'. The valley proper has groups and isolated examples of Viburnum lantana, Zelkova serrata and Hydrangea arborescens 'Annabelle', which divide up the area in a harmonious way. Different species of ground-covering creepers have been planted according to the light conditions. Shady spots are occupied by Fragaria vesca (Wild Strawberry) and Geranium macrorrhizum 'Spessart' (Cranesbill). Sunny spots are planted with a combination of two varieties of Bugle (Ajuga reptans 'Atropurpurea' and Ajuga reptans 'Catlins Giant').

Areas have been kept clear in the ground-cover to form small beds, each of which sports a well-chosen combination of bulbs and perennials. The species that make up the combination have naturally also been selected according to the amount of daylight received by the bed concerned. There are about fifteen beds in sunny locations and ten in the shade; enough to give the visitor ample ideas for combining bulbs and perennials.

Dieses Tal der seltenen Zwiebelgewächse liegt im Teilbereich 'am See' auf einem Hang an der Ostseite der Hauptroute und erstreckt sich über eine Fläche von über 1500 Quadratmetern. Der eigentliche Garten ist in mehrere Terrassen unterteilt, die etwa 4 m Höhenunterschied überbrücken. Eine eindrucksvolle Stahltreppe, die diese Terrassen zertrennt, bietet dem Besucher die Möglichkeit, das Tal aus unterschiedlichen Höhen zu betrachten. Aber man kann sich die überraschenden Pflanzenkombinationen auch aus der Nähe anschauen, da zwei Spazierwege das Tal in Längsrichtung durchqueren. Die bereits vorhandenen Bäume und Sträucher, darunter Pappeln und Haselbüsche, hat man möglichst überall stehen gelassen.

Die beiden Garteneingänge werden von dicken Buchsbaumbüscheln des Typs Semperflorens 'Rotundifolia' markiert. Im Tal selbst sorgen Büsche oder einzelne Exemplare von Viburnum lantana, Zelkova serrata und Hydrangea arborescens 'Annabelle' für räumliche Ausgewogenheit. Die Bepflanzung am Boden hängt von der einfallenden Lichtmenge ab. An schattenreichen Stellen wächst Fragaria vesca (Walderdbeere) und Geranium macrorrhizum 'Spessart' (Storchschnabel). An sonnigen Stellen wurde eine Kombination aus zwei Günselsorten (Ajuga reptans 'Atropurpurea' und Ajuga reptans 'Catlins Giant') angepflanzt.

In diesem bodenbedeckenden Bewuchs gibt es offene Stellen, kleine Gärtchen, in denen Zwiebel- und mehrjährige Pflanzen nebeneinander stehen, die gut zu einander passen. Da die Kombination natürlich auch wieder davon abhängt, wieviel Licht jeweils einfällt, gibt es ungefähr fünfzehn Beispiele für Sonnengärten und zehn Beispiele für Schattengärten. Das reicht in jedem Fall aus, um dem interessierten Besucher einen Eindruck davon zu vermitteln, wie viele Möglichkeiten der Kombination von Zwiebel- und Dauerpflanzen es gibt.

De aanwezige natuur met zijn flauwe hellingen naar het water is voor een deel gespaard gebleven maar hier en daar is er een verhoogd accent aangebracht met bastions, met klimop begroeide bordessen die overzicht verlenen op de beplanting op de hellingen en aan de oevers. En daar liggen verspreid quasi achteloos plakken natuursteen uit België, alsof ze van nature horen.

Peilloos diep is het meer, in het midden misschien wel vijfentwintig meter, het is dus eerder een gat dan een plas, waarover nu de notarisbootjes puffen en een pontonbrug is gelegd om de oevers met elkaar te verbinden. Anders had niet gekund vanwege die diepte. Een Hollandse plas met populieren eromheen, ware het niet dat we aan de zuidelijke oever ons eerder in Azië wanen. De architectuur van de paviljoens ademt de sfeer van het Verre Oosten, van de panelen komt een geur van tatami (gedroogd gras), bamboe en riet. Hier zijn we helemaal los van de context, aan een polder denken we niet eens meer. Juist door die paviljoens – een theehuis, een bouwsel van bamboe – komt de typische Aziatische beplanting zoals *Metasequoia* en *Taxodium* beter tot haar recht, anders waren ze wellicht verdronken in het oer-Hollandse populierenbos.

Het bos is zo gesnoeid dat er een *parkbos* is ontstaan, met open plekken waarop de bolgewassen zich uitstrekken, afgewisseld met moerasachtige stukken aan de noordoostzijde waar orchideeën voorkomen. We bevinden ons nu in de meest oostelijke hoek van de Floriade, en opnieuw lijkt de tuin niet ten einde. Om van dit ongerepte gebied rond de zandwinningsplas een *park* te maken, dat was nog het moeilijkste. Het snoeimes en de zaag als rechter. En de hoogteverschillen moesten worden aangezet, zodat de bezoeker meer perspectief, meer zicht op het geheel zou krijgen. Nu ziet het eruit alsof het altijd zo is geweest,

Le relief naturel en pente douce vers l'eau a été pour le mieux respecté, seuls de petits bastions et des perrons garnis de lierre accentuent ici et là les différences de niveaux et offrent une vue d'ensemble de la végétation sur les pentes et sur les rives. Et là, se prélassent des dalles de pierre naturelle venues de Belgique, parsemées et presque intégrées au reste comme si elles avaient toujours été là.

Le lac est d'une profondeur insondable de peut-être vingt-cinq mètres en son milieu. C'est en fait plus une cavité qu'un terrain en contrebas, d'élégantes embarcations y voguent aujourd'hui de part et d'autre d'un ponton jeté pour rejoindre les deux rives. Vu la profondeur, il n'y avait pas d'autre solution. Le plan d'eau, couché dans sa couronne de peupliers, est donc d'aspect très hollandais même si nous nous imaginons plutôt en Asie sur la rive sud. L'architecture des pavillons respire l'ambiance de l'Extrême-Orient, des parois émane l'odeur du tatami (herbe séchée), du bambou et des roseaux. Ici, complètement détachés du contexte, nous ne pensons même plus aux polders. Dans le cadre des pavillons avec entre autres un salon de thé et bambou, les sujets typiquement asiatiques tels que le *Metasequoia* et le *Taxodium* sont tout à fait dans leur élément et ressortent mieux qu'ils ne l'auraient fait sans doute dans le bois de peupliers très 'vieille Hollande'.

Le bois a été aménagé en *'bois de parc'*, avec des claires-voies où paradent les bulbes, avec en alternance au nord-est de petits marécages où fleurissent les orchidées. Nous sommes maintenant dans l'angle le plus à l'est de la Floriade et de nouveau, le jardin ne semble pas avoir de fin. Le plus difficile a été sans doute de faire un *parc* de ce coin sauvage autour de la carrière de sable, avec le sécateur et la scie pour juges prononçant la sentence. En plus, il a fallu créer des différences de niveaux pour que le

A good proportion of the natural vegetation that was already present has been preserved on the gentle slopes leading down to the water. Here and there, a raised bastion gives us a broad view over the plants on the slopes and banks. Here and there, too, we can see slabs of Belgian rock scattered around as though they had always been there.

The Lake is extremely deep, perhaps twenty-five metres at its centre. After all, it is an abandoned quarry and not just a watery dip in the gentle Dutch landscape. Now it has been civilized, with motor-boats chugging across its surface and a bailey bridge from one side to another (this was the only practical solution on such a deep lake). Apart from the unusual bridge, it would look very much like a typical Dutch lake fringed with Poplar trees, if it were not for the unmistakable patch of Asia on its south bank. The pavilions on the shore exude a distinctively Oriental atmosphere, and that we are really in a Dutch polder is quickly forgotten. The pavilions – a teahouse and a bamboo structure – provide a fitting setting for the typically Asian plants such as Metasequoia and Taxodium. Otherwise they could easily be lost in a background of Poplar trees, so redolent of Holland.

The woods have been selectively felled to produce a 'woodland park', with clearings rich in flowering bulbs and marshy areas on the north side where orchids bloom. We are now in the eastern corner of the Floriade, but the garden once more seems endless. It was hard work converting this wilderness around the waterlogged sandpit into a parkland.

The pruning hook and the chainsaw passed their judgement. Existing differences in ground level, such as they were, were exaggerated to offer the visitor a wider perspective and some grasp of the whole area. Now it looks as though it had always been like this, but only those intrepid

Die vorhandene Landschaftsform, die zum Wasser sanft abfällt, ist teilweise erhalten geblieben, aber hin und wieder wurden in Form von Erhebungen neue Akzente gesetzt, mit Efeu begrünte Podeste, die einen Überblick über die Bepflanzung der Hänge und der Ufer bieten. Die dort scheinbar achtlos verstreuten Natursteinscheiben aus Belgien wirken, als hätten sie schon immer so dagelegen.

Der See ist unergründlich tief, in der Mitte wohl an die fünfundzwanzig Meter, so dass es sich eher um ein Loch handelt. Jetzt tuckern elegante Boote über ihn hinweg, und eine Pontonbrücke verbindet die Ufer miteinander. Etwas anderes wäre wegen der Tiefe nicht gegangen. Ein holländischer See, umgeben von Pappeln, gewiss, aber dann kommt man zum Südufer und wähnt sich in Asien. Die Architektur der Pavillons verbreiten eine fernöstliche Atmosphäre, die Felder verströmen einen Duft von Tatami (getrocknetes Gras), Bambus und Riet. Der Besucher wird ganz aus dem Kontext gelöst und vergisst den Polder. Gerade diese Pavillons – ein Teehaus, ein Gebilde aus Bambus – bringen die typisch asiatische Bepflanzung aus *Metasequoia, Taxodium* u.ä., die sonst vielleicht im urholländischen Pappelwald untergegangen wäre, gut zur Geltung.

Der Wald wurde so zurecht gestutzt, dass ein Parkwald entstanden ist, in dem sich Lichtungen für die Zwiebelpflanzen mit sumpfigen Zonen an der Nordostseite, wo Orchideen wachsen, abwechseln. Hier sind wir im östlichsten Winkel der Floriade angekommen, wo der Garten immer noch nicht aufhören will. Die Umgestaltung dieses unberührten Geländes am Sandgewinnungssee in einen Park war alles andere als leicht. Da schwang die Baumschere und die Säge das Zepter. Man musste die Höhenunterschiede betonen, um dem Betrachter mehr Perspektive, mehr Überblick zu bieten. Jetzt wirkt es, als sei es immer so gewesen. Wer hier vor zehn Jahren

114

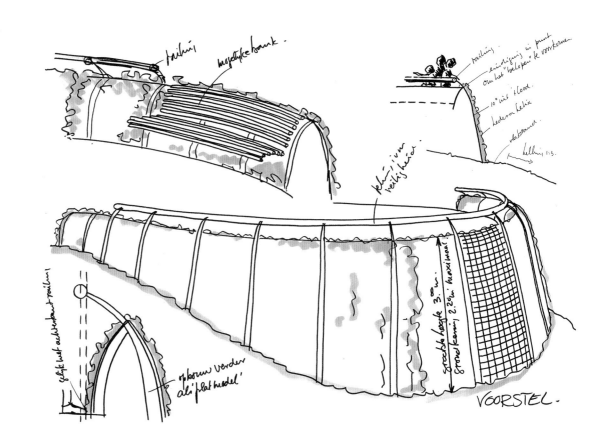

railing

mogelijke bank.

railing

eindiging in punt
om het "haleken" te voorkomen.

10° uit t lood.

hedera helix

afstand.

helling 1:3.

pleinium
veiligheid.

gelijke trek afstand railing

streefde hoogte 3 m.
grawrkani 2.20 m. maximaal

opbouw verder
als plat model.

VOORSTEL.

115

zoveel mogelijk radius volgen van bastions.

staal.

1.10

3

20 cm

Robinia kastanje bamboe

Let op ruimte rem voeten.

afstand houders

teak plelku laminere.

12

200

ovalen KVS buis

algemeen: voorkeur 'hout' omdat na de floriade deze parkachtige omgeving geen onderdeel is van het gecultiveerde landschap.

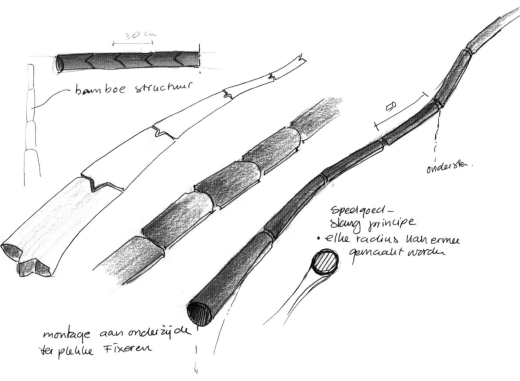

30 cm

bamboe struchuur

50

onderste.

Speelgoed-
slang principe
• elke radius kan ermee
  gemaakt worden

montage aan onderzijde
ter plekke Fixeren

Vingerhoedskruid, daglelie
en varen

**Digitale, hémérocalle et
osmonde**

Fingerhut, Taglilie und Farn

Foxglove, Day Lily and Fern

terwijl iedereen die hier tien jaar geleden de hond heeft uitgelaten, wel anders weet. Hoewel...

Zodra we ons over de voetbrug over de N205 voorbij een reusachtige kopie van de Zonnebloemen van Van Gogh, uitgestald op een schilders-ezel in het bos hebben begeven, zijn we ineens in een andere wereld. We hebben het formele park met zijn rechte tochten en vierkante eilanden verlaten, hebben ook de tuinbouw achter de rug – tuinbouw in een enclave van nut en noodzaak – en nu zijn we omringd door de sierteelt. Sierteelt in een romantisch, informeel decor, met hoog opschietend groen. Proefden we eerder de tong en de neus, dit is het rijk van het oog. Het zijn de scherpe contrasten die Floriade 2002 aanbiedt, tegen-stellingen in het landschap die elke keer ons in een andere beleving onderdompelen. Dit is niet een tuin met een concept, dit is een tuin met wel tien verschillende karakters en binnen die karakters nog eens uit-eenlopende nuances. Aan de oever van het Meer overbruggen we alleen al de wereld door een bezoek aan het moderne Duitsland dat zijn pavil-joen tot in het water heeft laten uitlopen, naar een traditioneel Tsje-chisch huisje dat zo uit een sprookje lijkt te zijn weggelopen terwijl we in de verte al de exotica van Azië zijn. A global village in enkele hecta-res bijeengebracht. Het parkbos verleidt je met slingerpaden door bos-schages, over hellingen, door besloten tuinen, en de namen die erbij horen, doen een appèl op de geheimzinnigste van de zintuigen: de psy-che. Wat ontroert ons, wat verstilt, en wat is juist dynamisch? In elke emotietuin wisselt de sfeer per minuut, aangesticht door de bloemen en struiken die er zijn geplant en op onverwachte momenten hun geur verspreiden of hun schaduw werpen. We zijn op het intiemste deel van Floriade aangekomen, weg van de grote gebaande paden.

visiteur puisse mieux voir l'ensemble. On pourrait croire maintenant qu'il en a toujours été ainsi mais celui qui venait y promener son chien il y a dix ans, sait que l'aspect a changé. Quoique ... Après avoir passé sur le pont au-dessus de la N205 et devant une reproduction gigantesque des Tourne-sols de Van Gogh exposée sur un chevalet au mileu du bois, nous atterris-sons subitement dans un autre monde. Nous avons quitté le parc formel avec ses promenades rectilignes et ses îles rectangulaires, l'enclave utile et nécessaire de l'horticulture est derrière nous. Nous sommes entourés à présent de végétaux d'ornement, dans un décor romantique et décontracté, dans une haute verdure. Si les narines et les papilles ont été éveillées plus tôt, tout le régal est maintenant pour les yeux. Ce sont là les contrastes flagrants que propose la Floriade, les paradoxes du paysage qui nous plongent à chaque fois dans de nouvelles aventures. Ce n'est pas un jardin mais un concept, un ensemble avec plus de dix caractères différents et au cœur de ces caractères, des nuances encore divergentes. Sur la rive du Lac, nous parcourons déjà le monde en passant de l'Allemagne, avec un pavillon moderne s'avançant dans l'eau, à une petite maisonnette tchèque traditionnelle et comme évadée d'un conte de fées alors que l'exotisme d'Asie se profile au loin: le monde entier réuni dans un village de quelques hectares. Le bois du parc nous séduit par ses sentiers tortueux passant à travers les buissons, sur des pentes, dans des jardins enclos, et nous fait découvrir des noms qui sollicitent en nous la plus secrète des perceptions: la psyché. Qu'est-ce qui nous émeut, nous apaise ou justement nous dyna-mise? Dans chaque jardin des émotions, l'ambiance change d'une minute à l'autre, portée par les fleurs propageant leurs senteurs à l'improviste et les arbustes projetant leurs ombres. Nous sommes arrivés dans la partie la plus intime de la Floriade, loin des grandes allées tracées.

enough to walk their dogs in this terrain ten years ago know otherwise. After crossing the footbridge over the N205 and passing a gigantic copy of Van Gogh's Sunflowers on a giant easel in the woods, we find ourselves in another world. We have left the formal park with its straight water chan-nels, square islands and its emphasis on utilitarian horticulture. Here it is the art of ornamental gardening that surrounds us – ornamental garden-ing in a romantic, informal decor, surrounding by tall trees. Before, the tongue and nose were the sense organs that served us best, but this is the realm of the eye. These are the sharp contrasts that Floriade 2002 offers us, variations in the landscape which continually immerse us in new atmospheres. The Floriade is not a park with a single concept, but a park with perhaps ten different characters, and with varied shades within each of those characters. Following the shore of the Lake, we traverse the globe, first with a visit to modern Germany whose pavilion extends out over the water, and then a traditional Czech house that seems to spring straight from a fairy tale. In the distance, the exotics of Asia await us. A global village has been condensed into a few hectares.
The parkland wood tempts us with its winding paths and labyrinths, with its slopes and enclosed gardens. The names that go along with it appeal to that most mysterious of our human capacities: the mind. What is it that moves us, that brings us tranquillity or enlivens us? The mood changes minute by minute in the Emotion Gardens, instigated by the herbs and shrubs that spread their perfume or cast their shadows at unexpected moments. We have arrived at the most intimate part of the Floriade, well away from the busy thoroughfares.

mit seinem Hund Gassi gegangen ist, weiß es besser. Obwohl...

Wenn wir die überführung über die N205 überquert haben und an einer rie-senhaften Kopie der van Goghschen Sonnenblumen, die mitten im Wald auf einer Staffelei steht, vorbei gekommen sind, landen wir plötzlich in einer anderen Welt. Wir haben den förmlichen Park mit seinen geraden Gräben und viereckigen Inseln verlassen, genau wie den Gartenbaubereich – diese Enklave des Nutzens und der Notwendigkeit – und stehen nun inmitten des Zierpflanzenanbaugebiets. Es liegt in einer romantischen, informellen Kulisse voller hochaufgeschossener Grünpflanzen. Während bisher Zunge und Nase genießen konnten, sind wir nun im Reich der Augen. Die Floriade 2002 konfrontiert uns mit scharfen Kontrasten, mit landschaftlichen Gegensätzen, die uns jedes Mal in ein anderes Erlebnis tauchen. Der Flo-riade-Garten hat nicht nur ein Konzept, sondern umfasst mindestens zehn verschiedene Gärten, die alle einen eigenen Charakter und außerdem noch unterschiedliche Nuancen besitzen. So wechselt man am Ufer des Sees von einer Welt in die andere über, indem man vom Pavillon des modernen Deutschland, der ins Wasser hinein reicht, in ein traditionelles tschechisches Haus gelangt, das aus einem Märchen stammen könnte, während man in der Ferne schon die Exotik Asiens erblickt. 'A global village' auf einigen wenigen Hektar. Der Parkwald verführt den Spaziergänger mit Schlängelwe-gen durch Baumgruppen, über Hänge, durch abgeschlossene Gärten, und die Namen, die dazu gehören, appellieren an den geheimnisvollsten unserer Sinne: die Psyche. Was rührt uns, was beruhigt uns, und was aktiviert uns? In jedem Garten der Emotionen wechselt die Stimmung von einer Minute zur anderen, da die Blumen und Sträucher so angeordnet wurden, dass sie plötzlich anfangen, Duft oder Schatten zu spenden. Wir sind im intimsten Teil der Floriade angekommen, der abseits der ausgetretenen Pfade liegt.

Orchidee, ratelaar
en waterlelie
**Orchidée, rhinante
et néuphar**
Orchidee, Klappertopf
und Seerose
**Orchid, Rattle and
Water Lily**

Emotietuinen

'The art of nature' openbaart zich soms op een heel subtiele manier: in de dauwdruppels op het zich ontvouwende blad van vrouwenmantel, in de zoete geur van lelies op een warme zomeravond en in het troostende gefluister van dikke toeven bamboe. Met de gedachte dat planten het vermogen hebben om te ontroeren en sluimerende emoties in de mens naar boven te halen hebben de verschillende sierteeltorganisaties een gezamenlijke inzending ontwikkeld die hierop gebaseerd is. Het resultaat is een drietal tuinen waarin emoties een hoofdrol spelen. De Tuin der Bezinning loopt over in de Tuin van de Romantiek en deze grenst weer aan de Tuin van de Dynamiek. Deze drie tuinen zijn gesitueerd in het deel 'aan het Meer', op een open plek in het bestaande populierenbos. Om ervoor te zorgen dat die plek toch een beschutte, intieme ruimte wordt, zijn rondom diverse hagen aangeplant, bestaande uit onder andere beuk, vuurdoorn en hulst.

Voor alle drie de tuinen geldt één gezamenlijk uitgangspunt dat bepalend is voor de sfeer: de basis van elke tuin bestaat uit bladhoudende en bladverliezende heesters en coniferen, hier en daar aangevuld met een niet te grote boom die geschikt is voor de partikuliere tuin. Slechts sporadisch doen bodembedekkende vaste planten mee in het geheel. Toch zit er een verrassingselement in deze tuinen, want in elk van de drie bloeit in het voorjaar een grote verscheidenheid aan vroege bolgewassen. Wanneer die uitgebloeid zijn daalt de rust even

Les jardins des émotions

'L'art de la nature' se manifeste parfois très subtilement: dans la rosée sur la feuille tout juste déployée de l'alchémille, dans le parfum sucré des lys par un beau soir d'été ou dans le murmure cajolant de grosses touffes de bambou. Partant de l'idée que les plantes ont le potentiel d'attendrir et de réveiller chez l'être humain des émotions somnolentes, les diverses organisations d'horticulture ornementale ont créé une présentation commune, avec pour résultat trois jardins où les émotions jouent un rôle primordial. Le Jardin de la Réflexion ouvre ses portes vers le Jardin du Romantisme qui lui-même voisine avec le Jardin du Dynamisme. Ces trois jardins sont situés dans la partie Au Bord du Lac, dans une clairière du bois de peupliers existant. Afin que cet endroit soit abrité et intime, des haies de caractère différent ont été plantées en pourtour, formées entre autres par des charmes, des pyracanthes et des houx.

Le même principe a été retenu pour les trois jardins et détermine l'ambiance qui y règne: chaque jardin se compose à la base d'arbustes à feuilles persistantes ou caduques et de conifères, avec ici et là un arbre de taille modeste convenant au jardin du particulier. De temps à autre, des plantes vivaces couvre-sol complètent le tout. Pourtant ces jardins nous réservent une surprise. Au printemps, fleurissent dans chacun d'entre eux des bulbes précoces d'une grande diversité. Puis, quand leur floraison est passée,

The Emotion Gardens

'The art of nature' sometimes reveals itself in very subtle ways: in a drop of dew on the unfolding leaf of a Lady's Mantle, in the sweet perfume of lilies on a warm summer evening or in the soothing rustle of clumps of bamboo in the breeze. The idea that plants are capable of touching our emotions and evoking dormant feelings inspired the participating ornamental plant cultivation organizations to prepare a joint contribution on this theme. The outcome is a group of three Emotion Gardens. The Garden of Reflection adjoins the Garden of Romance, and this in turn adjoins the Dynamic Garden. These three gardens are situated in the 'on the Lake' section of the park, in a clearing in the pre-existing poplar woods. Various hedges, consisting of species such as Beech, Pyracantha and Holly, have been planted to give this area a sheltered, intimate character. The three gardens have one feature in common that sets the general mood. Each garden is based on a mix of deciduous and evergreen shrubs and conifers, with a tree of not too large a size, suitable for the domestic garden. Ground-covering perennials play only a sporadic part in the effect. However, these gardens have an element of surprise, for each of them has its own spring glory with a diverse range of early flowering bulbs. When these have finished flowering, there is a short period of tranquillity, followed by the next wave of colour as the summer-flowering bulbs come into

Die Gärten der Emotionen

'The art of nature' offenbart sich zuweilen ganz subtil: in den Tautropfen auf dem sich entfaltenden Blatt des Frauenmantels, im süßen Duft der Lilien an einem warmen Sommerabend und im tröstlichen Gewisper der dicken Bambusbüschel. Aus dem Gedanken heraus, dass Pflanzen dazu imstande sind, den Menschen anzurühren und in ihm schlummernde Gefühle zu wecken, haben die verschiedenen Organisationen des Zierpflanzenanbaus einen Gemeinschaftsbeitrag konzipiert, der auf diesem Prinzip beruht. Das Ergebnis besteht aus drei Gärten, die den Emotionen gewidmet sind. Der Garten der Besinnung geht in den Garten der Romantik über, der wiederum an den Garten der Dynamik grenzt. Die drei Gärten liegen im Teilbereich 'am See', auf einer Lichtung im Pappelwald. Damit dieser Standort zu einer geschützten, intimen Lage wird, hat man mehrere Hecken angepflanzt, darunter Buche, Feuerdorn und Stechpalme.

Die Atmosphäre wird von einem übergreifenden Ausgangspunkt bestimmt: Grundlage jedes Gartens sind die immer- oder sommergrünen Sträucher und Koniferen, zu denen hin und wieder ein nicht allzu hoher Baum tritt, der auch für private Gärten geeignet ist. Bodenbedeckende Dauerpflanzen sind nur sporadisch vertreten. Dennoch enthalten diese Gärten ein Überraschungsmoment, da in jedem von ihnen im Frühjahr viele verschiedene frühe Zwiebelgewächse blühen. Wenn sie ausgeblüht haben, zieht wieder Ruhe ein, bis die nächste

De Emotietuinen

Les jardins des émotions

Die Gärten der Emotionen

The Emotion Gardens

neer tot het moment waarop een volgende golf van zomerbloeiende bloembollen het specifieke karakter van elke tuin nog eens extra benadrukt.

De Tuin der Bezinning

Uitgangspunten voor de Tuin der Bezinning zijn de volgende karakteristieken die samen zorgen voor een beeld van rust en stilte:

– de kleuren van de bloemen zijn koel en sober: wit, blauw of groenachtig. De bloemen zelf zijn, op een enkele uitzondering na, klein en niet al te opvallend. Geuren zijn subtiel en zacht.
– Het accent ligt vooral op de verschillende bladvormen en de kleur van de bladeren. Daarom is het voorjaar, wanneer het blad weer als eerste zichtbaar wordt, in deze tuin heel belangrijk.
– Het voornaamste zintuig in deze tuin is het gehoor: het oor dat gestreeld wordt door het ritselen en ruisen van de verschillende types blad.

Deze ingetogen tuin is typisch een tuin om in afzondering van te genieten en om in te mediteren. Een belangrijk element vormen de 'droompaden'. Dit zijn paden die vanuit een centrale grondwal weglopen in het omringende bos, waarbij het spel tussen licht en donker overgaat in een schemerwereld die nergens lijkt te eindigen. Opvallend is het voor deze paden gebruikte materiaal: grote platen Noordfranse leisteen die in elk pad op een andere manier naast of op elkaar gelegd zijn. In de gelaagdheid van deze platen komt een geschiedenis van duizenden jaren tot leven die tot nadenken stemt.

De beplanting van deze tuin bestaat grotendeels uit heesters met opvallend blad, slechts hier en daar afgewisseld door heesters met blauwe of witte bloemen. Acer palmatum (Japanse esdoorn) en Cornus alba 'Elegantissima'

Le calme règne brièvement avant qu'une vague de bulbes d'été vienne souligner le caractère spécifique de chaque jardin.

Le Jardin de la Réflexion

Plusieurs caractéristiques font du Jardin de la Réflexion un cadre de quiétude et de silence:

– **Les fleurs ont des couleurs pâles et sobres: elles sont blanches, bleues ou verdâtres. Sauf exception, les fleurs sont petites et discrètes. Les senteurs sont douces et subtiles.**
– **L'accent est surtout posé sur la diversité des formes des feuilles et leur couleur. Ce jardin excelle donc au printemps, quand les feuilles font leur apparition.**
– **Le principal sens éveillé dans ce jardin est l'ouïe, quand on prête l'oreille au bruissement et au frémissement des divers types de feuilles.**

Ce jardin pacifique s'apprécie par excellence dans l'isolement et la méditation. Les 'allées du rêve' ont un caractère spécial. Elles se dispersent à partir d'un terre-plein central vers le bois environnant où le jeu du clair-obscur s'engage vers une pénombre paraissant sans fin. Le pavage des allées est original: de grandes dalles d'ardoise du Nord de la France se juxtaposent ou se superposent de manière différente dans chaque allée. Le chevauchement de ces dalles fait renaître mille ans d'histoire et nous invite à la réflexion.

La végétation du jardin se compose principalement d'arbustes au feuillage marquant, agrémentés ici et là d'arbustes aux fleurs bleues ou blanches. L'Acer palmatum (érable du Japon) aux feuilles palmées et le Cornus

bloom; again, each garden has its own mix of varieties, selected to match its special character.

The Garden of Reflection

The point of departure for the Garden of Reflection consisted of the following characteristics, chosen to communicate a mood of quiet and tranquillity:
– **The colours of the flowers are cool and muted: white, blue or greenish. The flowers themselves are small and subdued, with one exception. The perfumes are subtle and soft.**
– **The emphasis is on the different shapes and colours of the leaves. Therefore the moment when the leaves first open in the spring is a very important one in this garden.**
– **The primary sense addressed in this garden is that of hearing. The ear is soothed by the rustling and murmuring of the different leaves.**

This demure garden is typically one which you might enjoy alone, a garden in which to meditate perhaps. The 'dream paths' are an important element in its layout. The paths spread out from a central embankment into the surrounding woods, so that the checkered light and shade of the garden merges into an endless-seeming twilight world. The material of the paths is a fascination one: large slabs of slate from northern France, laid in a different pattern for each path. The many layers of these slabs recalls a history of countless thousands of years, a worthy subject of reflection. The plantation of this garden consists mostly of shrubs with striking leaves, alternating only here and there with shrubs bearing blue or white flowers. Acer palmatum (Japanese Maple) with its five-fingered leaf

Welle der sommerblühenden Zwiebelpflanzen einsetzt und den individuellen Charakter der einzelnen Gärten extra unterstreicht.

Der Garten der Besinnung

Ausgangspunkte des Gartens der Besinnung sind folgende Merkmale, die alle zusammen für ein Bild der Ruhe und Stille sorgen:
– *Die Blumen haben kühle und schlichte Farben: Sie sind weiß, blau oder grünlich. Außerdem sind sie, von einigen Ausnahmen abgesehen, klein und nicht sehr auffällig. Ihr Duft ist subtil und mild.*
– *Der Akzent liegt vor allem auf den verschiedenen Formen und Farben der Blätter. Daher ist der Frühling, in dem die Blätter wieder hervorkommen, in diesem Garten die wichtigste Saison.*
– *Dieser Garten spricht von allen Sinnesorganen am meisten das Gehör an: Das Rascheln und Rauschen der verschiedenen Blattsorten umschmeichelt das Ohr.*

Dieser maßvolle Garten eignet sich gut zum zurückgezogenen Genuss oder zur Meditation. Wichtige Elemente des Besinnungshorts sind die 'Traumwege'. Diese Wege beginnen beim zentralen Erdwall und führen in den Wald, wobei das Spiel von Hell und Dunkel in eine Dämmerwelt übergeht, die im Nirgendwo zu enden scheint. Sie bestehen aus auffallendem Material: große Schieferplatten aus Nordfrankreich, die bei jedem Weg anders nebeneinander oder übereinander gelegt wurden. Die Schichtung dieser Platten stimmt nachdenklich, birgt sie doch eine tausendjährige Geschichte in sich. Die Bepflanzung besteht größtenteils aus Sträuchern mit auffälligen Blättern, zwischen denen nur hin und wieder Sträucher mit blauen oder weißen Blüten stehen. Acer palmatum (Japanischer Ahorn) und Cornus alba 'Elegantissima' (Hartriegel) gehören mit ihrem handförmigem beziehungsweise weiß-

(witte kornoelje) met respectievelijk handvormig en witbont blad behoren tot de beste vertegenwoordigers van dit type tuin, evenals Sorbaria grandiflora 'Fern Cascade' en Hydrangea quercifolia (eikebladhortensia). Deze laatste twee laten behalve decoratief blad ook een bijzondere bloemvorm zien. De coniferen hebben donkergroene of grijsblauwe tinten en daar zijn Picea abies 'Repens' (fijnspar) en Cedrus deodara (Himalayaceder) sprekende voorbeelden van. Overwegend groenblijvende bodembedekkers zoals Vinca minor 'Gertrude Jekyll' (maagdenpalm) en Pachysandra terminalis maken het geheel compleet.

Het vroege seizoensaccent in de Tuin der Bezinning komt tot uiting in bloembollen als Anemone blanda 'Blue Shades' (voorjaarsanemoon), Allium cowanii en Narcissus poeticus recurvus (fazantenoognarcis). Zij worden in de zomer opgevolgd door Galtonia candicans, Ornithogalum thyrsoides (zuidenwindlelie) en verschillende vormen van Eucomis (kuifhyacint).

De Tuin der Romantiek

In de Tuin van de Romantiek staan begrippen als liefde en tederheid centraal. Zij worden verbeeld door een weelderige, verleidelijke beplanting. Bloemen in hoofdzakelijk lila, roze en rode tinten spelen hier een hoofdrol; ze zijn in overvloed aanwezig en ruiken zoet en bedwelmend. Naast geur zijn smaak en tast belangrijk en dat is de reden dat vruchtdragende heesters ook deel uitmaken van het sortiment. Dat maakt dat deze tuin eigenlijk het hele seizoen door tot de verbeelding spreekt.

Het moge duidelijk zijn dat de Tuin der Romantiek bedoeld is voor mensen die zeer op elkaar gesteld zijn. Zij kunnen van elkaars nabijheid genieten in

alba 'Elegantissima' (cornouiller blanc au feuillage blanc panaché) se rangent parmi les meilleurs représentants de ce type de jardin, de même que le Sorbaria grandiflora 'Fern Cascade' et l'Hydrangea quercifolia (hortensia à feuilles de chêne) qui, en plus de leur feuillage décoratif, ont des inflorescences originales. Les conifères ont des tons vert foncé ou gris bleuté avec pour meilleurs exemples le Picea abies 'Repens' (épicéa rampant) et le Cedrus deodara (cèdre de l'Himalaya). Des plantes couvre-sol à feuillage persistant pour la plupart complètent l'ensemble: Vinca minor 'Gertrude Jekyll' (grande pervenche) et Pachysandra terminalis.

Le Jardin de la Réflexion fête la première saison de floraison avec des bulbes comme l'Anemone blanda 'Blue Shades' (anémone de printemps), l'Allium cowanii et le Narcissus poeticus recurvus (narcisse des poètes). La relève est prise en été par le Galtonia candicans, l'Ornithogalum thyrsoides (ornithogale) et diverses dormes d'Eucomis (fleur ananas).

Le Jardin du Romantisme

Le Jardin du Romantisme respire l'amour et la tendresse reflétés par une végétation aussi luxuriante que séduisante. Les fleurs notamment mauves, roses et rouges y jouent le rôle principal; elles sont abondantes et émanent des parfums sucrés et grisants. Et comme le goût et le toucher ne sont pas moins importants que l'odorat, des arbres porteurs de fruits complètent l'assortiment. Le jardin frappe ainsi l'imagination à tout moment.

Comme de bien entendu, le Jardin du Romantisme est l'endroit privilégié des gens qui s'aiment. Ils apprécient d'être ensemble, à l'écart du monde,

and Cornus alba 'Elegantissima' (White Cornel [/American Dogwood]) with a variegated white leaf are among the best representatives of this kind of shrub, as are Sorbaria grandiflora 'Fern Cascade' and Hydrangea quercifolia (Oak Leafed Hydrangea). The latter two not only have interesting leaves but unusual flowering forms. The conifers have dark green or greyish-blue tints, with Picea abies 'Repens' (Norway Spruce) and Cedrus deodara (Deodar Cedar) as excellent examples. Largely evergreen ground-covering plants such as Vinca minor 'Gertrude Jekyll' (Lesser Periwinkle) and Pachysandra terminalis (Japanese Spurge) round off the greenery.
The early seasonal climax in the Garden of Reflection is expressed by such bulbs as Anemone blanda 'Blue Shades' (Blue Winter Anemone), Allium cowanii and Narcissus poeticus v recurvus (Pheasant's Eye). Their summer successors are Galtonia candicans, Ornithogalum thyrsoides (Chincherinchee) and various forms of Eucomis (Pineapple Flower).

The Garden of Romance

In the Garden of Romance, love and tenderness are the key emotions. They are symbolized by a lush, sensual vegetation. Flowers play the starring role, predominantly in tints of lilac, pink and red. They grow in abundance and spread a sweet, intoxicating perfume. But taste and touch are also important, so fruit-bearing shrubs have been included too. This garden thus appeals to the senses throughout the seasons. The Garden of Romance is, as the name suggests, a garden for lovers. Fond couples can enjoy some seclusion in the shelter of a niche, an arbour or in one of the love-seats placed here (a modern alternative to the turf

buntem Blatt zu den besten Vertretern dieses Gartentyps, genau wie Sorbaria grandiflora 'Fern Cascade' und Hydrangea quercifolia (Eichenblatthortensie). Die beiden letzteren besitzen neben dem dekorativen Blatt auch eine außergewöhnliche Blumenform. Die Koniferen sind dunkelgrün oder graublau getönt, was insbesondere für die Picea abies 'Repens' (Fichte) und den Cedrus deodara (Himalajazeder) gilt. Überwiegend immergrüne Bodendecker wie Vinca minor 'Gertrude Jekyll' (Kleines Immergrün) und Pachysandra terminalis (Japanischer Ysander) komplettieren das Ganze.
In der Frühsaison setzen im Garten der Besinnung Blumenzwiebeln wie Anemone blanda 'Blue Shades' (Balkan-Windröschen), Allium cowanii und Narcissus poeticus recurvus (Poetennarzissen) Akzente. Im Sommer übernehmen Galtonia candicans (Kaphyazinthe), Ornithogalum thyrsoides (Milchstern) und verschiedene Eucomis-Sorten (Schopflilien) diese Rolle.

Der Garten der Romantik

Der Garten der Romantik kreist um Begriffe wie Liebe und Zärtlichkeit, die von dem üppigen, verführerischen Pflanzenwuchs symbolisiert werden. Hier dominieren Blumen in Lila-, Rosa- und Rottönen. Sie sind im überfluss vorhanden und strömen einen süßen und betäubenden Geruch aus. Neben dem Geruch wird der Geschmacks- und Tastsinn bedient, und daher gehören auch früchtetragende Sträucher zur Bepflanzung. Insofern reizt dieser Garten eigentlich die ganze Saison über die Sinne.
Dass der Garten der Romantik für Menschen bestimmt ist, die sich sehr mögen, dürfte inzwischen klar sein. Sie können sich in verborgenen Nischen, Lauben oder einem der im Garten aufgestellten Himmelssitze, einer modernen Version der mittelalterlichen Rasenbank, nahe kommen. Den Mittelpunkt des Gartens bildet ein Wasserbecken, das als Spiegel des Alls gestaltet wurde.

Duizendblad

Achillée millefeuille

Schafgarbe

Milfoil

de beslotenheid van een nis, een prieel of op een van de hier geplaatste 'hemelzitjes', een modern alternatief voor de middeleeuwse zodenbank. Een waterbassin als spiegel van het heelal vormt het middelpunt van deze tuin.

Het voorjaar laat een overdaad aan bloemen zien in Kolkwitzia amabilis 'Pink Cloud', Syringa vulgaris 'Monique Lemoine' en Deutzia rosea 'Carminea'. Maar de zomer laat zich evenmin onbetuigd. In een zoetgeurende beplanting ontbreken natuurlijk vlinderstruiken zoals Buddleia davidii 'Black Knight' en 'Nanho Blue' niet en even onmisbaar zijn hortensiasoorten waaronder Hydrangea macrophylla 'Bouquet Rose', 'Mariesii Perfecta' en 'Alpenglühen'.

De altijd-groene basis die ervoor zorgt dat een dergelijke tuin ook in wintertijd zijn specifieke karakter behoudt wordt in dit geval onder andere gevormd door buxusbollen in verschillende afmetingen en door Chamarecyparis pisifera 'Filifera', een van de elegantste coniferen.

Oude tulpenrassen zoals parkiettulpen ('Black Parrot', 'Fantasy', 'Rococo') en pioenbloemige tulpen ('Angélique', 'Uncle Tom', 'Carnaval de Nice') geven extra glans aan het voorjaar. Zij worden in de zomer opgevolgd door Freesia's, lelies en decoratieve dahlia's zoals 'Arabian Night' en 'Lavender Perfection'.

De Tuin van de Dynamiek

Dynamiek staat voor in beweging zijn, energie uitstralen, uitbundigheid, een sterk karakter tonen. Al deze begrippen zijn verenigd in de derde tuin die in tegenstelling tot de andere twee volop in het zonlicht baadt. Aandacht vragen en op de voorgrond treden zijn eveneens kenmerken die vereenzelvigd worden met het begrip 'dynamiek' en daarom is in de beplanting gekozen voor planten met een krachtig silhouet die elkaar door hun uitgesproken vorm versterken.

dans l'intimité d'une niche de verdure, sous une charmille ou sur l'un des 'petits bancs du paradis', une version moderne des bancs de gazon moyenâgeux. Un bassin se fait le miroir du ciel au centre du jardin.

Au printemps s'admire la floraison abondante du Kolkwitzia amabilis 'Pink Cloud', du Syringa vulgaris ' Monique Lemoine' (lilas commun) et du Deutzia rosea 'Carminea'. Mais le jardin ne perd en rien de sa beauté et de ses senteurs en été puisque les arômes sucrés sont ceux entre autres des arbustes à papillons comme le Buddleia davidii 'Black Night' et 'Nanho Blue' qu'il ne fallait surtout pas oublier, pas plus que diverses variétés d'hortensias dont l'Hydrangea macrophylla 'Bouquet Rose', 'Mariesii Perfecta' et 'Alpenglühen'.

Des boules de buis de diverses dimensions et des Chamarecyparis pisifera 'Filifera', l'un des conifères les plus élégants, forment la base de verdure persistante qui permet à ce type de jardin de garder son caractère spécifique même en hiver. De vieilles variétés de tulipes comme celles du type perroquet ('Black Parrot', 'Fantasy', 'Rococo') et celles à fleur de pivoine ('Angélique', 'Uncle Tom', 'Carnaval de Nice') apportent encore plus de brillant au printemps. Elles sont succédées en été par les Freesias, les lys, et plusieurs variétés de dahlias décoratifs telles 'Arabian Night' et 'Lavender Perfection'.

Le Jardin du Dynamisme

Le dynamisme, c'est aussi le mouvement, le rayonnement d'énergie, l'exubérance, la force de caractère. Toutes ces notions sont mises en scène dans le troisième jardin qui, contrairement aux deux autres, baigne en plein soleil. Attirer l'attention et se faire valoir sont aussi des traits de caractère qui vont souvent de pair avec le dynamisme, raison pour laquelle

seats of medieval gardens). A pool mirrors the cosmos and forms the centre point of this garden.

Spring is marked by a glut of flowers provided by Kolkwitzia amabilis 'Pink Cloud', Syringa vulgaris 'Monique Lemoine' and Deutzia rosea 'Carminea'. But summer is not far behind. A densely perfumed garden is not of course complete without Butterfly Bushes such as Buddleia davidii 'Black Knight' and 'Nanho Blue'. Nor can it do without sweet-smelling hydrangeas such as Hydrangea macrophylla 'Bouquet Rose', 'Mariesii Perfecta' and 'Alpenglühen'.

The evergreen basis that helps preserve the special character of this garden through the winter includes Box balls in various sizes, and Chamaecyparis pisifera 'Filifera' (Dwarf Cypress), one of the most elegant of conifers.

Old-fashioned tulip varieties, such as the Parrot Tulips ('Black Parrot', 'Fantasy', 'Rococo') and Peony Flowered Tulips ('Angélique', 'Uncle Tom', 'Carnaval de Nice') give the spring an extra shine. They are succeeded in summer by Freesias, Lilies and ornamental Dahlias such as 'Arabian Night' and 'Lavender Perfection'.

The Dynamic Garden

Dynamic stands for being on the move, energy, exuberance and an extrovert character. All these ideas have been combined in the third Emotion garden which, unlike the other two, bathes in full sunlight. Shouting for attention and being up-front are also aspects of a dynamic character, so the garden has plants with a decided profile which support one another with their emphatic shapes. The first candidates that spring to mind are conifers, for example the column-shapes of Juniperus scopulorum

Im Frühjahr prangen hier Unmengen von Blumen wie Kolkwitzia amabilis 'Pink Cloud', Syringa vulgaris 'Monique Lemoine' und Deutzia rosea 'Carminea'. Aber der Sommer kann durchaus mithalten. In einer Bepflanzung, die süßen Duft ausströmt, dürfen natürlich Sommerfliedersträucher wie Buddleia davidii 'Black Knight' und 'Nanho Blue' nicht fehlen, und Hortensien wie die Hydrangea macrophylla 'Bouquet Rose', 'Mariesii Perfecta' und 'Alpenglühen' sind ebenso unentbehrlich.

Die immergrüne Basis, die dafür sorgt, dass ein solcher Garten auch im Winter seinen speziellen Charakter behält, besteht in diesem Fall unter anderem aus Buchsbaumkugeln in verschiedenen Größen und aus Chamarecyparis pisifera 'Filifera', einer der elegantesten Koniferen.

Alte Tulpenarten wie Papageitulpen ('Black Parrot', 'Fantasy', 'Rococo') und gefüllte späte Tulpen ('Angélique', 'Uncle Tom', 'Carnaval de Nice') verleihen dem Frühling besonderen Glanz. Im Sommer werden sie von Freesien, Lilien und dekorativen Dahlien wie 'Arabian Night' und 'Lavender Perfection' abgelöst.

Der Garten der Dynamik

Dynamik steht für Beweglichkeit, Energie, Überschwänglichkeit, Charakterstärke. All diese Begriffe werden im dritten Garten vereint, der im Gegensatz zu den anderen beiden geradezu im Sonnenlicht badet. Die Aufmerksamkeit auf sich ziehen und in den Vordergrund treten sind weitere Aspekte des Begriffes Dynamik. In diesem Sinne wurden Pflanzen mit einer starken Silhouette ausgewählt, die sich durch ihre unverkennbare Form gegenseitig besser zur Geltung bringen. Da bieten sich Koniferen als erste an, so dass hier säulenförmige Gewächse wie Juniperus scopulorum 'Blue Arrow' oder Juniperus communis 'Suecica', kugelförmige Gewächse wie Thuja occidentalis 'Golden

Naast vormen hebben ook kleuren een bepaalde gevoels-waarde. Er zijn koele kleuren (blauw, groen, violet en wit, hoewel dat eigenlijk geen echte kleur genoemd mag worden) en warme kleuren (geel, oranje, rood en paars). Een groter contrast dan tussen koele en warme kleuren is er niet en met die combinatie moet dus voorzichtig omgegaan worden. Combinaties van kleuren onderling in de koele of warme afdeling zijn vaak zeer evenwichtig. Algemeen kan gesteld worden dat koele kleuren op hun mooist zijn op beschaduwde plekken en warme kleuren in de zon.

Outre les formes, les couleurs ont, elles aussi, une symbolique. Il y a des tons froids (le bleu, le vert, le mauve et le blanc, quoique le blanc ne soit pas vraiment une couleur) et des tons chauds (le jaune, l'orange, le rouge et le violet). Il n'est de contraste plus fragrant que celui enre les tons chauds et les tons froids, aussi les couleurs doivent-elles être combinées avec prudence. Les mélanges de tons chauds ou de tons froids sont souvent très équilibrés. En règle générale, les tons froids sont les plus beaux dans les endroits ombragés et les tons chauds au soleil.

Not only shapes but colours have definite emotional values. There are cool colours (blue, green, violet and white – if we may call that a colour for present purposes) and warm colours (yellow, orange, red and purple). The contrast between warm and cool is more intense than any other, so we must be very careful about using them in combination. A well-balanced colour scheme is usually only successful with either a combination of warm colours or a combination of cool colours. As a general rule, cool colours come out best in shady spots, and warm colours in the sun.

Nicht nur Formen, sondern auch Farben haben einen bestimmten Gefühlswert. Es gibt kühle Farben (blau, grün, violett und weiß, obwohl das eigentlich keine richtige Farbe ist) und warme Farben (gelb, orange, rot und lila). Der Kontrast zwischen kühlen und warmen Farben ist so groß, dass man mit deren Kombination vorsichtig sein muss. Dagegen sind Farbkombinationen innerhalb der kühlen oder der warmen Gruppe meist recht ausgewogen. Im Allgemeinen kann man sagen, dass kühle Farben an schattigen Stellen und warme Farben in der Sonne am besten wirken.

Ooievaarsbek en klokjesbloem
Bec-de-grue et campanule
Storchschnabel und Glockenblume
Cranesbill and Bellflower

Dan komen coniferen als eerste in aanmerking en dus zijn er zuilvormen van bijvoorbeeld Juniperus scopulorum 'Blue Arrow' en Juniperus communis 'Suecica', bolvormen van onder andere Thuja occidentalis 'Golden Globe' en 'Little Champion' en uitwaaierende vormen zoals die van Juniperus media 'Pfitzeriana'. Zij worden ondersteund door imposante bladverliezende en bladhoudende heesters, waaronder Clerodendron trichotomum fargesii, Hydrangea aspera 'Macrophylla' en Mahonia japonica 'Hivernant'. Bijpassende bodembedekkers zijn Cotoneaster procumbens 'Queen of Carpets' en Juniperus virginiana 'Grey Owl'.

Ook de bolgewassen laten zich niet onbetuigd. En omdat de hoofdkleuren in deze tuin geel en oranje zijn zal het geen verwondering wekken dat dubbele narcissen zoals 'Petit Four' en 'Unique' en spleetkronige narcissen zoals 'Tiritomba' en 'Orangery' zich op de voorgrond dringen naast keizerskronen (Fritillaria imperialis) en Eremurus 'Pinokkio' (woestijnkaars). Daarna is het de beurt aan opvallende zomerbollen. Canna, Crocosmia 'Emberglow' en Crocosmia 'Emily McKenzie' staan te stralen naast Begonia 'Flamboyant' en Begonia 'Crispa Marginata'. Dit festijn wordt afgesloten met een vuurwerk van dahlia's in het cactus- en semi-cactusassortiment: 'Clarion', 'Gold Crown', 'Promise', 'Vulkan' en 'Yellow Happiness'.

Het zal duidelijk zijn dat het oog in deze tuin alle waarnemingen moet doen,

ont été choisies des plantes qui se donnent la répartie par leurs silhouettes robustes et leurs formes spécifiques. Les principaux acteurs sont les conifères, tantôt en colonne comme le Juniperus scopulorum 'Blue Arrow' et le Juniperus communis 'Suecica' (genévriers), tantôt en boule avec entre autres le Thuja occidentalis 'Golden Globe' et 'Little Champion' (thuyas), tantôt au port étalé comme le Juniperus media 'Pfitzeriana'. Ils sont assistés par d'imposants arbustes à feuilles caduques ou persistantes, parmi lesquels le Clerodendrum trichotomum fargesii (clérodendron), l'Hydrangea aspera 'Macrophylla' et le Mahonia japonica 'Hivernant'. En figurants: le Cotoneaster procumbens 'Queen of Carpets' et le Juniperus virginiana 'Grey Owl' forment une végétation couvre-sol s'harmonisant au reste.

Les bulbes ne restent pas non plus en coulisse. Et comme le décor du jardin est dominé par le jaune et l'orange, rien d'étonnant à ce que les narcisses doubles comme les variétés 'Petit Four' et 'Unique' et les narcisses à couronne fendue telles que les variétés 'Tiritomba' et 'Orangery' n'occupent l'avant-scène à côté des couronnes impériales (Fritillaria imperialis) et des Eremurus 'Pinokkio' (lys des steppes). Après, de remarquables bulbes à floraison estivale font leur entrée: Canna (balisier), Crocosmia 'Emberglow' et Crocosmia 'Emily McKenzie'. Ils rayonnent à côté du Begonia 'Flamboyant' et du Begonia 'Crispa Marginata'. Le

'Blue Arrow' or Juniperus communis 'Suecica', the globe shapes of Thuja occidentalis 'Golden Globe' or 'Little Champion', and flared shapes such as that of Juniperus media 'Pfitzeriana'. They are supported by imposing deciduous and evergreen shrubs, including Clerodendron trichotomum fargesii, Hydrangea aspera 'Macrophylla' and Mahonia japonica 'Hivernant'. Ground cover plants that match these alternatives include Cotoneaster procumbens 'Queen of Carpets' and Juniperus virginiana 'Grey Owl'.

The flowering bulbs are equal to this energetic display. Since the main colours in this garden are yellow and orange, you will not be surprised to learn that Double Daffodils such as 'Petit Four' and 'Unique', and Split Collar Narcissi like 'Tiritomba' and 'Orangery' jostle for the footlights, alongside Crown Imperial (Fritillaria imperialis) and Eremurus Pinokkio (Desert Candle).

Then it is the turn of the vibrant summer-flowering bulbs. Canna, Crocosmia 'Emberglow' and Crocosmia 'Emily McKenzie' shine out alongside Begonia 'Flamboyant' and Begonia 'Crispa Marginata'. This feast of colour concludes with a firework-show of Dahlias from the cactus and semi-cactus range: 'Clarion', 'Gold Crown', 'Promise', 'Vulkan' and 'Yellow Happiness'. It will be clear that in this garden it is the eye that does all the perceiving, while in the previous

Globe' oder 'Little Champion' und fächerförmige Gewächse wie Juniperus media 'Pfitzeriana' stehen. Unterstützt werden sie von imposanten immer- oder sommergrünen Sträuchern, darunter Clerodendron trichotomum fargesii, Hydrangea aspera 'Macrophylla' und Mahonia japonica 'Hivernant'. Die dazu gehörigen bodenbedeckenden Pflanzen sind Cotoneaster procumbens 'Queen of Carpets' und Juniperus virginiana 'Grey Owl'.

Auch die Zwiebelgewächse tun ihr Bestes. Da Gelb und Orange die Hauptfarben dieses Gartens sind, ist es nicht verwunderlich, dass gefüllte Narzissen wie 'Petit Four' und 'Unique' und spaltblütige Narzissen wie 'Tiritomba' und 'Orangery' neben Kaiserkronen (Fritillaria imperialis) und Eremurus 'Pinokkio' (Steppenlilie) stark vertreten sind.

Danach sind auffällige Sommerblumen an der Reihe. Canna, Crocosmia 'Emberglow' und Crocosmia 'Emily McKenzie' prangen neben Begonia 'Flamboyant' und Begonia 'Crispa Marginata'. Den Abschluss dieses Spektakels bildet ein Feuerwerk aus Dahlien und ein Kakteen- beziehungsweise Kaktusdahlien-Sortiment: 'Clarion', 'Gold Crown', 'Promise', 'Vulkan' und 'Yellow Happiness'.

Dieser Garten regt also das Auge an, während die Wirkung der vorhergehenden Gärten auf das Ohr (Klang) und die Nase (Geruch) abzielte.

Der Garten der Dynamik ist auf Gruppen eingestellt, die etwas zusammen unternehmen möchten – ein Spiel, eine Grillparty oder ein Picknick. Ein mar-

135

waar in de vorige tuinen het oor (geluid) en de neus (geur) bepalend waren.

De Tuin van de Dynamiek is bestemd voor een groep mensen die samen iets willen ondernemen zoals een spel, een barbecue of een picknick. Dan mag een opvallend kunstwerk niet ontbreken. In dit geval is dat een spiraalvorm met grote bloemschalen, in zijn geheel uitgevoerd in metaal. De beplanting in deze schalen wordt regelmatig gewisseld: de tuin blijft in beweging.

Als we weer aankoersen in de richting van de plas, zwaait het bos open en zijn we getuige van een kom in het meer waar de planten het ritme van de dag volgen. Om dit te kunnen beleven zou je hier vierentwintig uur moeten verblijven en kunnen zien hoe kelken zich sluiten en ontsluiten, hoe ze hun palet aanpassen aan de weersgesteldheid. Een steiger van gecorrodeerd ijzer breekt de kom doormidden en hier lopen we dan, als op een catwalk, tussen de mooiste fotomodellen van de Floriade: waterlelies in onwaarschijnlijke kleurencombinaties. Geel, oranje, wit met gele harten, en natuurlijk alle tinten paars en rose.

De nieuwe Monet zou zich hier met een schildersezel op de oever moeten nestelen en de wisselingen van de kelken moeten vastleggen.

spectacle est clos par un feu d'artifice de dahlias dans un assortiment de cactées et semi-cactées: 'Clarion', 'Gold Crown', 'Promise', 'Vulkan' et 'Yellow Happiness'. Ce jardin est un délice pour les yeux alors que les oreilles et le nez ont été séduits dans les jardins précédents.

Le Jardin du Dynamisme est le cadre idéal pour les visiteurs venus à plusieurs et désireux d'entreprendre quelque chose ensemble: un jeu, un barbecue, un pique-nique, etc. Raison de plus pour y présenter une œuvre d'art originale: une forme de spirale en métal composée de grosses coupes de fleurs dont la garniture est régulièrement changée pour que le jardin soit comme en mouvement perpétuel.

En avançant vers le plan d'eau, le bois semble ouvrir ses rideaux pour nous faire découvrir dans le lac une coupe où les plantes vivent la journée à leur propre cadence. Pour vraiment s'en rendre compte, il faudrait rester là vingt-quatre heures afin de voir comment les fleurs ouvrent et referment leurs calices et s'adaptent aux caprices du temps. Une coursive en fer rouillé fend la coupe en son milieu et nous ouvre le passage, comme si une estrade avait été jetée pour une présentation de mode, à la seule différence que c'est le public qui défile entouré par les plus beaux mannequins de la Floriade que sont les nénuphars dans de fabuleux mélanges de couleurs: jaune, orange, blanc au cœur jaune et bien sûr, toutes les nuances de rose et de mauve. Si Monet ressuscitait, il planterait son chevalet sur la rive pour figer sur sa toile les évolutions des calices.

gardens the ear (sound) and the nose (perfume) were the main senses. The Dynamic Garden is meant for people who have their mind set on an activity, such as a game, a barbecue or a picnic. It would not of course be complete without a striking piece of sculpture, and here it is a spiral form with large, shallow flower bowls attached, all made of metal. The plants in these bowls are changed at intervals: the Dynamic Garden cannot stand still.

Resuming our path in the direction of the Lake, the wood spreads open to reveal a side-pool of the lake containing plants that mark the rhythm of the day. To appreciate it to the full, we would have to spend 24 hours here, watching the flower trumpets folding and unfolding, and adapting their palette to the weather conditions. A rusted iron jetty divides the pool in two, and we walk across it as on a kind of inverted catwalk, with the Floriade's most photogenic models gazing up at us. The is the pool of waterlilies, in countless improbable combinations of hues: yellow, orange, white with yellow hearts and, of course, every shade of pink and purple. A new Monet would surely settle down on this bank with his easel before him and record the changes of the blooms as the day passes.

kantes Kunstwerk darf dabei nicht fehlen. Hier erhebt sich ein spiralförmiges Gebilde mit großen Blumenschalen, das ganz aus Metall besteht. Die Bepflanzung der Schalen wird regelmäßig ausgewechselt: Der Garten bleibt in Bewegung.

Wenn wir wieder auf den See zusteuern, öffnet sich der Vorhang des Waldes, und wir stehen vor einer Art Becken im See, dessen Bepflanzung sich ganz nach dem Tagesrhythmus richtet. Eigentlich müsste man sich hier vierundzwanzig Stunden lang aufhalten, um zu verfolgen, wie sich die Kelche schließen und öffnen, wie sie ihre Palette auf die Wetterlage abstimmen. Ein Steg aus rostigem Eisen teilt die Wanne und führt wie ein Laufsteg zwischen den schönsten Fotomodellen der Floriade hindurch: Seerosen in unglaublichen Farbzusammenstellungen. Sie sind gelb, orange, weiß mit gelben Herzen und natürlich gibt es sie auch in allen möglichen Lila- und Rosatönen. Ein neuer Monet würde vermutlich seine Staffelei an diesem Ufer aufbauen, um die wechselnden Formen der Kelche zu erfassen.

Vaste planten zijn op hun mooist als ze niet gesteund of opgebonden hoeven te worden. Toch is er een aantal soorten dat de neiging heeft om in de loop van het seizoen om te gaan vallen. Dat zijn vooral soorten die in de zomer of in de nazomer bloeien zoals *Campanula lactiflora,* Phloxen, hoge Sedumsoorten, Asters, Chelone, Kalimeris en Artemisia. De beste remedie om deze planten overeind te houden is om ze tegen eind mei, maar in ieder geval vóór 21 juni, te halveren. Op het overgebleven deel van de stengel ontstaan al spoedig nieuwe stevige uitlopers die wel tegen een stootje kunnen.

Perennials are at their loveliest when they have no need of stakes or other supports. All the same, there are several kinds that have a tendency to flop over in the course of the season. The worst offenders are those that flower in the summer and early autumn, such as *Campanula lactiflora*, Phloxes, tall types of Sedum, Asters, Chelone, Kalimeris and Artemisia. The best method for keeping these plants upright is to halve them early in the summer, perhaps around the end of May or at the latest by midsummer's day. The remaining part of the stalk soon sprouts sturdy side-stems which stand up well to whatever the summer has in store for them.

Les plantes vivaces sont les plus belles quand elles n'ont pas besoin d'être tuteurées ou liées. Plusieurs espèces ont toutefois tendance à se courber au cours de la saison, notamment celles qui fleurissent en été ou en fin d'été telles que la *Campanula lactiflora*, le Phlox, les hautes variétés de Sedum, les Asters, le Chelone, le Kalimeris et l'Artemisia. Le meilleur moyen pour qu'elles gardent un port bien dressé est de réduire ces plantes de moitié vers la fin mai et en tout cas avant le 21 juin. De nouvelles pousses vigoureuses se forment alors sur les tiges taillées.

Dauerpflanzen sind am schönsten, wenn sie nicht gestützt oder aufgebunden werden müssen. Einige Sorten neigen aber mit dem Fortschreiten der Saison zum Umfallen. Das betrifft vor allem die Arten, die im Sommer oder im Altweibersommer blühen, also *Campanula lactiflora*, Phloxe, hohe Sedumarten, Astern, Chelone, Kalimeris und Artemisien. Gegen das Hängen hilft am besten, sie Ende Mai, unbedingt aber vor dem 21. Juni, zu halbieren. Auf dem restlichen Teil des Stängels bilden sich bald neue Triebe, die recht widerstandsfähig sind.

139

Klokjesbloem, ooievaarsbek, gebroken hartje, primula en ooievaarsbek
Campanule, bec-de-grue, cœur saignant, primevère et bec-de-grue
Glockenblume, Storchschnabel, Tränendes Herz und Orchideenprimel und Storchschnabel
Bellflower, Cranesbill, Bleeding Heart, Primula and Cranesbill

Vaste planten (en het ritme van de dag)

In het derde parkdeel van de Floriade, 'aan het Meer', is in en grenzend aan een zijarm van het meer ruimte gemaakt voor een gecombineerde vaste planten- en waterplanteninzending. Het thema van deze inzending is 'het ritme van de dag' en gaat uit van de gedachte dat bij het vroege, heldere ochtendlicht andere kleuren en bloemvormen passen dan bij het zachte, schemerige licht van de avond. Dit idee is tot leven gebracht in een reusachtige vasteplantenborder en in de waterlelie-inzending die door deze border omarmd wordt.

Hier ontwaakt vroeg in de morgen de tuin op het oosten in stralend zonlicht. Bij een dergelijke sfeer passen vaste planten met fijne bloemetjes in zachte tinten zoals Scabiosa columbaria 'Butterfly Blue', *(zachtblauw)*, Salvia nemorosa 'Blauhügel' *(blauw)*, Sidalcea 'Elsie Heugh' *(roze)* en Gillenia trifoliata *(wit)*. Naarmate de ochtend vordert en het licht wat 'harder' wordt is er meer behoefte aan heldere, sprekende kleuren. Een tuin op het zuiden, waarin de zon vanaf haar hoogste punt naar binnen schijnt, is op haar mooist wanneer zij is ingevuld met planten die vrij stevige bloemen in felle kleuren hebben: rood, diepgeel en oranje zijn vertegenwoordigd in soorten als Achillea 'Terracotta', Potentilla 'Gibson's Scarlet', en Hemerocallis 'Stella de Oro'. Grijsbladige planten waaronder Stachys- en Artemisiasoorten zijn op verschillende plekken toegevoegd om de felste brand enigszins te blussen.

De tuin op het westen komt tot leven in vaste planten in diepe, zondoorstoofde kleuren en in vaste planten met donker blad. De bloemen zijn wisselend van grootte, hoog opgroeiende planten zijn hier in de meerderheid. Imposante combinaties van Echinacea purpurea, Eupatorium rugosum 'Chocolate', Lavatera 'Burgundy Wine' en Iris sibirica 'Ruffled Velvet' worden afgewisseld door de ijle silhouetten van siergrassen, bijvoorbeeld die van Miscanthus 'Kleine Silberspinne' en Calamagrostis acutiflora 'Karl Foerster'.

Perennials (and the Rhythm of Daily Life)

The third section of the Floriade, on the Lake, includes a combined entry of perennials and water plants. An area bordering on a side-pool of the Lake has been reserved for it. The theme of this is the 'Rhythm of Daily Life', which is based on the idea that different colours and flower shapes are suited to the clear, early morning light than to the soft, muted light of the evening. The idea has been brought to life in the form of a huge perennial border and the water-lily pool which the border surrounds.

The east-facing part of the garden wakes to the bright morning sunshine. The mood is set by perennials with fine flowers in gentle colours, such as **Scabiosa columbaria 'Butterfly Blue'**, *(light blue)*, **Salvia nemorosa 'Blauhügel'** *(blue)*, **Sidalcea 'Elsie Heugh'** *(pink)* and **Gillenia trifoliata** *(white)*. As the morning progresses and the light becomes a little harsher, we feel a need for bright, expressive colours. A south-facing garden, onto which the sun shines from its zenith, is at its best when it contains plants with robust blooms in bright colours. Red, deep yellow and orange are represented by plants like **Achillea 'Terracotta'**, **Potentilla 'Gibson's Scarlet'**, *and* **Hemerocallis 'Stella de Oro'**. *Grey-leaved plants, including various kinds of* **Stachys** *and* **Artemisia**, *have been added here and there to quench the fiercest fires a little.*

The west-facing garden comes to life with perennials in deep, sun-baked colours and in perennials with dark-coloured leaves. The flowers vary in size, and tall plants predominate here. Imposing combinations of Echinacea purpurea, Eupatorium rugosum 'Chocolate', Lavatera 'Burgundy Wine' and Iris sibirica 'Ruffled Velvet' alternate with the slender silhouettes of ornamental grasses, e.g. **Miscanthus 'Kleine Silberspinne'** and **Calamagrostis acutiflora 'Karl Foerster'**.

Les plantes vivaces (et le rythme de la journée)

La troisième partie du parc de la Floriade, 'Au bord du Lac', héberge dans un bras latéral du lac et sur ses rives une présentation combinée de plantes vivaces et aquatiques. La présentation a pour thème 'le rythme de la journée', sachant que les inflorescences et les couleurs qui s'apprécient le mieux à la lumière pâle et précoce du matin sont différentes de celles qui exaltent au crépuscule. L'idée est concrétisée par un énorme massif de plantes vivaces embrassant la présentation de nénuphars. L'est du jardin s'éveille à l'aube sous les premiers rayons du soleil. Dans cette lueur matinale, les plantes vivaces sont de préférence à petites fleurs et aux tons de pastel: la Scabiosa columbaria 'Butterfly Blue', (bleu clair), le Salvia nemorosa 'Blauhügel' (bleu), la Sidalcea 'Elsie Heugh' (rose) et la Gillenia trifoliata (blanche). Au fur et à mesure que le soleil poursuit sa course et s'intensifie, les couleurs doivent être plus franches, plus opulentes. Le jardin exposé au sud, que le soleil baigne quand il est à son zénith, est d'autant plus beau que s'y manifestent des fleurs plutôt robustes et aux tons vifs allant du rouge, au jaune ardent et à l'orange. Ce sont entre autres les couleurs de l'Achillea 'Terracotta', de la Potentilla 'Gibson's Scarlet' et de l'Hemerocallis 'Stella de Oro'. Des plantes au feuillage grisâtre comme le Stachys (épiaire) et l'Artemisia (armoise) viennent adoucir ici et là l'effervescence des couleurs. Le jardin à l'ouest est le théâtre des plantes vivaces au feuillage foncé et aux fleurs de tons soutenus, comme tanées au soleil. Les fleurs sont de format variable et les plantes sont pour la plupart assez hautes. D'imposants mélanges d'Echinacea purpurea, d'Eupatorium rugosum 'Chocolate', de Lavatera 'Burgundy Wine' et d'Iris sibirica 'Ruffled Velvet' alternent avec la frêle silhouette de graminées d'ornement telles que le Miscanthus 'Kleine Silberspinne'.

Dauerpflanzen (und der Tagesrhythmus)

Im dritten Teilbereich der Floriade, 'am See', wurde in und an einem Seitenarm des Sees Platz für eine Einsendung gemacht, die aus Dauer- und Wasserpflanzen besteht. Sie kreist um das Thema 'der Tagesrhythmus' und basiert auf der Idee, dass zum frühen, hellen Morgenlicht andere Farben und Blütenformen als zum sanften Dämmerlicht des Abends passen. Dieses Konzept führte zu einer riesigen Rabatte voller Dauerpflanzen, die eine Seerosenkolonie gleichsam umarmt.

Am frühen Morgen erwacht ein Garten im Osten im strahlenden Licht der Sonne. Dazu passen Dauerpflanzen, die feine Blüten und zarte Farben haben, hier beispielsweise Scabiosa columbaria 'Butterfly Blue' *(zartblau)*, Salvia nemorosa 'Blauhügel' *(blau)*, Sidalcea 'Elsie Heugh' *(rosa)* und Gillenia trifoliata *(weiß)*. Wenn das Licht im Laufe des Vormittags etwas 'härter' wird, bekommt man Lust auf klare, lebendige Farben. Ein Garten in Südlage, in den die Sonne aus der Höhe einfällt, ist am schönsten, wenn in ihm Pflanzen mit kräftigen Blüten in grellen Farben wachsen. Das illustrieren hier rote, sattgelbe und orangefarbene Gewächse wie Achillea 'Terracotta', Potentilla 'Gibson's Scarlet' und Hemerocallis 'Stella de Oro'. An manchen Stellen wurden graublättrige Pflanzen wie Stachys- und Artemisiasorten eingestreut, um den allzu heftigen Brand ein wenig zu dämpfen.

Einen Garten in Westlage zieren Dauerpflanzen in tiefen, sonnengetränkten Farben oder mit dunklem Blatt besonders gut. Hier sind die Blumen unterschiedlich groß, aber hochgewachsene Pflanzen überwiegen. Eindrucksvolle Kombinationen aus Echinacea purpurea, Eupatorium rugosum 'Chocolate', Lavatera 'Burgundy Wine' und Iris sibirica 'Ruffled Velvet' wechseln sich mit den filigranen Silhouetten von Ziergräsern ab, darunter Miscanthus 'Kleine Silberspinne' und Calamagrostis acutiflora 'Karl Foerster'.

Het paviljoen van de Haarlemmermeer

De misschien wel economisch best renderende gemeente van Nederland, een gebied ook met de meest uiteenlopende infrastructuur, is vermoedelijk voor het publiek de grote onbekende. De Haarlemmermeer is als Zwitserland, je rijdt er doorheen. Je ziet de afslagen naar Hoofddorp en Nieuw Vennep aan de A4, zonder het gemeentebord tegen te komen. Je landt op Schiphol, en het enige dat bij een buitenlander de mond van verbazing doet openvallen, is dat hij 4,5 meter beneden zeeniveau is aangeland. Desondanks ziet hij groen om zich heen. Een dieptepunt in Nederland dat op allerlei vlakken een hoogtepunt is: kan het paradoxaler?

Het is dan ook meer dan logisch dat in 1994 de keuze gevallen is op de Haarlemmermeer voor de vestiging van de Floriade, omdat het de gemeente van zijn vage identiteit kan afhelpen. Sterker zelfs, de Floriade geeft een nieuwe richting aan de Haarlemmermeer. Een nieuwe kwaliteit. Per slot van rekening heeft de geschiedenis aangetoond dat een Floriade de overtreffende trap van een park is, een park dat een gemeente verplicht. Het groen is gevarieerder, unieker en beter dan dat in een doorsnee park. Daar moet je zuinig op zijn, ook als het festijn al lang is afgesloten, redeneert de gemeente.

De tuinbouwtentoonstelling ontkent het eenzijdige imago van de grootste polder van Nederland als doorvoerhaven voor auto's en vliegtuigen. Integendeel, het kan ook een aangename verblijfplaats zijn, een aaneengesloten groengebied van tweeduizend hectare, dat als een buffer tussen de kernen Haarlem, Heemstede en Hoofddorp wordt opgetrokken met de Floriade als snijpunt. Wie in 2007 op de fiets vanuit Amsterdam naar Leiden wil rijden, zou niet eens hoeven te merken

142

Le pavillon de l'Haarlemmermeer

C'est peut-être, économiquement parlant, la circonscription la plus rentable des Pays-Bas, la région avec aussi la plus grande diversité d'infrastructures, mais vraisemblablement la moins connue du public. En voiture, l'Haarlemmermeer est comparable à la Suisse. On rencontre les pancartes indiquant les sorties de l'autoroute A4 vers Hoofddorp et Nieuw Vennep mais pas de pancarte indiquant la commune. L'étranger qui arrive par avion à Schiphol est stupéfié et apprenant qu'il atterrit à 4,5 m au-dessous du niveau de la mer alors qu'il se voit entouré de verdure. C'est à la fois l'un des points les plus bas du pays et celui qui culmine dans bien des domaines: quoi de plus paradoxal?

Il est donc tout à fait logique que le choix soit tombé en 1994 sur l'Haarlemmermeer pour y implanter la Floriade et donner ainsi l'occasion à la commune d'affirmer son identité. Mieux encore, la Floriade donne un nouveau sens à l'Haarlemmermeer, une nouvelle qualité puisque finalement le passé témoigne qu'une Floriade est le superlatif d'un parc, qu'elle engage une commune. La végétation y est plus variée, plus exceptionnelle et de meilleure qualité que dans un parc normal. La commune hôte en déduit donc qu'il faut en prendre soin, même longtemps après les festivités.

L'exposition horticole nie l'interprétation simpliste qui ne ferait du plus grand polder néerlandais qu'un lieu de transit pour les voitures et les avions. Au contraire, cela peut être un lieu où il fait bon séjourner, un site de verdure ininterrompue de deux mille hectares formant une zone tampon entre les noyaux Haarlem, Heemstede et Hoofddorp, avec La Floriade pour carrefour. Le promeneur et vélo qui se rendra en 2007 d'Amsterdam à Leyde ne remarquera même pas qu'il traverse un polder urbanisé. Il est

The Pavilion of the Municipality of Haarlemmermeer

With perhaps the most flourishing economy in the Netherlands and a huge range of transport infrastructure, Haarlemmermeer is probably a great unknown for the public at large. It's the kind of place you normally drive through without noticing. You see exits to Hoofddorp and Nieuw Vennep but without seeing a sign for Haarlemmermeer itself. Or you land at Schiphol and rush off wherever you are going; only the occasional foreign visitor feels a sense of surprise at being $4^1/_2$ metres below sea level while seeing green countryside all around. It's low point topographically, but a high point in all kinds of other respects. Paradoxical, isn't it?

So it was perfectly logical when, in 1994, the choice fell on Haarlemmermeer as the location of the next Floriade, for this could help the municipality shake off its vague image. Indeed, the Floriade could give Haarlemmermeer a new sense of direction, a new quality. History has after all shown that a Floriade is a park raised to a superlative degree, a park that puts certain obligations on the municipality that houses it. The greenery is more varied, rarer and better than in an average park. The municipality has to take special care of it, long after the show is over.

The horticultural exhibition contradicts the one-sided image of the Netherlands' largest polder prior to the 20th century, a port of transit for cars and planes. On the contrary, it could also be fine place to explore, a continuous green area measuring two thousand hectares which is earmarked as a rural buffer between the towns of Haarlem, Heemstede and Hoofddorp with the Floriade Park at its heart. A cyclist travelling from Amsterdam to Leiden in 2007 will not even necessarily notice that he or she is riding through an urbanized polder, but will be surrounded by greenery almost all the way, unaware of being a character in a scenario

Der Haarlemmermeer-Pavillon

Der Name der wirtschaftlich wohl erfolgreichsten Gemeinde der Niederlande, die zugleich über die vielseitigste Infrastruktur des Landes verfügt, sagt dem Publikum vermutlich wenig. Mit Haarlemmermeer ist es wie mit der Schweiz: Man fährt nur durch. Man sieht die Abfahrt nach Hoofddorp oder nach Nieuw Vennep an der A4, ohne das Ortsschild zu Gesicht zu bekommen. Man landet auf Schiphol, und das Einzige, dass den Reisenden staunen macht, ist die Tatsache, dass er 4,5 Meter unter dem Meeresspiegel steht. Dabei ist er trotzdem von Grün umgeben! Ein Tiefpunkt der Niederlande, der in mancherlei Hinsicht ein Höhepunkt ist – paradoxer geht es wohl kaum.

Es ist also ganz logisch, dass man Haarlemmermeer 1994 zum Standort der Floriade ernannt hat. Das dürfte der Gemeinde zu einer klareren Identität verhelfen, wenn nicht sogar neue Richtung geben. So entsteht eine neue Qualität. Schließlich ist historisch erwiesen, dass eine Floriade die Steigerungsstufe eines Parks darstellt, die der jeweiligen Gemeinde eine Verpflichtung auferlegt. In einem Floriade-Park ist das Grün variierter, einzigartiger und besser als in einem Stadtpark. Das sollte man sich auch nach dem Fest erhalten, denkt die Gemeinde dann.

Die Gartenbauausstellung negiert das einseitige Image des größten Polders der Niederlande, der als Durchfahrtsgebiet für Autos und Flugzeuge gilt. Sie demonstriert, dass es sich hier auch um einen angenehmen Aufenthaltsort handeln kann, eine ununterbrochene, zweitausend Hektar große Grünzone, die als eine Art Puffer zwischen den Orten Haarlem, Heemstede und Hoofddorp entsteht. Die Floriade bildet den Schnittpunkt. Wer im Jahre 2007 mit dem Fahrrad von Amsterdam nach Leiden fahren will, braucht gar nicht zu merken, dass er sich durch einen verstädterten

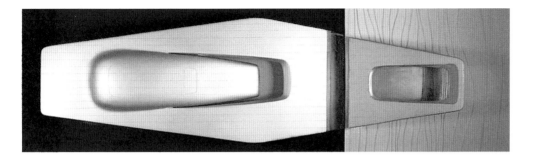

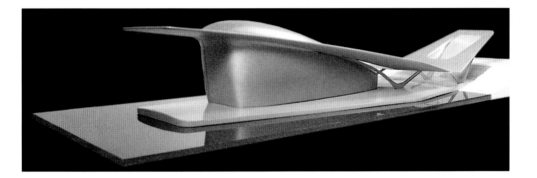

Het paviljoen van de Haarlemmermeer

Le pavillon de l'Haarlemmermeer

Der Haarlemmermeer-Pavillon

The Pavilion of the Municipality of
Haarlemmermeer

143

dat hij door een verstedelijkte polder trekt. Hij is een met het groen. Hij beseft niet dat hij een personage is in een scenario waarvoor de basis ruim tien jaar geleden werd gelegd, een scenario dat in het teken stond van de duurzaamheid. Wat werd gebouwd en werd aangelegd, zou niet meer moeten verdwijnen. Littekens in het landschap zijn er al genoeg.

Het moderne park kan niet volstaan met bosschages en ligweiden, het mag geen *private party* zijn voor hazen en konijnen, het moet zo attractief zijn, dat de bezoeker er uitstapt op de twee haltes van de Zuidtangent. Na de sluiting van de Floriade blijft daarvan vermoedelijk een halte bestaan, die toegang geeft tot het Meer en zijn paviljoen, waarmee een einde komt aan een geïsoleerd en provisorisch recreatiegebied zonder veel voorzieningen.

De Haarlemmermeer mag dan 150 jaar jong zijn, dat betrekkelijk prille verleden heeft sporen achtergelaten, het Cruquius-gemaal en zijn consorten die als wachters aan de Ringvaart staan. Pioniers spelen de hoofdrol in de geschiedenis van de Haarlemmermeer. Allereerst de boeren die de schippers vervingen, en die hier de vette klei hebben ontgonnen met de modernste landbouwvoertuigen. Na hen volgden de vliegtuigbouwers, Anthony Fokker voorop, die vanaf Schiphol-Oost de wereld veroverden. En nu lijkt de polder opnieuw overstroomd te wor-

en pleine nature et ne réalise pas qu'il est le personnage d'un scénario dont la base a été posée dix ans plus tôt, un scénario placé sous le signe de la durabilité. Ce qui a été réalisé et planté ne devrait plus jamais disparaître. Le nombre de cicatrices dans le paysage est déjà bien suffisant.

Ce parc moderne doit être plus qu'un ensemble de bosquets et de pelouses pour s'y allonger, plus qu'un lieu de 'surprise-partie' pour les lièvres et les lapins; son attrait doit être tel qu'il fascine le visiteur qui descend à l'une des deux haltes de la Zuidtangent. Après la fermeture de la Floriade, l'une d'entre elles sera vraisemblablement conservée pour donner accès au Lac et à son pavillon, mettant ainsi fin à l'époque où le plan d'eau n'était qu'une aire de loisirs isolée et à caractère provisoire sans grands aménagements.

L'Haarlemmermeer a beau n'avoir que 150 ans, les marques de ce passé relativement récent sont là: la station de pompage Cruquius et ses consœurs se dressent comme des gardes le long de la Ringvaart. L'histoire de l'Haarlemmermeer est celle de pionniers. Les premiers furent d'abord les agriculteurs venus remplacer les pêcheurs et qui ont travaillé cette terre grasse et argileuse avec les machines agricoles les plus modernes. Ensuite, arrivèrent les constructeurs d'avions, Anthony Fokker en tête, allant à la conquête du monde à partir de Schiphol-Est. Et maintenant, le polder semble de nouveau envahi, cette fois par des multinatio-

which was initiated almost ten years previously and is dominated by ideas of sustainability. There was no need to get rid of buildings and other human structures that were already present; there were already enough scars in the landscape.

A modern park cannot suffice with coppices and lawns, nor must it be a private picnic for rabbits and hares. It must be so attractive that the visitor gets of at one of the two bus stops along Zuidtangent, and enters a swirling zone of greenery with amenities like the exhibition hall under the solar roof at the North Entrance and the pavilion at the southern entrance. The former waterlogged sandpit was an ad hoc recreational area with little to offer except perhaps to intrepid swimmers in the lake and nothing in the way of amenities – not even toilets. Now it has been swallowed up by the Floriade Park, and this imposes obligations of maintenance.

The Haarlemmermeer polder may only be 150 years old, but it has gathered some historic relics in its short history, such as the Cruquius pumping station and its confrères which stand like sentries along the ring canal around the polder. That history can be told in terms of a succession of pioneers. Firstly there were the farmers who came in place of the fishermen, and who first cultivated the recalcitrant clay with the latest agricultural machinery of 1910s and 20s. These were followed by the aeroplane builders, with Anthony Fokker in the lead, who conquered the world from

Raum bewegt, denn er geht ganz im Grün auf. Ihm dürfte gar nicht bewusst sein, dass er eine Figur aus einem Drehbuch ist, das mehr als zehn Jahre zuvor geschrieben wurde, ein Drehbuch im Zeichen der Dauerhaftigkeit. Die darin konzipierten Bauten und Anlagen sollten nicht mehr weichen müssen. Die Landschaft hat schon genug Narben.

Ein moderner Park braucht mehr als Baumgruppen und Liegewiesen. Er sollte auch nicht als *'private party'* für Hasen und Kaninchen fungieren, sondern so viel zu bieten haben, dass der Besucher an den beiden Haltestellen der Südtangente aussteigt. Nach der Schließung der Floriade bleibt dann vermutlich eine Haltestelle, die eintrit zum See und seinem Pavillon bietet. Damit wird einem isolierten und provisorischen Erholungsgebiet ohne viele Einrichtungen ein Ende bereitet.

Haarlemmermeer ist zwar erst 150 Jahre alt, weist aber dennoch schon Spuren der Vergangenheit auf – das Cruquius-Schöpfwerk und seine Ableger, die an der Ringvaart Wache halten. Die Geschichte von Haarlemmermeer wurde von Pionieren geprägt. Erst lösten die Bauern die Schiffer ab und bearbeiteten den fetten Lehmboden mit modernsten landwirtschaftlichen Geräten. Ihnen folgten die Flugzeugbauer, allen voran Anthony Fokker, und eroberten von Schiphol-Ost aus die Welt. Zur Zeit breiten sich im Polder internationale Betriebe wie Sony, Hotels und Kongresszentren, Wohnungsbausiedlungen und – im Zuge der Floriade – Grünzonen aus. Über die alten

den, met internationale bedrijven als Sony, met hotels en congres-centra, met bewoners van Vinex-wijken en met de groenstructuur waarvan de Floriade het hart vormt. De oude rechte vaarten, de Ringvaart incluis, worden op drie plaatsen overbrugd, door futuristische bruggen van de Spaanse architect Santiago Calatrava, die een verdere betekenis hebben dan het ontsluiten van de polder alleen. Ze dingen mee naar de status van symbool van de moderne dynamische polder. Voor vijftienduizend nieuwkomers worden wijken uit de grond gestampt, Stellinghof in Vijfhuizen, Getsewoud in Nieuw-Vennep, Floriande in Hoofddorp, en uiteindelijk zullen de twee kernen wel een keer versmelten. Tot Meerstad, wat beter past bij de statuur van een poldermetropool.

Over paradoxaliteiten gesproken: het paviljoen van de Haarlemmermeer is ontworpen door een Amerikaan van Egyptische afkomst, Hani Rachid. Proef zijn naam op de tong, bedenk de betekenis en zie wat hij heeft bedacht, waarna de conclusie alleen kan zijn: de wereld staat op zijn kop. Een Egyptenaar, geboren in een van de droogste delen der aarde, staat aan de wieg van een van de natste paviljoens. (En op een steenworp afstand staat nota bene een heuvel waarvan de maat correspondeert met de piramide van Cheops in zijn land). Het water stroomt over het dak van het scheepsvormige huis dat meterslang het meer insteekt, zonder het wateroppervlak echt aan te raken. Je loopt tussen twee watervallen door en betreedt het 10 meter hoge paviljoen dat wat de architect betreft een doel heeft: de architectuur voor zichzelf laten spreken. Wat er aan informatie over de gemeente geboden wordt, is summier. Immers, de meeste gasten hebben al een stevige wandeling achter de rug.

nales comme Sony, par des hôtels et des centres de congrès, par les habitants des quartiers Vinex et par la verdure dont la Floriade est le cœur battant. Les trois cours d'eau rectilignes, y compris la Ringvaart, sont traversés en trois endroits par des ponts futuristes de l'architecte espagnol Santiago Calatrava qui non seulement donnent accès au polder mais contribuent aussi à symboliser le statut moderne et dynamique du polder. La construction de nouveaux quartiers permettra d'accueillir quinze mille nouveaux venus: Stellinghof à Vijfhuizen, Getsewoud à Nieuw-Vennep, Floriande à Hoofddorp, qui finiront bien par se fondre pour former Meerstad, au statut d'une métropole de polder.

A propos de paradoxes: le pavillon de l'Haarlemmermeer est l'œuvre d'un Américain d'origine égyptienne, Hani Rachid. Ecoutez la résonance de ce nom, imaginez le cadre qu'il évoque et regardez la création de cet homme... vous ne pourrez qu'en conclure que c'est le monde à l'envers. Un Egyptien, né dans l'une des parties les plus sèches du monde, se tient au berceau de l'un des pavillons les plus humides. (Et qui plus est, à quelque pas se dresse une colline au format de la pyramide de Cheops dans son pays). L'eau coule sur le toit de la construction en forme de coque de bateau qui s'avance sur plusieurs mètres dans le lac sans toucher la surface de l'eau. Nous passons entre deux cascades pour entrer dans le pavillon de 10 m. de haut qui, selon l'architecte, à un seul objectif: laisser parler l'architecture. La documentation proposée sur la commune est succincte. En effet, la plupart des visiteurs ont déjà arpenté pas mal de terrain et apprécient de se reposer dans ce 'pavillon d'accueil' du polder.

Vivre l'art de la nature alors que le regard se pose sur du métal et du verre. Comment faire rimer l'un et l'autre? Rachid s'est posé la question,

146

their base in Schiphol East. Now the polder seems to be undergoing a new deluge of development, with multinational companies such as Sony, hotels, conference centres, new housing developments and the green network of which the Floriade Park forms the central link. The old straight navigable canals and the ring canal have been bridged in three places. The futuristic bridges were designed by the Spanish architect Santiago Calatrava and have a significance which goes beyond providing access to the polder. They compete for status as symbols of the modern, dynamic polder. New residential districts, known as VINEX developments, are being knocked up to provide homes for some fifteen thousand new residents of Haarlemmermeer. The developments are Stellinghof in Vijfhuizen, Getsewoud in Nieuw-Vennep, Floriande in Hoofddorp. Ultimately the latter two towns will fuse into a single city: Meerstad, as people have been speculatively calling it, a name considered fitting for a true polder metropolis.

The Floriade is park full of paradoxes. The Pavilion of the Municipality of Haarlemmermeer was designed by an American of Egyptian extraction, Hani Rashid. It is odd to think of the dry deserts of Egypt as an antecedent to this most watery of pavilions (not forgetting that it is only a stone's throw from Big Spotters' Hill, with its dimensions based on the Pyramid of Cheops). Water flows over the roof of this ship-shaped building, which projects over the lake by several metres without actually touching the water. We pass between two waterfalls and enter the 10-metre tall pavilion. From the architect's point of view, it has only one purpose, to let the architecture speak for itself. The pavilion offers us only brief information about the municipality of Haarlemmermeer. After all, like most visitors we have had long walk by the time we reach here, and

geradlinigen Kanäle einschliesslich der Ringvaart werden an drei Stellen Brücken gebaut. Es handelt sich dabei um futuristische Entwürfe des spanischen Architekten Santiago Calatrava, die nicht nur der Erschließung des Polders dienen. Sie beteiligen sich am Wettbewerb um den Symbolstatus eines modernen, dynamischen Polders. Für fünfzehntausend neue Bewohner entstehen Neubausiedlungen: Stellinghof in Vijfhuizen, Getsewoud in Nieuw-Vennep, Floriande in Hoofddorp, und im Endeffekt werden die beiden Bebauungskerne wohl zu einer Seestadt verschmelzen, die dem Status einer Poldermetropole besser gerecht werden kann.

Weil wir gerade von Paradoxen sprechen: Entworfen wurde der Haarlemmermeer-Pavillon von Hani Rachid, einem Amerikaner ägyptischer Herkunft. Wenn man seinen Namen auf der Zunge zergehen lässt, über seine Bedeutung nachdenkt und den Entwurf betrachtet, ist nur eine Schlussfolgerung möglich: Die Welt steht auf dem Kopf. Ein Ägypter, geboren in einem der trockensten Erdteile, ist der Schöpfer eines ausgesprochen nassen Pavillons. (Hinzu kommt, dass sich ganz in der Nähe des Pavillons ein Hügel erhebt, dessen Maße denen der Cheopspyramide entsprechen...) Über das Dach des schiffsförmigen Baus, der meterweit in den See hineinreicht, ohne wirklich dessen Oberfläche zu berühren, fließt Wasser. Man geht zwischen zwei Wasserfällen hindurch und betritt den zehn Meter hohen Pavillon, mit dem der Architekt nur das eine Ziel verfolgt: Die Architektur soll für sich sprechen. An Information über die Gemeinde wird nur wenig geboten. Die Besucher haben ja meist schon einen Rundgang hinter sich, wenn sie am Pavillon ankommen. In diesem 'Gasthaus' des Polders können sie ein wenig verschnaufen.

'Feel the art of nature', aber dennoch sehen wir Stahl und Glas. Wie passt das zusammen? Im Einvernehmen mit den Auftraggebern hat sich Rachid

Zij kunnen in dit 'gasthuis' van de polder even op adem komen. *Feel the art of nature*, desondanks zien we staal en glas. Hoe is dat te rijmen? Rachid heeft zich in samenspraak met de opdrachtgever de vraag gesteld wat natuur nog is, zeker in de Nederlandse omstandigheden. De natuur is door mensen gemaakt en gevormd. Dat er vliegtuigen landen in een polder is een 'mooi vormgegeven technologie' waarvan de elementen in een natuurlijke omgeving worden ingepast. Symbolischer kan een paviljoen niet zijn, want hier komt alles samen: de wording van de Haarlemmermeer, de manier waarop de polder opnieuw contact zoekt met zijn bron, het water, en de ruimte die het paviljoen biedt. Ruimte en technologie, als basis voor de gemeente Haarlemmermeer. Je kunt bijkomen op het voorplein, want je hoeft niet naar binnen, maar als je daar bent, ervaar je fysiek de omgeving. Inderdaad, meters onder zeeniveau, in een gemeente die zich wel lijkt weg te cijferen, maar waarvan de cijfers boekdelen spreken.

Het paviljoen van de Haarlemmermeer is een gongslag. Het scheidt de oever van het meer, het breekt de noordkant van het Meer los van de zuidkant. Het is steen en vloeibaar tegelijk. En het blijft: als een uitspanning voor de recreanten. Het paviljoen van de Haarlemmermeer is daarmee – onbewust – een monument voor het derde leven dat de

en concertation avec le donneur d'ordre, de savoir ce que la nature signifie d'autre, surtout dans le cas des Pays-Bas. La nature y est réalisée et formée par les hommes. Si des avions atterrissent dans un polder, il faut y voir une 'technologie esthétique' dont les composantes ont été intégrées à un entourage naturel.

Un pavillon ne saurait être plus symbolique, car c'est ici que tout se rejoint: la genèse de l'Haarlemmermeer, la façon selon laquelle le polder cherche à retrouver ses sources, l'eau et l'espace qu'offre le pavillon. Espace et technologie sont les notions de base de la circonscription Haarlemmermeer. On peut se reposer sur l'esplanade si l'on n'a pas envie d'entrer; mais quand on est là, on éprouve physiquement l'entourage. En effet, à des mètres et en dessous du niveau de la mer, dans une commune qui semble vouloir se dissimuler mais qui en dit long par ses chiffres.

Le pavillon de l'Haarlemmermeer est comme un coup de gong. Il sépare la rive du lac, il dissocie le côté nord du Lac du côté sud. Il marie le solide et le fluide. Et il reste: pour la distraction des promeneurs. A ce titre, le pavillon de l'Haarlemmermeer est, inconsciemment, un monument pour la troisième vie qu'entame le polder, une vie qui passe de l'effort à la dilettante.

Si les rives sud et ouest du Lac accueillent les présentations internatio-

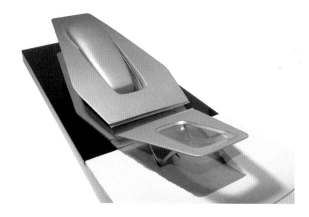

Het paviljoen van de Haarlemmermeer

Le pavillon de l'Haarlemmermeer

Der Haarlemmermeer-Pavillon

The Pavilion of the Municipality of Haarlemmermeer

this 'guest house' in the polder offers us a chance to get our wind back. 'Feel the art of nature' is the motto, but we see steel and glass before us; how can we reconcile this paradox? Hani Rashid thought hard about the concept of nature, particularly in the Dutch context, and discussed it at length with his client, the Haarlemmermeer local government. Here, he argued, 'nature' has been made and shaped by people. The fact that planes land on a former seabed is a 'well-designed technology' whose components have evolved in adaptation to the natural environment. A pavilion could hardly be more symbolic, because everything comes together here: the genesis of Haarlemmermeer, the way the polder seeks renewed contact with its origins, the water, and the spaciousness of the pavilion interior. Green space and technology form the basis for the Municipality of Haarlemmermeer. We can take a break in the pavilion forecourt, for there is no need to go inside – we can survey the whole environment from here. The water flows above our heads, reminding us that here we are several metres below sea-level.

The Pavilion of the Municipality of Haarlemmermeer is as sudden as the beat of a gong. It separates the shore from the Lake, it detaches the north side of the Lake from the south side. It is masonry and fluid at the same time. And above all it is a place for visitors to unwind. The Pavilion of the

die Frage gestellt, was denn Natur heute noch ist, vor allem unter den Bedingungen der Niederlande. Die Natur wurde hier von Menschenhand geschaffen und gestaltet. Dass Flugzeuge in einem Polder landen, ist eine 'Technologie mit schöner Formgebung', deren Elemente sich ins natürliche Umfeld eingliedern.

Symbolischer kann ein Pavillon gar nicht sein, denn hier kommt alles zusammen: die Entstehung von Haarlemmermeer, die Art und Weise, wie der Polder wieder zu seinen Ursprüngen zurückkehrt, das Wasser und die Raumwirkung des Pavillons. Raum und Technologie als Grundlage der Gemeinde Haarlemmermeer. Man kann auch auf dem Vorplatz bleiben, aber wenn man den Pavillon betritt, hat man ein physisches Erlebnis des Raums und der Umgebung. Und das ein paar Meter unter dem Meeresspiegel, in einer Gemeinde, die sich nicht zu wichtig nehmen will, obwohl sie Dinge tut, die Aufmerksamkeit verdienen.

Der Haarlemmermeer-Pavillon ist ein Paukenschlag. Er trennt das Ufer vom See, er bricht die Nordseite des Sees von der Südseite ab, er ist aus Stein und zugleich flüssig. Und er wird bleiben: als Ausflugslokal für die Erholungssuchenden. Damit wird der Haarlemmermeer-Pavillon – unwillkürlich – zum Denkmal des dritten Lebens, das im Polder einzieht – die Erholungs- und Entspannungsfunktion.

Aan het Meer
Au bord du Lac
Am See
On the Lake

polder ingaat, een leven dat van spanning overgaat in ontspanning. Worden de zuid- en westkant van het Meer in beslag genomen door de internationale inzendingen, aan de noordkant roeren de beste kwekers van Nederland zich, de meesters van de heesters, de rozenexperts maar ook de varentuin van de gemeente Amstelveen die bijna sluipenderwijs zich tussen de populieren heeft genesteld. Amstelveen presenteert zich met natuur en Cobra, logisch voor een gemeente die niet alleen heemtuinen maar ook een gespecialiseerd museum binnen zijn grenzen heeft. Zoals de deelnemers van Cobra het landschap opzochten met hun dierlijke beelden en kleurrijke, wilde vormen, zo verwelkomt het landschap hen hier, in een harmonieuze verstrengeling.

nales, sur le côté nord se manifestent les producteurs des Pays-Bas, les maîtres des arbustes, les experts en roses ainsi que la municipalité d'Amstelveen avec un jardin de fougères qui s'est capricieusement niché entre les peupliers. Amstelveen se présente par la nature et par Cobra, logique puisque cette ville héberge sur son territoire non seulement des jardins naturels mais aussi un musée spécialisé. A l'inverse des participants de Cobra qui allaient à la rencontre du paysage avec leurs sculptures, leurs riches couleurs et leurs formes sauvages, le paysage les accueille maintenant ici dans un entrelacement harmonieux.

Municipality of Haarlemmermeer is thus unintendedly a monument to the third phase of life which the polder is now entering, a life in transition from tension to relaxation. The south and west shores of the Lake are occupied by the international contributions to the Floriade, but the north side is home to some of the best plant breeders in the Netherlands – masters of shrubbery, experts on roses, and last but not least the greenery department of the municipality of Amstelveen, whose fern garden has nestled almost surreptitiously between the poplars. The town of Amstelveen presents itself with a combination of nature and the Cobra art movement. Perfectly logical for a municipality which has not only botanical gardens but also a specialized museum within its borders. Just as the members of Cobra interpreted the landscape with animalistic images and wild, colourful forms, the landscape welcomes them here in a harmonious patchwork.

Während die Süd- und Westseite des Sees den internationalen Einsendungen vorbehalten ist, zeigen an der Nordseite die besten Züchter der Niederlande ihr Können. Es ist das Terrain der Meister der Sträucher, der Rosenexperten, aber auch der Farngarten der Gemeinde Amstelveen hat sich hier fast unmerklich zwischen den Pappeln eingenistet. Amstelveen präsentiert sich als Heimstatt der Natur und der Künstlergruppe Cobra. Schließlich besitzt diese Gemeinde Naturlehrgärten und ein Cobra-Museum. Die Cobra-Künstler, die sich mit ihren Tiermotiven und den bunten, wilden Formen von der Landschaft inspirieren ließen, werden hier ihrerseits von der Landschaft vereinnahmt.

Rozentuin

Er is geen plant die, als het gaat om het opeisen van de aandacht, kan wedijveren met de roos. Al ver vóór de jaartelling was de roos, samen met de druif en de Madonnalelie, de belangrijkste plant in Perzische en Egyptische tuinen. Wat daarin zeker een rol gespeeld heeft is dat de roos altijd beschouwd is als het enige ware symbool van de liefde. Er is dan eigenlijk ook geen tuin die zonder haar kan.

In de rozentuin bij het meer staat dat romantische karakter van de roos centraal. Nu eens geen stijve perken waarin het alleen gaat om de schoonheid van de bloem, maar een evenwichtige tuin met een natuurlijk karakter. Deze tuin biedt rozen de gelegenheid te fungeren als volwaardige partners van vaste planten en bloembollen. Een perfect voorbeeld voor een particuliere tuin waarin rozen op dezelfde manier toegepast zouden moeten worden. Rozen komen immers pas in juni op gang en zullen daarvóór, maar ook tijdens en na hun bloeitijd alleen maar profijt hebben van ondersteunende buurplanten. In dit samenspel is de roos op haar best en voor de bezoeker zal er een wereld van tot op heden verborgen gebleven mogelijkheden opengaan.

Deze rozentuin is gesitueerd op een kleine heuvel die glooiend afloopt naar het water. Op het hoger gelegen deel is gekozen voor een beplanting met gele, abrikooskleurige en koperkleurige rozen, afgewisseld met oranje en rode rozen. Soorten als 'Amber Queen', 'Golden Celebration', 'Just Joey' en 'Scarlet Pavement' zijn hier verwerkt tussen vaste planten in bijpassende kleuren. In het voorjaar bloeien daar Waldsteinia ternata, Alchemilla erythropoda (vrouwenmantel) en Euphorbia amygdaloides robbiae (wolfsmelk), gevolgd door onder meer Potentilla tongei (ganzerik) en Foeniculum vulgare

Le jardin aux roses

Aucune plante ne saurait attirer plus d'attention qu'un rosier. Bien avant notre ère, le rosier était déjà, avec la vigne et le lys Madonna, la plante la plus importante dans les jardins de Perse et d'Egypte. Le fait que la rose ait toujours été considérée par excellence comme le symbole de l'amour y a certainement contribué. Aucun jardin ne peut donc s'en passer.

Le romantisme de cette fleur joue un rôle crucial dans le jardin aux roses près du lac: cette fois, pas de massifs guindés où il n'y va que de la beauté de la fleur, mais un jardin équilibré de caractère naturel. Ce jardin permet aux rosiers de se présenter en partenaires idéaux des plantes vivaces et des bulbes. C'est un parfait exemple montrant comment les rosiers peuvent être utilisés dans le jardin du particulier. En effet, les rosiers qui ne se manifestent qu'en juin, ne peuvent qu'y gagner avant, pendant et après la floraison s'ils sont dans le voisinage d'autres plantes. La rose se montre sous son meilleur jour dans cette mise en scène qui fait découvrir au visiteur une multitude de possibilités encore inexplorées.

Le jardin aux roses s'étend sur une petite colline plongeant vers l'eau. En haut de la colline fleurissent des roses jaunes, abricot et cuivre intercalées avec des roses orange et rouges. Les variétés 'Amber Queen', 'Golden Celebration', 'Just Joey' et 'Scarlet Pavement' y ont été plantées parmi des plantes vivaces de couleurs assorties. Au printemps s'épanouissent le Waldsteinia ternata, l'Alchemilla erythropoda (manteau-de-Notre-Dame) et l'Euphorbia amygdaloides robbiae, suivis entre autres par la Potentilla tongei (herbe aux oies) et le Foeniculum vulgare 'Giant Bronze' (fenouil à feuille rouge). Et comme le

The Garden of Roses

When it comes to claiming attention, there is surely no plant to rival the rose. In far-off times, the rose, the grape-vine and the White Lily were the most important plants in the gardens of ancient Persia and Egypt. Then, as now, the rose was regarded as the only true symbol of love. So no garden is complete without roses.
The Floriade Garden of Roses, on the shore of the Lake, has more to offer us than the romance of the rose. Not now in tidy beds where the beauty of the flower is everything, but in a balanced garden with a naturalistic character. This garden gives roses an opportunity to function as fully-fledged partners of perennials and flowering bulbs. It offers a perfect example for domestic gardens, in which roses are best applied in a similar way. Roses have little to show us until June, and until then they can only profit from the support of other plants nearby; and this supporting role continues through the flowering period of the rose and beyond. The rose looks its best in combined display of this kind. At the Floriade, a world of hitherto unexpected possibilities will open up.

The Garden of Roses is sited on a hillock which slopes gently down to the lake shore. The higher part has been chosen for the display of yellow, apricot and copper-coloured roses, interspersed with orange and red. Varieties like 'Amber Queen', 'Golden Celebration', 'Just Joey' and 'Scarlet Pavement' have been intermixed with perennials in harmonizing colours. Waldsteinia ternata, Alchemilla erythropoda (Lady's Mantle) and Euphorbia amygdaloides robbiae (Wood Spurge) bloom in spring, followed by Potentilla tongei (Cinquefoil) and the red-leaved fennel Foeniculum vulgare 'Giant Bronze'. And since red leaves only add to

Der Rosengarten

Keine Pflanze erregt mehr Aufmerksamkeit als die Rose. Schon vor unserer Zeitrechnung war die Rose neben der Traube und der Madonnenlilie die wichtigste Pflanze in persischen und ägyptischen Gärten. Dabei spielte gewiss eine Rolle, dass die Rose immer als das einzige wahre Symbol der Liebe betrachtet wurde. Im Grunde kommt kein Garten ohne sie aus.
Im Rosengarten am See dreht sich alles um den romantischen Charakter der Rose. Hier gibt es keine ordentlichen Beete, die die Schönheit der Blume unterstreichen, sondern eine ausgeglichene, natürliche Gartenlandschaft. Die Rosen dürfen in diesem Garten als vollwertige Partner von Dauerpflanzen und Blumenzwiebeln fungieren. In privaten Gärten könnten sie genauso eingesetzt werden. Da die Rosen ja erst im Juni auf den Plan treten, können sie in der Zeit davor, aber auch während ihrer Blütezeit, die Unterstützung anderer Pflanzen gut gebrauchen. In diesem Zusammenspiel kommt die Rose am besten zur Geltung. Dem Besucher eröffnet sich damit eine Welt bisher verborgener Möglichkeiten.

Der Rosengarten liegt auf einer Anhöhe, die zum Wasser hin sanft abfällt. Im höheren Gartengelände stehen gelbe, aprikosen- und kupferfarbene Rosen, die sich mit orangefarbenen und roten Exemplaren abwechseln. Arten wie 'Amber Queen', 'Golden Celebration', 'Just Joey' und 'Scarlet Pavement' sind in Dauerpflanzen mit harmonisierenden Farben eingebettet. Im Frühling blühen dort zunächst Waldsteinia ternata, Alchemilla erythropoda (Frauenmantel), Euphorbia amygdaloides robbiae (Wolfsmilch), später unter anderem Potentilla tongei (Fingerkraut) und Foeniculum vulgare 'Giant Bronze', der rotblättrige Fenchel. Weil rotes Blatt die oben genannten Farben noch lebendiger macht, sind auch Heuchera micrantha 'Palace

Het beste moment om rozen voor een boeket te knippen is 's ochtends vroeg, als de knoppen nog maar net open gaan. Verwijder dan doorns en bladeren tot op minstens de helft van de stengel. Snij de steel aan de onderzijde zo schuin mogelijk af zodat het oppervlak waarmee de roos water moet opzuigen op zijn grootst is. Vul een vaas tot bijna aan de rand met vers, lauwwarm water waaraan snijbloemenvoedsel is toegevoegd.

Le meilleur moment de couper les roses pour en faire un bouquet est le matin de bonne heure, quand les boutons commencent à s'ouvrir. Eliminez les épines et les feuilles sur la moitié de la tige. Coupez la tige en biseau de façon à ce que la surface d'absorption soit la plus grande possible. Remplissez presque jusqu'au bord un vase avec de l'eau fraîche contenant un produit pour fleurs coupées.

The best time of day to cut roses for a bouquet is early in the morning, when the buds are just beginning to open. Remove thorns and leaves from at least the lower half of the stem. Cut off the bottom of the stem at as steep an angle as possible, to maximize the surface through which the rose can suck up water. Fill the vase almost to the brim with lukewarm water in which you have dissolved some cut flower crystals.

Der beste Zeitpunkt, um einen Rosenstrauß zusammenzustellen, ist der frühe Morgen, wenn die Köpfe gerade erst aufgehen. Entfernen Sie dann die Dornen und Blätter bis mindestens in halber Höhe des Stängels, schneiden Sie den Stiel ganz schräg ab, so dass die Fläche, mit der die Rose das Wasser aufsaugt, möglichst groß ist, und füllen Sie eine Vase fast bis zum Rand mit frischem, lauwarmen Wasser. Fügen Sie Schnittblumendünger hinzu.

153

'Giant Bronze', de roodbladige venkel. En omdat rood blad de eerder genoemde kleuren nog sprekender maakt zijn Heuchera micrantha 'Palace Purple' en Euphorbia amygdaloides 'Purpurea' ook van de partij.

Op de glooiïng naar het water gaan de tinten van de rozen over in wit en roze en vervolgens in lila, paars en dieprood. Hier zijn rozen te vinden in soorten als 'Pearl Drift', 'The Fairy', 'Escapade' en 'Rosy Carpet'. Zij worden vergezeld door met zorg gekozen vaste planten zoals Verbena bonariensis, Knautia macedonica, Artemisia schmidtiana 'Nana' en Salvia officinalis. De laatste twee zijn gekozen om hun rustgevende zilvergrijze blad dat het wisselende kleurenspel in balans moet houden.

In het voorjaar, wanneer de rozen pas in het stadium van blad- en knopvorming zijn, gaat alle aandacht naar de bloembollen. Ook zij zijn geplant op een manier die overeenstemt met het ongedwongen karakter van deze tuin: in luchtige groepen tussen de aanwezige vaste planten. Veel tulpen met sfeerbepalende namen als 'Blushing Bride', Spring Green' en 'Purissima' die hun naam zeker eer aandoen. Daarnaast narcissen zoals 'February Gold' en 'Golden Dawn'. Blauwe druifjes, boshyacintjes en vogelmelk hebben een bescheidener rol toebedeeld gekregen en zijn vooral te vinden in randjes langs de paden en in de overgang naar het omringende bos.

feuillage rouge fait encore plus ressortir les couleurs nommées plus haut, l'Heuchera micrantha 'Palace Purple' et l'Euphorbia amygdaloides 'Purpurea' sont aussi au rendez-vous.

Sur la pente allant vers l'eau, les roses passent d'abord aux tons de blanc et de rose puis au mauve, au violet et au rouge foncé. Les variétés telles que 'Pearl Drift', 'The Fairy', 'Escapade' et 'Rosy Carpet' sont en compagnie de plantes vivaces choisies avec soin: Verbena bonariensis, Knautia macedonica, Artemisia schmidtiana 'Nana' et Salvia officinalis. Les deux dernières ont été choisies pour le gris argenté de leur feuillage qui équilibre le jeu des couleurs.

Au printemps, lorsque les rosiers n'en sont qu'au stade des feuilles et des boutons, toute l'attention se porte sur les bulbes. Ils ont été plantés, eux aussi, et en harmonie avec le caractère nonchalant du jardin: en groupes aérés parmi les plantes vivaces. On y trouve de nombreuses tulipes faisant honneur à leurs noms enchanteurs de 'Blushing Bride', 'Spring Green' et 'Purissima', à côté de narcisses tels que le 'February Gold' et le 'Golden Dawn'. Le muscari, les jacinthes sauvages et l'ornithogale ont un rôle plus discret et se rencontrent surtout dans de petites bordures le long des allées conduisant vers le bois et pourtour.

the expressive power of the colours mentioned above, Heuchera micrantha 'Palace Purple' and Euphorbia amygdaloides 'Purpurea' are also in on the act.

On the slope down to the water's edge, the hues of the roses shift to white and pink, and then to lilac, purple and crimson. They include such varieties as 'Pearl Drift', 'The Fairy', 'Escapade' and 'Rosy Carpet'. These too are accompanied by thoughtfully selected perennials like Verbena bonariensis, Knautia macedonica, Artemisia schmidtiana 'Nana' and Salvia officinalis. The last two were chosen for the gentle coolness of their silvery-grey leaves, which help keep the shifting colour combinations in balance.

In spring, when the roses are still busy forming their leaves and buds, all attention goes to the flowering bulbs. They too were planted in a scheme that matches the informal character of the Garden of Roses, in scattered groups between the perennials. Many Tulips with evocative labels such as 'Blushing Bride', Spring Green' and 'Purissima' do their names justice. Daffodils such as 'February Gold' and 'Golden Dawn' keep them company. Grape Hyacinths, Wood Hyacinths and Star-of-Bethlehem have been cast in a more modest role. They appear mainly in borders along the paths and near the margins of the surrounding woodland.

Purple' und Euphorbia amygdaloides 'Purpurea' *mit von der Partie.*
Auf dem Abhang an der Seeseite werden die Rosen weiß und rosa und schließlich lila, violett und tiefrot. Hier wachsen Rosensorten wie 'Pearl Drift', 'The Fairy', 'Escapade' *und* 'Rosy Carpet'. *Ihre Begleiter sind sorgfältig ausgewählte Dauerpflanzen wie* Verbena bonariensis, Knautia macedonica, Artemisia schmidtiana 'Nana' *und* Salvia officinalis. *Die beiden letzten wurden wegen ihrer Ruhe spendenden silbergrauen Blattfarbe ausgewählt, die das abwechslungsreiche Spiel der Farben im Gleichgewicht halten soll.*
Im Frühjahr, wenn die Rosen noch Blätter und Knospen treiben, ziehen die Zwiebelpflanzen alle Blicke auf sich. Auch sie wurden so gesteckt, dass es zum ungezwungen Charakter dieses Gartens passt: in luftigen Büscheln zwischen die bereits vorhandenen Dauerpflanzen. Viele Tulpen machen ihren stimmungsvollen Namen wie 'Blushing Bride', Spring Green' *und* 'Purissima' *alle Ehre. Daneben gibt es Narzissen des Typs* 'February Gold' *und* 'Golden Dawn'. *Traubenhyazinthen, Spanische Hasenglöckchen und Milchsterne müssen sich mit unauffälligeren Stellen begnügen und stehen meist am Wegrand und im Übergang zum Wald.*

Biotopia, het ecologisch
geweten van Nederland
**Biotopia: la conscience
écologique des Pays-Bas**
Biotopia, das ökologische
Gewissen der Niederlande
**Biotopia, the ecological con-
science of the Netherlands**

Voorbij de rozentuin lijken we te zijn beland in het ruigste deel van het bos, met een klein moeras, een gebied om door heen te dwalen, langs pergola's, over bruggetjes, totdat we uitkomen bij Biotopia, het ecologisch geweten van Nederland. Biotopia is het hier en nu van de milieuorganisaties (Natuurmonumenten, Vogelbescherming, de Waddenvereniging, Goois Natuurreservaat, IVN, De Landschappen, het Wereldnatuurfonds, de Nationale Postcodeloterij en de Stichting Doen). Het is een spraakmakend onderdeel van de Tuinbouwtentoonstelling, een soort kashba dat aanvankelijk zelfs liefderijk de bomen in zijn midden zou opnemen maar zich nu heeft gewurmd tussen bomen. De boodschap is hoe de mens evenwicht kan vinden met de natuur in een land waar om elke meter gevochten moet worden. De reis door Biotopia gaat door negen kubusvormige huisjes die met elkaar verbonden zijn door loopbruggen. De gevelbekleding is opzienbarend, met gras, veren en andere natuurlijke materialen. En het eerste paviljoen brengt ons binnen in het heelal. Maar we dalen geleidelijk af van de kometen op aarde en bevinden ons na verloop van tijd op ooghoogte met de ons omringende plantenwereld, alsof we in een science fiction-roman zijn verzeild. Dan wordt het spannend, want we ondervinden bijna fysiek hoe het is om van elkaar afhankelijk te zijn, de natuur van de mens en omgekeerd ook de mens van de natuur.
Daarmee lijkt de puzzel van de Floriade gelegd. Wil je de kunst van de natuur kunnen aanvoelen, dan moet de natuur een kans krijgen, levensvatbaar zijn door het ingrijpen van de mens. Die moet zich daarna op gepaste afstand houden om de natuur zijn gang te laten gaan zodat de planten, bloemen en struiken ook voor de toekomstige

En quittant le jardin aux roses, nous arrivons semble-t-il dans la partie la plus sauvage du bois; un dédale au cœur d'un petit marécage, longeant des pergolas, traversant des petits ponts, nous amène à Biotopia: la conscience écologique des Pays-Bas. Biotopia est le rendez-vous à la pointe de l'actualité des organismes pour la sauvegarde de l'environnement (Natuurmonumenten: pour les sites classés, Vogelbescherming: pour la protection des oiseaux, Waddenvereniging: pour la sauvegarde des îles Wadden, Goois Natuurreservaat: parc naturel du Gooi, IVN: pour la défense de la nature et de l'environnement, De Landschappen: pour la sauvegarde du paysage, la Fondation mondiale pour la Nature, la loterie 'Nationale Postcodeloterij' et l'association 'Stichting Doen'). C'est l'une des parties les plus frappantes de l'exposition horticole, une sorte de casbah qui devait en premier lieu chaleureusement accueillir les arbres entre ses murs mais qui, en définitif, s'est logée parmi eux. Le message est clair: comment trouver l'équilibre entre l'Homme et la Nature dans un pays à l'affût de chaque mètre carré. Le parcours de Biotopia passe par neuf petits bâtiments en forme de cubes reliés entre eux par un pont. Les parois sont remarquablement tapissés de graminées, de plumes et autres matériaux bruts. Et le premier pavillon nous transporte dans l'espace extraterrestre, puis nous quittons petit à petit les comètes pour redescendre sur la terre et nous retrouver ensuite face au monde végétal qui nous entoure. C'est comme si nous étions entrés dans un roman de science fiction, avec tout le suspense de circonstance car nous éprouvons presque physiquement le phénomène de l'interdépendance entre la Nature et l'Homme et réciproquement.
Ainsi le puzzle de la Floriade semble-t-il achevé. Pour pouvoir ressentir l'art de la nature, il faut lui donner une chance et veiller à ce que l'inter-

Beyond the Garden of Roses, we land in the wildest part of the wood, with a small bog, an area for rambling, past pergolas, over little bridges, until we find ourselves at Biotopia, the ecological conscience of the Netherlands. Biotopia is the display of the environmental organizations (The Dutch Association for the Preservation of Monuments, The Society for the Protection of Birds, the Wadden Society, the Gooi Nature Reserve, IVN, De Landschappen, the Worldwide Fund for Nature, the National Postcode Lottery and Stichting Doen). It is the largest single building apart from the Solar Roof in the horticultural show. Originally it was planned to lovingly enclose trees within its embrace, but now it wriggles its way between the trees. The message is about how people can strike a balance with nature in a country where every square metre of space has to be fought over. The journey through Biotopia takes us through nine cube–shaped pavilions linked together by a bridge. The first pavilion launches us into the cosmos. Then we descend slowly from the realm of comets to planet Earth, and eventually find ourselves face-to-face with the plant kingdom that surrounds us, as though we were in a sci-fi storey. The excitement mounts as we experience almost physically what it is like to be mutually dependent, mankind on nature and nature on mankind. This would seem to be the final piece in the puzzle of the Floriade. If we are to 'feel the art of nature', then we must give nature a chance. Deliberate action is needed to keep nature alive. But then we must keep a respectful distance and let nature take its own course, so that the plants, flowers and wild creatures will retain their vitality and diversity for future generations. Meanwhile, people breed plants and cultivate the land, in the conviction that they must create a bridge between the garden and the landscape, between town and country.

Hinter dem Rosengarten beginnt der wildwüchsigste Teil des Waldes. Beim Durchqueren kommt man an einem kleinen Sumpf vorbei, irrt durch Laubengänge und über Stege, bis man schließlich bei Biotopia herauskommt. Biotopia ist das ökologische Gewissen der Niederlande, das Hic et Nunc aller Umweltorganisationen (Naturschutz, Vogelschutz, Wattenverein, Naturreservat der Gooiregion, IVN, De Landschappen, Weltnaturfonds, Nationale Postleitzahl-Lotterie und Stiftung Doen). Es handelt sich dabei um einen spektakulären Teil der Gartenbauausstellung, eine Art Kasbah, die ursprünglich sogar Bäume in sich aufnehmen sollte, sich nun aber selbst zwischen die Bäume gezwängt hat. Es will zum Ausdruck bringen, wie der Mensch in übereinstimmung mit der Natur leben kann, und das in einem Land, in dem man um jeden Meter Boden kämpfen muss. Die Reise durch Biotopia führt durch neun kubusförmige kleine Häuser, die eine Brücke miteinander verbindet. Der erste Pavillon nimmt uns ins Weltall auf. Aber allmählich steigen wir von den Kometen wieder auf die Erde herab und stehen nach einiger Zeit wieder auf gleicher Höhe mit der uns umgebenden Flora, als hätten wir uns in einen utopischen Roman verirrt. Dann wird es spannend, denn wir erleben fast körperlich, wie es sich anfühlt, wenn man voneinander abhängig ist – die Natur vom Menschen und umgekehrt.
Damit ist das Floriade-Puzzle wohl komplett. Wenn der Mensch die Kunst der Natur fühlen will, muss er der Natur eine Chance geben, muss er so eingreifen, dass sie lebensfähig ist. Dann aber muss er gehörigen Abstand halten, damit die Natur ihren Gang gehen kann, damit die Pflanzen, Blumen und Sträucher auch auf künftige Generationen intensiv einwirken können. Inzwischen züchtet der Mensch aus der überzeugung heraus, dass er eine Brücke zwischen dem Garten und der Landschaft, zwischen Stadt und

generaties hun intensiteit houden. Intussen kweekt en teelt de mens, vanuit de overtuiging dat hij een brug moet slaan tussen de tuin en het landschap, tussen de stad en het land. Niet toevallig gebeurt dat in 2002 op het snijpunt van de Randstad.

Terug bij de ingang met treurwilgen aan de zuidelijke ingang en de kei met waterbron aan de noordkant, hebben we een gevoel gekregen dat we net als Alice in een betoverde tuin zijn rondgeleid. We werden verleid en vermaakt, alle zintuigen zijn beroerd en we weten een ding zeker dat de volgende dag, de volgende maand die tuin weer anders is. Dat is misschien wel de meest onbevredigende gedachte: dat de leukste tuin van Nederland zich nooit laat betrappen. Dat het een momentopname was.
We zijn om de tuin geleid. Dat was voor een keer geen onprettige ervaring.

vention de l'Homme la rende viable. L'Homme doit ensuite savoir se tenir à distance et donner libre cours à la nature afin que les plantes, les fleurs et les arbres gardent toute leur intensité pour les générations futures. Entre-temps, l'Homme continue de développer, de cultiver et de produire, convaincu de devoir jeter un pont entre le jardin et le paysage, entre la ville et la campagne. Et le fait que cela soit concrétisé en 2002 au carrefour de la Randstad (conurbation) n'est pas le fruit du hasard.

De retour auprès des saules pleureurs de l'entrée sud ou à la source jaillissant des rocs de l'entrée sud, nous avons le sentiment de nous être promenés dans un jardin enchanté comme Alice au pays des merveilles. Nous avons été séduits et divertis, tous nos sens ont été éveillés et nous sommes tout à fait conscients que l'aspect du jardin sera déjà différent le lendemain et le mois suivant. Et c'est peut-être ce qui nous chagrine le plus: le fait de savoir que le jardin le plus passionnant des Pays-Bas ne se montre pas sous toutes ses facettes, que l'impression n'est que celle du moment présent.
En fait, le jardin nous a fait marcher aux sens propre et figuré... Ce qui, pour une fois, était loin d'être déplaisant.

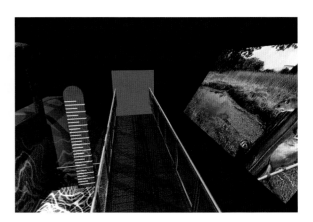

This is what is happening in 2002, aptly at a crossroads of the densely urbanized Randstad.

Returning to the south entrance with its weeping willows, or the north entrance with its rocky fountain, we feel like Alice that we have traversed a wonderland, an enchanted garden. We were tempted and stimulated. All the senses were gratified. One thing is certain though, and that is that if we come back tomorrow, or next month, the garden will be different. The thought is a little sobering: Holland's most gorgeous garden refuses to be pinned down and changes provocatively from day to day. This visit was just a momentary snapshot. We have been led up the garden path, perhaps. But that wasn't so bad, was it?

Land schlagen muss. Dass das anno 2002 auf einem Schnittpunkt des Ballungsgebiets geschieht, ist kein Zufall.

Wieder am Eingang mit den Trauerweiden auf der Südseite und mit dem Felsbrocken mit Wasserbrunnen auf der Nordseite angelangt, ist uns wie Alice nach ihrem Gang durch den Zaubergarten zumute. Wir wurden verführt und unterhalten, all unsere Sinnesorgane wurden angeregt, und uns ist völlig klar, dass dieser Garten jeden Tag, jeden Monat ganz anders aussehen wird. Der Gedanke, dass sich der schönste Garten der Niederlande nie wirklich festlegen lässt, dass wir immer nur eine Momentaufnahme von ihm zu sehen bekommen, ist ein wenig unbefriedigend.
Er hat uns nicht nur Spaß gemacht, sondern auch seinen Spaß mit uns getrieben. Aber unangenehm war uns das nicht.

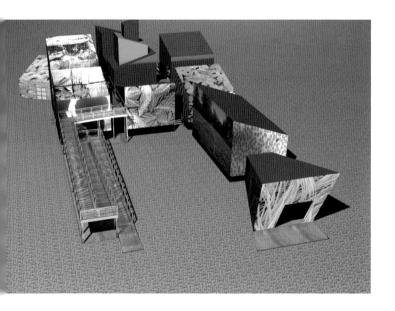

Colophon

Editorial concept and design
Cees de Jong and Jan Johan ter Poorten,
V+K Design, Blaricum

Authors
Jaap Huisman, Amsterdam
Jacqueline van der Kloet, Weesp

Photography
Jan den Hengst, Aarlanderveen
Annelies Roozen, Bennebroek

Illustrations and maps
DP⁶ architectuurstudio, Delft
Hypsos, Soesterberg
Kuiper Compagnons, Rotterdam
NUON, Arnhem
Oosterhuis.nl, Rotterdam
Perspekt Studio's, Haarlem
Niek Roozen tuin- en landschapsarchitecten,
Weesp

Translations
Victor Joseph, Amsterdam (English)
Helga Marx and Rosi Wichmann, Amsterdam (German)
Claudine Vogels-Priou, Naaldwijk (French)

Lithography and printing
Snoeck Ducaju & Zoon, Ghent

Internet
www.floriade.com

© 2001 V+K Publishing
in cooperation with Floriade 2002
ISBN 90 74265 29 4

V+K Publishing
Meentweg 37c
1261 XS Blaricum
Phone +31 (0)35 533 44 55
Fax   +31 (0)35 533 44 33
Email vk@euronet.nl

**Floriade 2002 has been made possible
due to the support of**